The Metaphysicians of Meaning

Bertrand Russell and Gottlob Frege are universally acknowledged as the founding fathers of Analytic Philosophy. Russell's essay 'On Denoting' and Frege's 'On Sense and Reference' propose theories which are arguably their authors' most remarkable contributions to philosophy. Both remain at the forefront of contemporary discussion in philosophy of language and philosophical logic.

The Metaphysicians of Meaning takes a fresh look at these two seminal essays, challenging much of the accepted understanding of them. It forces us to reconsider their author's grounds for advancing them which, as Gideon Makin argues, have been generally misunderstood. Why did Russell and Frege abandon their former theories? What, in their views at the time, were the theoretical alternatives and reasons for adopting these new solutions? Even when these questions have been clearly distinguished they have received only partial answers.

Through a careful and historically sensitive examination of key passages in both essays, as well as of earlier work – in Russell's case including material published only recently – Makin offers new perspectives on both theories. He proposes that Russell's and Frege's deliberations concerning key notions such as 'proposition', 'sense' and 'thought' are a novel form of *doing* metaphysics, and not of circumventing it by shifting attention to language. He also argues that these are inseparable from their authors' occupation with the logicist enterprise in the philosophy of mathematics. Finally, the volume concludes that the shared ground between Russell and Frege is far greater than their differences.

The Metaphysicians of Meaning presents new insights into Russell and Frege and offers a new comparative discussion of their work. It will be essential reading for all students of philosophy of language and logic.

Gideon Makin is Research Fellow at Wolfson College, University of Oxford.

International Library of Philosophy
Edited by José Bermúdez, Tim Crane and Peter Sullivan

Advisory Board: Jonathan Barnes, Fred Dretske, Frances Kamm, Brian Leiter, Huw Price and Sydney Shoemaker

The Metaphysicians of Meaning

Russell and Frege on sense and denotation

Gideon Makin

London and New York

First published 2000
by Routledge
11 New Fetter Lane, London EC4P 4EE

Simultaneously published in the USA and Canada
by Routledge
29 West 35th Street, New York, NY 10001

Routledge is an imprint of the Taylor & Francis Group

© 2000 Gideon Makin

Typeset in Times by
The Running Head Limited, Cambridge
Printed and bound in Great Britain by
TJ International Ltd, Padstow, Cornwall

British Library Cataloguing in Publication Data
A catalogue record for this book is available from the British Library

Library of Congress Cataloging in Publication Data
Makin, Gideon, 1954–
    The metaphysicians of meaning : Russell and Frege on sense and denotation / Gideon Makin.
        p. cm. – (International library of philosophy)
    Includes bibliographical references and index.
        1. Meaning (Philosophy) 2. Russell, Bertrand, 1872–1970. 3. Frege, Gottlob,
    1848–1925. I. Title. II. Series.

    B840.M29 2000
    121′.68′0922–dc21   00–055320

    ISBN 0–415–24225–8 (hbk)
    ISBN 0–415–24226–6 (pbk)

Contents

List of abbreviations   ix

Introduction   1

PART I
Russell   9

1   Russell's first theory of denoting   11

   I   *The elements 11*
   II   *The mathematical context 13*
   III   *Denoting, definition and identity 16*
   IV   *Three essential elements 17*
   V   *Post-PoM developments 20*

**2   The collapse of the first theory and the discovery of the theory
of descriptions**   22

   I   *Introduction: the obscure passage in 'On Denoting' 22*
   II   *The argument: the 'substantial' round 24*
          (i)   C2 is a different entity from C1 25
          (ii) C1 cannot be a constituent of C2 26
          (iii) 'But this cannot be an explanation', I 28
          (iv) The third charge 32
   III   *The argument: the 'symbolic' round 33*
          (i)   The twin phenomena 34
          (ii) Use and mention 37

IV   'But this cannot be an explanation', II 38
        (i)   The burden of proof 38
        (ii)   A survey of theoretical possibilities 38
        (iii) C2 as a description of C1 39
        (iv)   Denoting and other logical relations 41
V   The transition 42
VI   The discovery of the theory of descriptions 45

3   The place of 'On Denoting' in Russell's development   52

I   'On Denoting' and Russell's ontological development:
            some preliminaries 53
II   Russell's case against Meinong 58
III   Russell's ontology in PoM reconsidered 61
IV   Methodological developments: 'every word must have
            some meaning' 66
V   Contextual definition 68
VI   The notion of an incomplete symbol 69
VII   The role of language 73
VIII   Some positive remarks 76

PART II
Frege   79

4   From *Begriffsschrift* to sense and reference   81

I   Introduction 81
II   The problem 82
III   Frege's solution in Bs. 90
IV   'Sinn und Bedeutung': the collapse of the first theory 94
V   'Sinn und Bedeutung': the new solution 101

5   Further considerations regarding sense and reference   106

I   The priority of the distinction for proper names 106
II   Sense and indirect speech 109
III   Sense as a route and empty senses 112
IV   Sense determines reference, I: the question of relativization 117
V   Sense determines reference, II: the conceptual model 121
VI   The application of Russell's argument in OD to Frege's
            distinction 127

PART III
Russell and Frege   133

6   **Russell and Frege compared**   135

   I   *Introduction: the strategy 135*
   II   *The PoM theory of denoting and the theory of sense
            and reference: some preliminaries 137*
   III   *The common ground: propositionalism, sensism and
            the implied metaphysical model 139*
   IV   *The differences, and further similarities, in relation to
            the metaphysical model 144*
   V   *An apparent gap in Frege's argument 148*
   VI   *Can all expressions have sense? 151*
   VII   *The taxonomic difference: a diagnosis of Frege's
            position 155*
   VIII   *Frege's suppressed premise: are all names on a par? 157*
   IX   *The theory of descriptions versus sense and reference:
            an adjustment on the Russellian side 164*
   X   *Frege's description operator and the theory of
            descriptions 169*
   XI   *The progression towards transparency 173*

7   **The Russell–Frege enterprise and natural language**   179

   I   *Introduction 179*
   II   *Ordinary names and logically proper names 180*
   III   *What morals can we draw from illustration? 182*
   IV   *The revisionary nature of the Russell–Frege enterprise 187*
   V   *Logic as metaphysics 191*
   VI   *The latency of the metaphysical facet 197*
   VII   *Concluding remarks: the nature of the enterprise 199*

   Appendix A   203

   The text of the obscure passage from 'On Denoting'   203

   Appendix B   206

   *Russell's example in the latter half of paragraph (D) of
   the obscure passage   206*

Appendix C   **208**

Some recent discussions of the obscure passage 208
I   Searle, Blackburn and Code, and Hylton 208
II   Pakaluk 210
III   Kremer 213
IV   Noonan 219

Bibliography   223
Index   227

Abbreviations

Bs.	*Begriffsschrift* ('Conceptual Notation', Frege)
Bynum	*Conceptual Notation and Related Articles*, edited by T. Bynum (Frege)
CPR	*The Collected Papers of Bertrand Russell*
CPF	*Collected Papers on Mathematics, Logic, and Philosophy* (Frege)
EIP	'The Existential Import of Propositions' (Russell)
FOP	*Frege and Other Philosophers* (Dummett)
FPL	*Frege: Philosophy of Language* (Dummett)
Furth	*The Basic Laws of Arithmetic,* translated and edited by Montgomery Furth (Frege)
G&B	*Translations . . . Gottlob Frege* edited by P. T. Geach and M. Black
Gl.	*Grundlagen der Arithmetik* ('The Foundations of Arithmetic', Frege)
Gg.	*Grundgesetze der Arithmetik* ('The Basic Laws of Arithmetic', Frege)
IFP	*The Interpretation of Frege's Philosophy* (Dummett)
KAKD	'Knowledge by Acquaintance and Knowledge by Description' (Russell)
Lackey	*Essays in Analysis*, edited by D. Lackey (Russell)
Marsh	*Logic and Knowledge*, edited by R. C. Marsh (Russell)
OD	'On Denoting' (Russell)
OF	'On Fundamentals' (Russell)
OMD	'On Meaning and Denotation' (Russell)
PM	*Principia Mathematica* (Russell, with Whitehead)
PMC	*Philosophical and Mathematical Correspondence* (Frege)
PoM	*The Principles of Mathematics* (Russell)
PW	*Posthumous Writings* (Frege)
ROD	'Russell's Ontological Development' (Quine)
SuB	*Über Sinn und Bedeutung* ('On Sense and Reference', Frege)

Introduction

Imagine someone who had mastered the technical aspects of the theory of types but who was unaware of the contradiction ('Russell's paradox') which prompted it, or someone who knew Tarski's theory of truth while knowing nothing of the Liar's paradox. Would we be willing to credit them with an understanding of these theories? Surely something fundamental is missing, and yet what is missing is not strictly part of the theory itself. It concerns, rather, the theory's context, its author's rationale of putting it forth; we might even say, the theory's whole point.

Roughly a century after they were first introduced, Russell's theory of descriptions and Frege's distinction between sense and reference remain unequalled paradigms in the philosophy of language and philosophical logic; and in view of the extensive secondary literature regarding them, any claim to having something new to say about them is bound to sound suspect. However, if understanding a philosophical theory requires understanding why it was called for, and this, in turn, is only possible when it is known what exactly was wrong with the earlier view, then something substantial is lacking in our understanding of these theories.

It is surprising to discover how few serious attempts were ever made to approach these theories from this perspective. In the first place, most writers seem not to have thought the matter important. Others were content with plausible-sounding answers which a little further examination reveals as false. Yet others have offered their own views where it is Russell's or Frege's view that is called for. I do not pretend that finding the correct answers is easy, but I do think the task important, and that it has been generally overlooked.

The following chapters will, I hope, reveal just how important; but even before entering into any detail, it is easy to see how ignorance of Russell's or Frege's reasons for abandoning his former theory might obscure what is distinctive about the new theory he put in its place. One might unknowingly play down features which, in the light of the author's diagnosis of the old theory's faults, emerge as most fundamental; or mistake the new theory's success in handling a problem, which the former theory handled quite adequately, for a chief asset. Moreover, we are in danger of unconsciously investing the situation with our own philosophical concerns and interests, letting them take the place of what can only be unravelled by the careful examination of the texts.

The present work proposes a revisionary view of Russell's theory of descriptions and of Frege's distinction between sense and reference by setting them in a somewhat different philosophical context than they are usually in, which in turn affects the view of what *kind* of theories they are. I will first tell the tale of how I came to adopt such a view, and then try to characterize my differences with what I will be referring to as 'the prevailing view' about them more sharply.

My initial intention was to obtain a clear view of the differences between Russell's and Frege's views on singular terms. Early on I was drawn to examine a notoriously obscure passage from 'On Denoting' (sometimes dubbed 'the Gray's *Elegy* passage'), where Russell appears to be arguing against Frege's distinction. Like many readers before me, I found that the kind of repeated rereading one would ordinarily apply to a difficult passage would not do, and I sought help in discussions of this passage in the secondary literature then available. I found little comfort there, however. In some cases the difficulty lay in the implausibility of the argument proposed indeed being Russell's, but more often the interpretation proposed either simply failed to fit the text, or upon closer inspection accounted only for a fraction of it. In short, none of those discussions appeared to me to provide any sensible account of Russell's text. In view of the status of 'On Denoting' in the analytic tradition and the extent of the secondary literature dealing with it, this state of affairs struck me as being nothing short of a scandal. It was like encountering a patch of uncharted land in the heart of a capital city. (Readers who wish to obtain a glimpse of the problem can do no better than read through this passage, reproduced in Appendix A, and see what sense they can make of it.)

Since not knowing what the argument in that passage is allows one to only speculate about its significance for the essay as a whole, acknowledging this gap gave rise, at first, only to a vague suspicion. But then I came across another piece of evidence which strongly suggested, apparently on independent grounds, that something was substantially amiss with the prevailing view of 'On Denoting' and the theory of descriptions.

The theory is most commonly presented, first and foremost, as Russell's solution to the problem of empty denoting phrases, that is to say, as a way of avoiding any ontological commitment to putative objects like the present King of France, without thereby dismissing sentences in which such a phrase occurs as meaningless. Although the theory of descriptions does indeed provide a solution to this problem as well, which is probably why this explanation appears so plausible, it by no means follows that this was the problem which called it into being. Rather clear evidence suggests, in fact, that it could not have been. In a brief polemical paper written shortly *before* OD, Russell wrote that 'the present King of France' is a complex concept denoting nothing, and that 'these words have a *meaning*, . . . but they have not a *denotation*: there is no entity, real or imaginary, which they point out'.[1]

This piece of evidence was bewildering, because that essay was written *before* Russell discovered the theory of descriptions, when he was clearly still within the bounds of his former theory of denoting. Yet he is squarely denying that 'the present King of France' has a denotation. Why then did he need the theory of descriptions? And if avoiding a commitment to the present King of France was not OD's chief purpose, then what was its purpose? Despite the abundance of discussions aiming to reconstruct this problem, none seemed to fit the available evidence. It is natural to take the three puzzles discussed in OD as embodying this problem, but this does not bear scrutiny. At least one of the three appears not to be genuine;[2] it is doubtful whether the theory really solves another;[3] the third seems to have been resolved by Russell's former theory which is repudiated in OD.

The exegetical problem thus created cannot be simply ignored: in the absence of an alternative answer to put in its place, removing the wrong answer leaves us with an intolerable lacuna. There is a host of (mainly historical) reasons which might explain why this situation *vis-à-vis* the theory of descriptions remained concealed from so many for so long, but the lacuna remains nonetheless. It is tempting at this point to switch to other reasons which might have been Russell's, or to explaining why *we* should prefer the theory of descriptions to Russell's former theory. But the question at stake is why *Russell* should have preferred it – answering which requires quite a different set of resources.

In the absence of (at least) a plausible suggestion regarding the latter question, the implication seems to be that Russell struck upon his theory with no real understanding of the grounds in its favour.[4] Since I was not inclined to believe that Russell, at the height of his powers, was such a fool, or that the theory of descriptions might be a discovery one could stumble upon by accident, I set out to find a better answer. This pointed me back to the obscure passage. Fairly early in the course of my study of it, it transpired that Russell is arguing against his own former, PoM, theory of denoting, and this gave hope that a reconstruction might supply the missing argument. The results of my quest, which provide a *comprehensive* interpretation of this passage

---

1 EIP: p. 100.
2 R. M. Sainsbury, *Russell* (London: Routledge and Kegan Paul, 1979) pp. 106–8.
3 L. Linsky, *Referring* (London: Routledge and Kegan Paul 1969) Chapter 5.
4 See G. Evans, *The Varieties of Reference* (Oxford: Clarendon Press 1982) pp. 51–3; Sainsbury, *Russell*, pp. 100–12; and especially J. A. Coffa, 'Russell as a Platonic Dialogue: The Matter of Denoting', *Synthese* 45 (1985), 43–70, where this seems to be the chief point of the whole paper.

from 'On Denoting', are recorded in the first two chapters. The third is an attempt to follow through the implications of this reconstruction for our understanding of OD as a whole, and of its place within Russell's broader philosophical development.

By the time this exercise was carried through I found that many of my former assumptions regarding the theory of descriptions – which were, I suppose, quite typical – had to be revised, regarding not only the local matter of why Russell needed a new theory of denoting, but also, more importantly, my view of Russell's general philosophical outlook and OD's place within it. It is these indirect effects of the inquiry that now seem to me the more profound. The attempt to make sense of the passage led me to study Part I of *The Principles of Mathematics*, Russell's principal work of that period, and four (then as yet unpublished) manuscripts from the period between the *Principles* and OD.[5] The more I delved into these sources the clearer it became that the prevailing view of what the theory of descriptions was about was on a wrong footing. What had previously been explained away as quirks or loose metaphors for which Russell should be graciously excused[6] began to make perfect sense when interpreted quite literally in the light of the pre-OD material. Formerly baffling but isolated remarks in OD transpired, when seen in the context of Russell's other writings, to be the tips of a comprehensive and carefully worked out theoretical framework.

One of the most surprising changes was that the theory of descriptions no longer appeared to be a theory about language – at least not in any substantial sense. The notion of 'proposition', which the whole discussion in OD revolves around, is expressly *not* a linguistic (or language-dependent) one. Second, OD could hardly mark Russell's extricating himself from a Meinongian ontology, because he never endorsed one in the first place. Third, OD marks no major revolution in Russell's thinking. All the essential ingredients that came together in this solution were already at hand, and it transpires that the transition from his former theory to the theory of descriptions was a more local affair than was formerly thought. There were, however, some positive results gained as well. Chief among them was the recognition of just how deeply rooted the theory of descriptions was in the logicist enterprise. It is the logicist enterprise, rather than latter-day concerns of the philosophy of language, that provided the motivation and the theoretical setting at large. Logicism not only put denoting on Russell's agenda in the first place, it also provided him with criteria which enabled him to

---

5 'On the Meaning and Denotation of Phrases'; 'Points About Denoting'; 'On Meaning and Denotation' and 'On Fundamentals', which have since been published in *The Collected Papers of Bertrand Russell*, Volume 4. The first three are dated by the editors of this volume to 1903. The fourth is undoubtedly from 1905. All that matters for my purposes is that they were from the period between the *Principles* and 'On Denoting'.

6 See e.g. Evans, *Varieties*, p. 82.

recognize this solution as definitive when he struck upon it (which he might not have if he were considering it as a theory of natural language).

One of the questions to which the study of the obscure passage gave rise was whether Russell had intended the argument contained in it as an attack on Frege's distinction between sense and reference and, if so, whether this attack was successful. Consider-ing these questions revealed that Russell had understood Frege in a peculiar way, roughly as engaged in the same kind of inquiry as himself. This seemed at first clear evidence that Russell had radically misunderstood him – and this indeed is the conclusion drawn by some writers. But upon further reflection and consideration of both the appendix in PoM devoted to Frege, and the Frege–Russell correspondence, Russell's understanding of Frege came to look increasingly plausible. A process of unlearning, similar to that experienced in relation to Russell and the theory of descriptions, began in relation to Frege too. It was not so much a question of taking Russell as an authority on what Frege said, as of trying to see how far one could get on the assumption that Frege's broader outlook is essentially similar to Russell's. In some respects Frege provided an even clearer case than Russell, because the evidence was more abundant, and there is no Fregean analogue of the later (say, post-1910) Russell to confuse us.

It will come as no surprise that by this time I was inclined to take a fresh look at Frege's reasons for proposing the sense/reference distinction. Here there was no obscure passage standing in the way as there had been in Russell's case, but I did find, to my surprise, that the available accounts had been insufficiently attentive to detail in the few sentences where, in SuB, Frege explains his reasons for rejecting his former view. Having a 'Russellian' view of Frege in mind made me particularly attentive to something in Frege's text, to which other commentators had turned a blind eye. (Unfortunately, this was made more likely by a mistake in the English translation which obscures Frege's intention.) As with Russell and OD, I found that the available account of the matter had been insufficiently careful in keeping what might be *our* grounds for rejecting that theory apart from what might be Frege's. One important aspect of my account of Frege's case, set forth in Chapter 4, is that Frege's attitude towards language appears to be quite strikingly at odds with his being an author of a 'linguistic turn' in philosophy.

If in Russell's case my course took me from a specific exegetical problem to a revision of the broader theoretical context, in Frege's case the move was in the opposite direction. The revision of the broader context, inspired by what I had learned from Russell's case, made me more sceptical of generally accepted views. I then went on to pursue the implication of this new view of Frege's route to the distinction for the understanding of the distinction itself. Though I found no need to revise my view on what ingredients the notion of sense has, some of them appeared to me now more central, and others more peripheral, than in other, highly influential, accounts of the matter. I thus ended up contesting the accepted wisdom regarding both writers' grounds for, and routes to, their respective theories.

It should be clear by now that when I returned, at last, to my initial interest of comparing Russell's and Frege's views on singular terms, the positions confronting me were quite different from those I had had in mind at the outset. The comparison required forming generalizations which would capture both positions and these, I discovered, served as a useful guide in discerning what is deeper and more stable in each. In view of the perspective on each of the theories developed in the earlier chapters, it no longer seemed obvious that one should plunge straight into the comparison of the theory of descriptions and the sense/reference distinction. The line I adopted instead was to take advantage of the substantial similarities between the PoM view and Frege's distinction, and use these as the benchmark for describing the differences which were to come about with the advent of the theory of descriptions. When all the relevant views are taken into account, I found Russell and Frege to be far closer than is customarily supposed. This is not to say that the remaining differences between them are insignificant, but only that they are far outweighed by the common ground. This common ground is by no means confined to platitudes everyone would agree to, and it involves rather strong assumptions which would probably be unacceptable to most subsequent analytic philosophers.

In the final chapter I try to delineate this common ground at a more programmatic and abstract level than that adopted in the discussion of these authors up to that point. Russell and Frege were not concerned in any fundamental way with language. On the contrary, for anything to qualify as a meaning in the context of their discussions it would have to be *independent* of language or anything specifically human. On the other hand, their shared view is distinguished by a peculiarly metaphysical view of logic. In the final chapter I address the questions of what precisely the place of language is in an investigation of the kind they were engaged in, and how we should understand the evidence which seems to give their theories a quasi-linguistic appearance.

My choosing to discuss Russell before Frege calls for some comment. Chronologically, most of Frege's work, and certainly the sense/reference distinction, were complete before Russell ever came onto the scene, so discussing Frege first would seem to be the natural way to proceed. However, Frege worked in relative isolation, and his work became known to Russell, at least in any detail, only after Russell had completed his *Principles* – which is why Frege is dealt with there only in an appendix. Russell would be the first to admit that Frege had anticipated many of his discoveries, but by historical accident this came to his notice too late for it to have influenced him. So although chronology would have made it possible for Russell to be of a subsequent philosophical generation (as, for example, Wittgenstein relates to Russell and Frege), circumstances made them, in effect, into contemporaries whose philosophical developments ran parallel to each other. Dealing with Russell first does not therefore falsify things, and I have chosen this course because that was the order in which things occurred to me.

I need to address some remarks to the nature of this study. Although my discussion is characterized by a more historical approach to this material than is common, I am still not as thoroughly historical as some. I have confined my attention to the writings of the authors in question and avoided the consideration of broader intellectual atmospheres and possible sources of influence. While I would not wish to deny that studies of the latter kind have a place, at least in relation to Russell's or Frege's reasoning in this particular area, I confess not to have found the drawing of parallels with other writers particularly illuminating. By the time Russell and Frege reached the stage in their careers we are concerned with, each had primarily his former self as adversary. Although I am admittedly more historical than most, I do not conceive of this study as merely setting the context, or supplying the historical backgrounds, of theories whose 'philosophical content' has already been settled. I see it, rather, as contesting what this philosophical content is.

This brings me to a matter which is not discussed in the present work, but which the work as a whole may be said to point to, and in which I would like to think part of its value lies. The question pointed to is this: what light does the revisionary stance developed in the present study shed on subsequent analytic philosophy?

The present study sets out to establish that Russell's and Frege's theories belong to an enterprise which is radically different in *kind* from what current practitioners of the philosophy of language profess to be doing. The two enterprises are not just different ways of doing the same thing. When this is acknowledged, one is deprived of the comforting assumption that the (at least implicit) justification for thinking that language has some central and new role in philosophy lies in the works of Russell and Frege. One needs, on the contrary, to argue *against* them to justify it.

The present work began life as a D.Phil. thesis submitted in Oxford University in the spring of 1995. Although its general structure and main thrust remain unchanged, in the course of the following three years it was revised to such an extent that probably not a single paragraph of the original remains intact.

Of the many people and institutions to whom I owe a very substantial debt for support, both material and moral, as well as valuable criticism, I would like to mention in particular John Campbell, Edward Harcourt, Hugh Miller, Adrian Moore, Benito Mueller, Mark Sacks, Lucy O'Brien, Roger Teichmann and Stephen Williams. I would also like to thank: the presidents (both past and present), fellows and staff of Wolfson College, Oxford where I was a D.Phil. student when this study began, and a research fellow when it was completed. The college provided a consistently friendly, supportive and stimulating working environment. Thanks are also due to colleagues at Bolton Institute of Higher Education, where I was a research fellow for most of the period spent on revision. But most of all I wish to express my gratitude to Peter Sullivan who encouraged me in this work from the very early stages and continued to follow its progress, providing both support and invaluable criticism, reading and commenting on more drafts and versions than either of us can remember. My debt to him is incalculable.

Some of the material presented here has appeared elsewhere, in article form. 'Making sense of "On denoting"' (*Synthese*, 102 (1995) pp. 383–412) and 'Why the theory of descriptions?' (*The Philosophical Quarterly*, 46 (1996) pp. 158–67) are early ancestors of the central sections and the final section, respectively, of Chapter 2. 'Some Prevalent Misconceptions Regarding the Theory of Descriptions', which won the annual essay competition of the Bertrand Russell Society for 1996, and was read at its annual meeting (at Drew University, Madison, New Jersey), is similarly an ancestor of the earlier sections of Chapter 3.

I would like to thank both Routledge and W. W. Norton for kind permission to reprint extracts from Bertrand Russell, *The Principles of Mathematics*, and Routledge for kind permission to reprint extracts from Bertrand Russell's 'On Denoting'.

Finally, a note about citations and typographical conventions. To provide the desired flexibility in the indication of emphasis within quotes, I have used italics when the emphasis is in the original, and boldface when it is my addition. References to the works referred to most often make use of abbreviations, the list of which is provided on a separate page.

G. M.
Oxford, December 1998

Part I

Russell

Chapter 1

Russell's first theory of denoting

The present chapter introduces Russell's first theory of denoting, namely the one he put forth in *The Principles of Mathematics* and endorsed up until the time he struck upon the theory of descriptions in 1905. Two intermingled tasks are involved: one is to explain the distinctive features of the theory itself – primarily to facilitate the discussion in the following chapter. This will be done just about in full. The other is to introduce the broader theoretical setting in which Russell's discussion of denoting is couched. Here I will merely point out some of the most salient features, without attempting to answer all the questions it gives rise to. Some of them will be touched upon at various points in the following chapters, but their more direct discussion will have to wait until Part III, after the discussion of Frege.

1 The elements

Russell's first theory of denoting can be wrapped into a single sentence: 'a concept denotes when, if it occurs in a proposition, the proposition is not *about* the concept, but about a term connected in a certain peculiar way with the concept' (PoM: § 56). But unless we know what precisely is meant by 'proposition', 'term', 'denote' and 'about' such a statement is hardly illuminating and part of our task, therefore, is to clarify these notions.

To begin with propositions, it is crucial to bear in mind that they are not, nor are they abstracted from, symbolic or linguistic or psychological entities (PoM: § 51). On the contrary, they are conceived of as fundamentally independent of both language and mind. Propositions are first and foremost the entities which enter into logical relations of implication, and hence also the primary bearers of truth. Their other role is to be the objects certain relations to which constitute belief and knowledge.

But even when the non-linguistic conception of propositions is acknowledged at the outset, it is in constant danger of being obscured when following particular discussions. Not only do 'truth' and 'implication' apply, in their primary senses, to propositions and only derivatively to the sentences expressing them, but there is a host of related notions – 'term' (meaning 'entity'),[1] 'verb', 'adjective', 'subject', 'concept', 'substitution', 'description' and 'occurrence' – which one is inclined to regard as relating to linguistic entities, but which Russell uses in a non-linguistic sense. On this view the application of these notions to linguistic items reflects their propositional sense rather than the other way around. The matter is both delicate and fundamental: propositions are specified primarily by appeal to sentences expressing them, and though in PoM Russell often seems to be flipping between a linguistic and a non-linguistic mode of speech, he never goes back on the fundamental point that the inquiry is concerned with propositions and their constituents, not with sentences or anything linguistic. It is crucial to bear this in mind despite the discussion often *appearing* to be linguistic.

I come now to the problem which gave rise to the notion of denoting as it is presented in Chapter 5 of PoM. So long as we confine our attention to the propositions expressed by sentences which do *not* contain denoting phrases (i.e. phrases composed of 'the', 'a', 'some', 'any', 'all' or 'every', followed by a word for a class concept), the account of what it is for a proposition to be *about* an entity is straightforward enough. 'Socrates preceded Plato', for example, is the verbal expression of a proposition which has Socrates and Plato (the men), and *preceding* (the relation) as constituents;[2] and the entities such propositions are about will always be among their constituents – more specifically, those entities occupying a subject position or positions (as there may be more than one). But the case is different with the proposition expressed by, e.g. 'I met a man'. When that proposition is true, then there is a particular man I met – let it be Jones. But what is affirmed in 'I met a man' is not the same as what is affirmed in 'I met Jones'. From this it seems to follow that the two sentences express different propositions. But while we have a reasonably clear notion of the proposition expressed by 'I met Jones', it is not at all clear what the *proposition* expressed by 'I met a man' is. It would seem that Jones himself does not occur in it – at least not in the same manner as in 'I met Jones' – but what, then, occurs in his place?

The answer to this would also have to explain the familiar phenomenon whereby any given name has a privileged set of associated denoting phrases (of the 'the . . .' kind) which may be substituted for it without affecting the sentence's truth value (and similarly for the other types of denoting phrases, e.g. 'a man' and 'a featherless biped'). Obviously enough, these are just those

---

1 'Whatever may be an object of thought, or may occur in any true or false proposition, or can be counted as *one*, I call a *term*' (PoM: § 47). This notion ought not to be confused with 'term-of-a-proposition' (indicating an entity's position in a proposition), which is explained below. The non-linguistic employment of some of the notions listed above is illustrated throughout Chapter 4 of PoM.

2 Ultimately we might wish to withdraw the claim that persons are terms in Russell's sense (see PoM: § 47; this will be discussed explicitly in Chapter 7, section II); but this consideration may be ignored at present.

phrases for which an identity sentence of the form '[proper name] = [denoting phrase]' is true; but this can hardly be an answer, since these sentences are merely a special case of the problem. Linguistic evidence suggests that *something* is substituted for Jones – just as Smith might be said to have been substituted for Jones (the man) to obtain the proposition expressed by 'I met Smith'. But it is not at all clear, at least in the first instance, what this something is.

It is worth noting the dichotomy underlying this manner of posing the problem: if the difference between two sentences is logically significant, then they express distinct propositions. If, on the other hand, we do not think that the propositions expressed are distinct, then the difference between the sentences is dismissed as merely linguistic or psychological.

Russell's solution to this problem in PoM invokes the allied notions of a denoting concept and the relation of denoting. A denoting concept is the special kind of propositional constituent which occurs in a proposition whose expression involves a denoting phrase; the relation this concept has to the entity the proposition is about (i.e. the denotation) is the logically primitive relation of denoting.

A great deal of attention and space in the chapter on denoting in PoM are devoted to the attempt to characterize the different kinds of *objects denoted* (called 'combinations') by the different kinds of denoting concepts.[3] But this problem can here be set aside, because it can be detached from our chief concern, namely the problems which give rise to the relation of denoting. The different kinds of combination need to be distinguished even when we confine our attention to finite domains – where the relation of denoting is in principle dispensable (PoM: § 61); while the relation of denoting is called for even when (as with 'the'-phrases in the singular) the denotation is a single entity, and hence there is no question of combinations. I mention the issue of combinations only to set it aside, and in what follows attention will be focused on 'the'-phrases in the singular.

II The mathematical context

From what has been said so far it remains unexplained why the discussion of denoting should occur in a work on the philosophy of mathematics, to

---

3 For example: assuming that the extension of 'man' consists of only Smith and Jones, then 'all men' denotes the combination {Smith *and* Jones} (which Russell calls a 'numerical conjunction'); while 'a man' denotes the combination {Smith *or* Jones} (called a 'variable disjunction'). In PoM §§ 59–60 Russell devised some very subtle distinctions in this regard, which we need not enter into here. Part of the point of these distinctions is to establish that each kind of denoting concept has a distinct kind of denoted object, which entitles us, in turn, to the assumption that denoting is a *single* relation in all cases (cf. the opening remark of § 59), which is particularly significant in view of denoting's status as a primitive notion.

which the relevance of establishing the correct account of 'I met a man' is hardly obvious. The answer provides us with a first glimpse of the broader theoretical context of Russell's discussion. To begin with, we may give a rather short answer, namely that Russell's logicist account of mathematics led him to recognize denoting as an indefinable logical relation, a logical constant, and Part I of PoM deals with the fundamental concepts of mathematics (i.e. logic); concepts which, on this account, are indefinable. This reply, though true as far as it goes, only raises further questions: is 'logical constant' being used in the modern sense and, if so, what led Russell to give denoting this status?

We might begin by removing one possible source of perplexity. The absence of any primitive *symbol* for a relation of denoting in the logical calculus is *not*, on Russell's view, in any tension with recognizing it as a logical constant. For reasons shortly to be explained, Russell viewed the division between logical notions which do occur in the calculus (and hence the symbolism) and others which do not occur as a matter of mere convenience, bearing no theoretical significance.[4] This in turn enabled him to regard a notion as indefinable for the purpose of the technical development of the calculus, and then to proceed to its *logical* analysis without appeal to the symbolism. The notion of formal implication, i.e. of propositions of the form $\forall x\ (Fx \rightarrow Gx)$, is regarded as indefinable for technical purposes, but it then gives rise to a number of indefinables in the course of its analysis (PoM: §§ 12 and 17, and Chapter 8, especially § 93), among which is denoting.

Though the fact that Russell recognized denoting as a logical constant is beyond dispute (see PoM: §§ 31, 56, 93 and 106),[5] his rationale for so doing is not immediately clear. Making it clear brings us back to the consideration of the foundations of mathematics. Despite the fact that the examples discussed in the chapter on denoting suggest a linguistic setting, the broader context in which the whole discussion occurs, i.e. its placement immediately before the chapter on classes, as well as remarks on denoting elsewhere in PoM, make it plain that the chief consideration for recognizing denoting as a logical constant is its role in relation to infinite classes.

---

4 However, readers who believe the occurrence of a symbol in a formula is absolutely essential can find a 'den' relation and a 'Dn' function occurring in formulae in Russell's 1903 'Dependent Variables and Denotation' (CPR Volume 4, pp. 299 and 301 ff.), as well as occurrences of 'denotes' in formulae in OF (which we will come to in the final section of the following chapter).

5 Strictly speaking, a logical constant can be definable (PoM: § 12), but for present purposes the term is used interchangeably with 'indefinable' (Russell uses 'fundamental idea'). What is important here is not so much the indefinability of denoting as its being a logical relation – a matter that will be elaborated upon below. Its status as a logical constant also throws light on Russell's preoccupation (see the beginning of § 62, and again in § 65) with whether a *single* relation of denoting will suffice.

With regard to infinite classes, say the class of numbers, it is to be observed that the concept *all numbers*, though not itself infinitely complex, yet denotes an infinitely complex object. This is the inmost secret of our power to deal with infinity. An infinitely complex concept, though there may be such, can certainly not be manipulated by the human intelligence; but infinite collections, owing to the notion of denoting, can be manipulated without introducing any concept of infinite complexity.

(PoM: § 72)[6]

Because infinite classes cannot be specified by mentioning each of their members singly, a purely extensional view of classes, Russell reasons, becomes untenable, and we must assume that in dealing with classes it is class concepts rather than the classes themselves that we deal with directly – though the view as to the *identity* of classes remains purely extensional (PoM: §§ 71–2). Denoting is the relation which obtains between the class concept and the class itself,[7] and is essentially the same as the 'determining' involved in saying that a concept *determines* a class.

Another consideration requiring the relation of denoting derives from the need to recognize the null class. After repeating the above consideration from infinite classes Russell continues, 'The consideration of classes which results from denoting concepts is more general than the extensional consideration . . . it introduces the null concept of a class' (PoM: § 72). This is because 'what is merely and solely a collection of terms cannot subsist when all the terms are removed' (§ 73).

From what has been said so far Russell's motivation for devising the theory of denoting may appear to stem from two quite different sources: the discussion in Chapter 5 of PoM seems to be concerned primarily with locutions from natural language, while the whole context in which it occurs, as well as references to it elsewhere in the *Principles*, points to a consideration of mathematics and infinite classes. How are these two sources to be reconciled? The answer points us to one of the most fundamental and to my mind most interesting features of Russell's outlook, but since its discussion belongs more properly to Chapter 7, I confine myself here to a provisional statement.

From Russell's perspective there is no need to reconcile the two sources, because there is no tension between them in the first place. The key to this

---

6 Other statements to the same effect occur, first, when explaining why a purely extensional view of classes is untenable, and thus that 'the point of view of intension is essential', Russell adds, 'It is owing to this consideration that the theory of denoting is of such great importance' (PoM: § 66); and earlier, in the chapter on denoting, where he writes, 'the possibility of giving a collection by a class-concept is highly important, since it enables us to deal with infinite collections' (§ 60).

7 More precisely we might use 'concept-of-a-class' (as opposed to 'class concept'), appealing to Russell's distinction in PoM § 67.

unitary view is the notion of proposition. The underlying assumption is that *both* in mathematics and in natural language we express propositions, and that it is of no theoretical significance what we choose to express in natural language and what in a symbolic language. It is therefore immaterial, when addressing the question of propositions expressed by means of denoting concepts (or, more to the point, propositions which cannot contain what they are about), whether the proposition is mathematical or not. The discussion of denoting is thus pitched at a level of generality which transcends the distinction between the philosophy of mathematics and the philosophy of language.

Having set out the bare essentials of Russell's first theory it remains for us, first, to note two applications that Russell found for it; second, to highlight three of its most essential features; and third, to note some developments the theory had undergone between PoM and OD.

III Denoting, definition and identity

Although there can be little doubt that denoting concepts were introduced by Russell first and foremost to handle the problem of how we can deal with infinite totalities (we may label this the 'primary case' in that respect), once the device had been made available Russell found it useful in solving two further and closely related puzzles for the sake of which alone he would probably not have introduced denoting concepts (we may thus regard them as 'secondary cases'). The same pair was revisited in OD – though there with a different solution. The first, which concerns definitions, can hardly be better introduced than by citing Russell's own words:

> It is a curious paradox, puzzling to the symbolic mind, that definitions, theoretically, are nothing but symbolic abbreviations, irrelevant to the reasoning and inserted only for practical convenience, while yet, in the development of a subject, they always require a very large amount of thought, and often embody some of the greatest achievements of analysis. This fact seems to be explained by the theory of denoting. An object may be present to the mind, without us knowing any concept of which the said object is *the* instance; and the discovery of such a concept is not a mere improvement in notation. The reason why this appears to be the case is that, as soon as the definition is found, it becomes wholly unnecessary to the reasoning to remember the actual object defined, since only concepts are relevant to our deductions. In the moment of discovery, the definition is seen to be *true*, because the object to be defined was already in our thoughts; but as a part of our reasoning it is not true, but merely symbolic, since what the reasoning requires is not that it should deal with *that* object, but merely that it should deal with the object denoted by the definition.
>
> (PoM: § 63)

We might, to take a familiar example, initially regard the equivalence of ∃x (Fx) (or 'something F') and ~∀x (~Fx) (or 'it is not the case that everything doesn't F') as a discovery. But when we adopt the latter as a *definition* of the former, then this equivalence may be said to have become merely symbolic. The appeal to denoting concepts seems here to offer a plausible account of a puzzling phenomenon associated with definition. It reconciles the role of definitions in the finished theory as essentially notational abbreviations, with their appearing, from an epistemic point of view, as significant discoveries.

The other case is essentially the same as the familiar puzzle from OD about George IV's wanting to know whether the author of *Waverley* was Scott while not wanting to know whether Scott was Scott. Russell asks, 'Why is it ever worth while to affirm identity?' (which might just as well be put, how can a true identity-statement fail to be tautological?), and he goes on to answer,

> This question is answered by the theory of denoting. If we say 'Edward VII is the King,' we assert an identity; the reason why this assertion is worth making is, that in the one case the actual term occurs, while in the other a denoting concept takes its place . . . When a term is given, the assertion of its identity with itself, though true, is perfectly futile, and is never made outside the logic-books; but where denoting concepts are introduced, identity is at once seen to be significant.
>
> (PoM: § 64)

In both these passages one discerns – despite the changing terminology – the underlying contrast between what will later come to be known as 'acquaintance' and 'knowledge by description' – the latter being correlative to denoting concepts. This brings the epistemic role of denoting to the fore. The problem facing both these secondary cases and the primary case may now be put thus: how can a proposition be *about* an entity which is not among its constituents? Denoting concepts are the device which makes this possible.

It is a curious fact that both the secondary cases deal exclusively with 'the'-phrases in the singular, which, since they involve neither classes nor combinations, were clearly the odd ones out in Russell's discussion of denoting in PoM. It is by no means obvious that 'the'-phrases belong with the other kinds of denoting phrases (rather than, say, with proper names). Yet Russell's grouping is laid down with no special justification. This classification, as will be seen in Chapter 7, is arguably the most pregnant feature of Russell's discussion of denoting in PoM.

IV Three essential elements

Before we turn to the post-PoM developments of this theory, it may be useful to take stock of, and underline, its most essential features. The first of these is the property of denoting concepts of making the propositions in which they occur be *about* an entity other than themselves. I shall be referring to this as 'aboutness-shifting'. This feature of denoting concepts is *sui generis* and is the key to their theoretical utility.

The second feature I wish to underline relates to the fact, noted earlier, that a whole range of *different* denoting phrases can replace a name without altering what the propositions expressed is about. Different denoting concepts may therefore have the very same denotation; in other words the relation of denoting is many–one. (This is not peculiar to 'the'-phrases, but in the other kinds of phrases the denotation will be a combination.) Now although introducing aboutness-shifters which relate one to one with their denotations would not be incoherent, it would undermine their utility in accounting for the phenomena in question.

The third feature, the logical nature of the relation of denoting, calls for special elaboration because it is particularly prone to misunderstanding. Russell took care to point this out no later than the second sentence of the chapter on denoting in PoM:

> There is a sense in which *we* denote, when we point or describe, or employ words as symbols for concepts; this, however, is not the sense that I wish to discuss. But the fact that description is possible – that we are able, by the employment of concepts, to designate a thing which is not a concept – is due to a logical relation between some concepts and some terms, in virtue of which such concepts inherently and logically *denote* such terms. It is this sense of denoting that is here in question.
>
> (PoM: § 56)

The contrast between the logical and the linguistic sense of 'denote' is brought out even more clearly in the intermediate 'On Meaning and Denotation', where 'meaning' (of a denoting phrase) replaces 'denoting concept' in the PoM nomenclature:[8]

> There are phrases which have to do with denotation only, others which have to do with meaning only, and yet others which have to do with both. The phrases which have to do with both have a different relation to the two: the denotation is what they designate . . . and the meaning may be said to be what they *express*. **But both designating and expressing have to do with language: the logically important matter is the relation**

---

8 This interchangeability – to which 'denoting complex' will be added as a third element – will be discussed only in the next chapter, and must be taken on faith for the time being; but its source can be traced back to PoM (§ 51 and, though not as immediately apparent, §§ 65 and 476). Russell's use of 'phrase' and 'name' does not here discriminate between proper names and denoting phrases (and accordingly between the verbs 'name' and 'designate').

between what is expressed and what is designated. For when one name both designates and expresses, this is not arbitrary, but is due to a relation between the objects designated and expressed. This relation is what I shall call *denoting*. Thus it is the meaning, not the name, which denotes the denotation; and denoting is a fact that concerns logic, not the theory of language or naming.

(OMD: pp. 317–18)

One reason why it is particularly important to have this distinction clearly in mind is that it recurs, though in a more concise form, as a preamble to an argument concerning this theory in OD (to be discussed in the next chapter), to wit: 'The relation of meaning and denotation is not merely linguistic through the phrase: there must be a logical relation involved, which we express by saying that the meaning denotes the denotation' (Marsh: p. 49).

If the relation between the meaning and the denotation was 'merely linguistic through the phrase', then it would consist in nothing more than the meaning's being expressed by the same phrase as that which denotes the denotation; there would be no *intrinsic* and direct relation between the two. The relation would then go via the phrase, and the duality of meaning and denotation would resemble cases of plain lexical ambiguity – like the unrelated senses of 'bank'.

What saying 'the meaning denotes the denotation' means, by contrast, is that when the meaning is given, the denotation is thereby determined, i.e. *logically* determined.[9] This makes the phrase's relation to its denotation, i.e. the sense in which a phrase may be said to 'denote', derivative: its relation to the denotation goes via the meaning.

The need to emphasize this point derives from an acute awareness of the crucial difference between logical and linguistic considerations. In this particular case the difference is between, on the one hand, relations, such as are supposed to hold between words and what they stand for – which, if they are not *purely* conventional as in the case of simple names, at least depend in part upon convention – and, on the other hand, *logical* relations, which are supposed to hold independently of any contingent matter of fact. The relation of denoting, it must be borne in mind, is operative in mathematical contexts as well, and it cannot therefore be allowed to depend on 'the way the world is'. It remains to discuss the theory's development after PoM. I pick the one particular feature which is crucial for understanding Russell's argument in OD.

---

9 The relation of a concept to its extension, or of a function, given an argument, to its value, illustrate this kind of determining. The crucial point here is to *exclude* the involvement of any linguistic or conventional element.

V Post-PoM developments

In PoM, denoting concepts were surmised to be simple[10] (though nothing was made to depend on this). But starting in the intermediate papers, probably as a result of considering denoting phrases of greater complexity than those considered in PoM, Russell came to notice that denoting phrases could be nested within each other (e.g. 'the Solar System' in 'the centre of mass of the Solar System'), and came to regard their meanings (i.e. denoting concepts), like propositions, as complexes whose constituents are the entities indicated by the words comprising the phrase. This conception is clearly expressed in the following passage from OMD regarding the phrase 'the present Prime Minister of England' ('designate' is here deliberately neutral between the name–bearer relation and the phrase–denotation relation), which is also a crystal-lized expression of the rationale for this conception of denoting complexes:

> The fact from which our discussion starts is embodied in this, that the whole phrase designates something of which the designations of the parts are not parts. There is *some* object involved, of which England, etc., are parts; but this object is not the designation of the phrase, since England is not part of Mr. Arthur Balfour. Thus we were led to assume an object, called the *meaning* of the phrase, or that which the phrase expresses, of which England, etc., were parts.
>
> (OMD: p. 320)

This line of reasoning rests on two assumption to which it is worth drawing attention. First, it is assumed that each of the individual words the phrase is made of (other than 'the', 'a', 'of' and their like) has a role. This assumption may not be absolutely necessary, but if it is not made we would be dealing with an unstructured expression, not with what gives rise to the logical prob-lem of denoting phrases. (We need not deny that in some cases such an account is indeed apt, but then these are not the cases we are concerned with.) Second, it is assumed that the component words have the same role as when they occur in other contexts. Here, too, other views are possible, but short of allow-ing the choice of words comprising the phrase to be arbitrary, one would

---

10 In PoM § 72 Russell writes, 'It would seem, then, that 'all *u*'s' is not validly analysable into *all* and *u*, and that language, in this case as in some others, is a misleading guide. The same remark will apply to *every, any, some, a,* and *the*'. Perhaps even more decisive is the *absence* of denoting concepts from the discussion of whole and part (PoM: Chapter 16). On the view Russell takes of denoting complexes in OF, he would not have said (as he does in PoM § 135) that the kind of wholes he calls 'unities' are *always* propositions, because in OF he treats denoting complexes as unities as well. Since it is barely credible that even in PoM he should have maintained that a denoting concept derived from a complex concept could be simple, it is plausible to suppose that Russell, rather than having changed his mind, simply shifted his interest from simple denoting concepts to complex ones.

need to systematically relate any other role they might have to the usual one. Clearly, our understanding of the whole phrase – as with a complete sentence – depends as a rule on our understanding of the constituent words.

This more elaborate conception of denoting concepts led Russell to investigate the rules governing substitutions of their constituents along lines familiar from the case of propositions, and thus to recognize their functional character. This endeavour led him to devise a very intricate system of distinctions between types of occurrences within a complex, covering both propositional and denoting complexes. The most fundamental distinction was between an occurrence 'as meaning' and 'as entity', which was already implicit in PoM. It is in this context too that these meanings came to be called 'denoting *complexes*' (though 'meaning' was never dropped altogether) – a label which underlines both their affinity with and distinctness from *non-denoting* complexes, i.e. propositions.[11] Indeed, much of the discussion in 'On Fundamentals' treats denoting complexes and propositional complexes as two species of a single logical genus. This richer conception of denoting concepts, as will be seen in section V of the following chapter, is important for understanding a particularly obscure statement in the obscure passage from OD.

To sum up, we noted in this chapter the theoretical setting which called for the notion of denoting. We found that it was deeply rooted in the needs of the logicist programme and in Russell's account of classes in particular, but that its scope was not therefore confined to mathematical propositions. Once denoting concepts were available, they provided (thanks to the inclusion of 'the'-phrases), solutions to two further puzzles. Three essential features of the theory were pointed out: the 'aboutness-shifting' nature of denoting concepts; the fact that the relation of denoting is many–one; and the logical nature of this relation. Lastly, we noted that after PoM denoting concepts came to be regarded as complexes – thus resembling propositions in some important respects.

On the first page of the chapter on denoting in PoM, when explaining the need to distinguish the denoting concept from its denotation, Russell wrote, 'Of the *concept* "any number," almost all the propositions that contain the *phrase* "any number" are false. **If we wish to speak of the concept, we have to indicate the fact by italics or inverted commas**' (PoM: § 56).

This indeed was Russell's practice (with regard both to concepts *simpliciter*, and denoting concepts) in PoM. But three years later he would have reason to reflect upon this comment as unduly naive, and inattentive to a problem which, as we shall see, led to the theory's collapse.

11 Although the affinity between both kinds of complexes came to the fore only after PoM, it was already implicit in the PoM terminology where 'propositional concepts' is used for *un*asserted propositions (see §§ 55, 60, 478, 498). Thus besides concepts *simpliciter*, we have denoting concepts and propositional concepts.

Chapter 2

The collapse of the first theory and the discovery of the theory of descriptions

I Introduction: the obscure passage in 'On Denoting'

Given that, as explained in the preceding chapter, denoting complexes are aboutness-shifters, how can there possibly be a proposition *about* a denoting complex? When trying to spell out the answer to this question Russell noticed that this involved what in OD he describes as 'certain rather curious difficulties, which seem in themselves sufficient to prove that the theory which leads to such difficulties must be wrong' (Marsh: p. 48). The exposition of these difficulties – which amount to a decisive argument against the theory expounded in the last chapter – occupies a notoriously obscure passage in OD (pp. 48–50; often dubbed the 'Gray's *Elegy*' passage). Deciphering this passage and exploring its argument form the chief objectives of the present chapter, and they will occupy us in all but its final section. Making sense of this passage may also be desired on more purely textual grounds: it occurs at the heart of one of the most influential and thoroughly studied essays of the analytic tradition, and so long as we have no satisfactory account of its content and role in the broader scheme of OD, our grip on that essay's argument as a whole remains precarious.

Before examining how the question of propositions about denoting concepts might be answered, we may first ask what exactly hinges on it: what would follow if the theory failed to provide for this possibility? At first blush such a failure seems awkward indeed: since propositions are what we think or say, failure to provide an adequate answer would mean that the theory has posited a kind of entity which, by the theory's own strictures, cannot *in principle* be either thought or spoken of. Further scrutiny, however, reveals the difficulty to be even more radical.

When one's conception of truth is as some kind of correspondence, the idea of a state of affairs (or whatever truth-bearers correspond to) which defies representation, or is epistemically inaccessible, is difficult but not quite incoherent. But on a view such as Russell's, where the truth of a proposition is *not* a matter of correspondence to anything outside it, to concede the impossibility of propositions about some class of entities means there cannot even *be* anything true (or false) about them either.[1]

To put it another way, if two denoting complexes are distinct, then there must be a true proposition to that effect. But a proposition in which those two complexes occur as constituents is one whose truth depends upon the distinctness *of their denotations*, which is quite a different matter. So unless propositions about such complexes are possible, the very contention that they are distinct becomes incoherent. Surely, to posit a kind of entity of which nothing *is* true must be incoherent. This is no side issue for which it would merely be nice to have an answer, but one which could bring down the whole theory.

At first it may seem as if the problem concerns the possibility of *speaking* about denoting complexes (that is to say, with the possibility of something linguistic, a representation), but when all is considered it transpires that this is only a derivative form of the problem. The essential point concerns *propositions* about denoting complexes – a matter which does not essentially involve language. To see this difference more clearly, imagine we possess a name for a denoting complex. Now a sentence in which this name occurs will express – as is always the case with names – a proposition in which the name's bearer occurs. But such a proposition will not be about the complex, but rather about its denotation, so whether complexes can be named is, upon reflection, irrelevant to the problem at stake. Having made these preliminary remarks, we can now turn to Russell's text.

To explain the course of our discussion in the present chapter an outline of the text's geography – provided in full in Appendix A – is called for. Using '(A)' to '(H)' to indicate the eight paragraphs composing the passage, the present reading distinguishes two rounds of argument. The first (occupying (D)) which I call 'symbolic', presents a difficulty facing attempts to introduce a symbol for speaking about meanings. The second, which by contrast I call 'substantial', begins in paragraph (F) and approaches the difficulty directly in terms of the entities which the symbolism is designed to represent. The transition between the two rounds takes place in (E). Paragraphs (A) to (C) I regard as a header: they provide the initial setting and sum up the problem at large. The two rounds are not independent arguments: they both aim at what is at bottom one and the same problem. But while the symbolic round only demonstrated that *something* is amiss with the theory, the substantial round attempts to unravel the source of this fault.

Driving straight to the core difficulty, I discuss the substantial round first (section II), then the symbolic round (section III), and only after returning to

---

1 For Russell's (chiefly negative) conception of truth at that time see PoM §§ 38, 52, 479; 'Meinong's Theory of Complexes and Assumptions', pp. 75–6; and the 1905 paper 'The Nature of Truth', in CPR Volume 4, pp. 492–506, which ought not to be confused with a paper from 1910 with a similar title.

the substantial round (in section IV) do I come to the transition (section V). Discussion of the header is dispersed. The core difficulty is explored initially in section II, but then returned to for further consideration after the exposition of the symbolic round in section IV. The final section (VI) employs the proposed interpretation of the passage to shed light on the few lines of manuscript (only recently published) which record Russell's discovery of the theory of descriptions. The acclaimed solution emerges as a direct consequence of Russell's attempts to circumvent the difficulty exposed in the obscure passage.

Although my dissatisfaction with other readings of the passage was a chief reason for beginning to study it, I thought it best to leave these to one side when presenting my own reading. My discussion of some of these other reading will be found in Appendix C.[2]

II The argument: the 'substantial' round

Returning now to the problem of propositions about denoting complexes, it is important for an understanding of Russell's argument that we focus on one *particular* instance, though it does not matter which. Let us take Russell's first pair of examples (to avoid confusion with use and mention I replace Russell's inverted commas with '<' and '>'):

(1) The centre of mass of the Solar System is a point, not a denoting complex.
(2) <The centre of mass of the Solar System> is a denoting complex, not a point.

Let us use 'C1' to indicate the entity occurring in subject position in the proposition expressed by (1), and 'C2' for the entity (whatever it may be) in subject position in the proposition expressed by (2) (as noted earlier, talk of 'subject position' carries no implication of a language-dependent entity).[3] C1, on the theory in question, is a meaning or denoting complex which denotes a particular point and whose constituents are indicated by the individual words of the corresponding phrase. (2), it is assumed, expresses a proposition *about* C1, but what precisely occurs in its subject position? What *is* C2?

Russell begins his principal argument by establishing two negative results concerning C2. First, that it must be a different entity from C1; and second, that C1 cannot be one of its constituents. The difficulty with these restric-

2 The appendix contains some brief comments on three earlier accounts (by Searle, Blackburn and Code, and Hylton), and a more detailed discussion of three more recent ones (by Kremer, Pakaluk and Noonan). It does not presuppose familiarity with subsequent chapters, and may be read immediately after the present chapter.
3 Ultimately it is precisely our entitlement to expressions such as 'C1' and 'C2' that is challenged, but some provisional device for speaking about a *propositional constituent* (as opposed to phrases and names) is indispensable for expository purposes.

tions is not so much to recognize their truth, as to understand why Russell feels the need to establish them with such care. These matters will be discussed presently (subsections (i) and (ii) below). He then goes on to argue that on account of these restrictions the theory ends up with no adequate explanation of what C2 is, which in turn undermines it altogether (this will be taken up in subsections (iii) and (iv)).

(i) C2 is a different entity from C1

That C1 and C2 are distinct entities might be thought not to require any argument, does it not follow from the fact that (1) and (2) express propositions about different entities? The answer is 'no', and the reason why becomes clear by contrasting our case with that of concepts *simpliciter*. Regarding the pair 'Socrates is human' and 'humanity characterizes Socrates', we might dismiss the *difference* between these sentences as merely linguistic or psychological – which is tantamount to saying that they express one and the same proposition. Alternatively, we might dismiss their *relatedness* – which is tantamount to denying any intrinsic relation between the propositions they express. The difficulty begins when, wishing to avoid both of these conclusions, we consider the linguistic difference as reflecting a *logical* difference such that the two sentences express distinct, yet logically related, propositions. (The question concerns, of course, the propositional reality underlying 'human' and 'humanity'; the occurrence of Socrates in both propositions is assumed to be unproblematic.)

We can either maintain, at this point, that one and the same entity occurs in both propositions – which puts the onus on explaining the *difference* between them; or we can argue that two distinct entities are involved – in which case the onus falls on explaining the (logical) *connection* between them.

Russell's position on concepts in PoM exemplifies the first of these courses. While holding that the propositions expressed by 'Socrates is human' and 'humanity characterizes Socrates' contain one and the same concept, he insists that only the second is *about* that concept (and hence expresses a distinct proposition). The difference is accounted for by invoking the notion of a *type of occurrence* of a constituent in a proposition. The same concept, namely 'human', may occur either 'as term', as in the latter proposition, or not, as in the former (by the time of OD the terminology had changed to occurrences 'as entity' or 'as being' as opposed to 'as meaning'). So despite different types of occurrence, the identity of the constituent remains intact.[4]

---

4 See PoM §§ 49 and 52 for verbs. In those discussions the only distinction is between occurrence as (logical) subject and as predicate or verb. Despite further and more finely grained distinctions (as well as the *phrase* 'mode of occurrence') being introduced after PoM, the opposition between an occurrence 'as entity' (or 'as being') and occurrence 'as meaning' remained the most fundamental.

This makes concepts (as opposed to 'things') 'twofold' in Russell's phrase – a locution which will resurface later in our discussion. A term is 'twofold' if it can have both kinds of occurrences.

Whatever its merits or demerits on other counts, this gives at least a prima facie account both of the relatedness and of the difference between the two propositions. Before discovering the problem we are concerned with, Russell seems to have tacitly assumed that the same would apply to denoting concepts, and that in the proposition about it, a denoting concept would have a different kind of occurrence than it has in a proposition about its denotation. Indeed, in PoM he employs the same notational devices, italicization and inverted commas, for speaking about both denoting and non-denoting concepts (see § 67 ff.).

But can such a line apply in our case? Could C2 be explained as a different kind of occurrence of C1? It would seem not: since the fact that C1 is its denotation is the *only* thing assumed regarding C2, conceding its identity with C1 would entail that C1 and *its* denotation were also one and the same, and hence to a general collapse of meanings and denotations. We cannot have all of

- C2 denotes C1,
- C2 is identical with C1 (and hence C1 denotes C1),
- C1 denotes (e.g.) a point and
- C1 is not a point.

So if (1) and (2) are *about* distinct entities, what occurs in their respective subject positions must *be* distinct entities. Moreover, by contrasting '. . . is a point' and '. . . is not a point', Russell's example serves to show that there is absolutely no case for thinking of the respective subjects of (1) and (2), whatever they may be, as having different types of occurrence. These considerations underlie Russell's move in paragraph (*F*) of the obscure passage culminating in 'what we use when we want to speak about the meaning must be not the meaning, but something which denotes the meaning'.

Our problem, then, is how to account not for the difference between C1 and C2, but rather for their relatedness. In the header to our passage it is put thus: 'we cannot succeed in *both* preserving the connexion of meaning and denotation *and* preventing them from being one and the same'. Having seen how preserving the connection leads to their being one and the same, we turn next to observe how recognizing their distinctness leads to severing the connection between them altogether.

(ii) C1 cannot be a constituent of C2

Consider the denoting complex <the Prime Minister>. When it occurs as a constituent of another denoting complex, e.g. <the father of the Prime

Minister>, only its *denotation* is relevant to determining the denotation of the whole. This is evidenced by the fact that the denotation of the entire complex remains unchanged when a constituent complex is replaced with another with the same denotation. The denotation of a denoting complex is thus a function only of the *denotations* of denoting complexes occurring in it (if any) – the meaning is irrelevant.

An important consequence of this is that C2 *cannot* contain C1 as a constituent. If it did that would make its denotation a function of the denotation of C1. But since C2's denotation is supposed to *be* C1 itself, it would follow that C1 is a function of its own denotation (i.e. a certain point). But this can be ruled out a priori because we know that the relation of meaning to denotation (i.e. denoting) is many–one, and hence that there cannot possibly be such a function, or to use Russell's phrase, there is no 'backward road' from denotations to meanings.[5]

The move just recounted occupies the latter part of paragraph (*F*), where it is said, 'if *C* occurs in the complex, it will be its denotation, not its meaning, that will occur'. In other words, if C1 is to occur as a constituent of C2 then (as is generally the case when one denoting complex is embedded in another) only its *denotation* will be relevant to determining the denotation of C2, but in that case the remainder of C2 would be a function from denotation to meaning. Since no such function is possible, C1 cannot be a constituent of C2. Ruling out this possibility is particularly important in view of its being precisely what the notation adopted at the outset leads one to expect. Unless we can come up with some alternative proposal for what C2 might be, our grip on it is in serious doubt.[6] I discuss this further below.

To sum up, in (1), where C1 is in subject position, or has an entity-occurrence, we get a proposition about its denotation, while in (2), which contains a *different* complex, we have a proposition about *that complex's* denotation. I will speak of a complex like C2, i.e. one whose denotation is a denoting complex, as a 'second-level' complex (the denoted complex must *not* denote yet another denoting complex).

---

5 This tenet has been regarded as the principal claim of the whole passage (S. Blackburn and A. Code, 'The power of Russell's criticism of Frege: "On Denoting"' pp. 48–50', *Analysis* 38 (1978) pp. 73–4; IFP, p. 87); but its role in the argument, though crucial, is only to support the claim that C1 cannot be a constituent of C2.

6 Russell's talk of the denotation (of the embedded complex) actually *occurring* cannot be interpreted literally without going against both everything else he had said about the subject up until then, and the evidence of the passage from which our text derives (OF: § 36). It is far more plausible to suppose this is a slip, particularly understandable in view of the terminology he uses in the preceding sections of OF. *C* (our C1) is said there to occur 'as entity' (i.e. not 'as meaning') and, at any rate, what the remark leads up to, namely 'there is no backward road from denotations to meanings', makes Russell's intention plain.

(iii) 'But this cannot be an explanation', I

The theory appears then to tell us *no more* about C2 than this: that it is a complex distinct from C1 which does not contain C1, but which denotes it (this is stated at the opening of (*G*)). What comes under attack is not the *truth* of this result, as far as it goes, but rather its blatant inadequacy as an explanation. But it is far from clear, at least at first blush, what kind of explanation *is* being called for, and why its absence is regarded by Russell as undermining the whole theory. Answering this question is not a matter of interpreting any single passage of the text, but calls for broader reflection on the standards of explanation Russell's argument invokes. This will be given in two instalments: the first follows immediately, the other after the discussion of the symbolic round in section IV.

Before going any further we might wish to lay aside three charges which could be mistaken for the one Russell is making. First, the argument's aim is *not* to establish that propositions about denoting complexes are impossible, but rather to expose a fundamental flaw in the theory which appears when its account of such propositions is scrutinized. Second, Russell is *not* challenging the legitimacy of second-level meanings as such, nor does he find fault in the implied (harmless) infinite hierarchy of higher-level meanings to which they open the way.[7] Third, it is *not* being argued that some principled obstacle bars us from finding second-level complexes to match a given first-level complex presented to us: one of Russell's examples in the obscure passage ('the denoting complex occurring in the second of the above instances', in (*D*)) ought to dispel suspicion that the difficulty might be to provide such an instance in an ad hoc manner. What, then, *is* wrong with the above account of C2?

Russell's complaint is expressed initially in two brief remarks. The first points out that the said account of C2 leaves its relation to C1 'wholly mysterious'. The second asks, 'where are we to find the denoting complex "*C*" [i.e. <*C*>] which is to denote *C*?' Whether or not the latter was intended as a distinctly epistemic (rather than metaphysical) point, we might begin with the epistemic difficulty because it serves as a useful springboard for the cardinal and more fundamental problem.

In understanding (1) we supposedly grasp, on the view in question, a particular denoting complex whose constituents (centre, mass, Sun and so on) we are able to enumerate. Switching now to (2) (and hence C2) – which we are also supposed to understand – if we ask, 'what are *its* constituents?', we find ourselves at a loss for an answer. Our earlier considerations have already made it plain that it cannot be a function of the original complex – as the '< . . . >' notation suggests.

---

7 Cf. P. Hylton *Russell, Idealism and the Emergence of Analytical Philosophy* (Oxford: Clarendon Press, 1990) p. 251.

The difficulty becomes even more evident if we consider complexes of higher levels (reiterating the '< >' brackets). Starting from a first-level meaning which we do unquestionably grasp, the third-level meaning will be mysterious not only with respect to its constituents, but also with respect to its denotation. Two steps up the ladder and we have no foot on the ground.[8] The very contention that we had really understood anything in (2) thus crumbles under scrutiny.

Since understanding why the theory's account of C2 is untenable – what Russell means by 'this cannot be an explanation' – is the crux of the matter, we may interrupt our commentary on the text and pause to consider it in greater detail. If we could say what *kind* of explanation *would* satisfy Russell, then, surely, we would be very close to our destination. Since *ex hypothesi* the explanation is not available in the case of denoting, we must seek it in some analogous case. Such a case seems to me to be provided by the relation of *correspondence* in Russell's multiple relation theory of judgement (henceforth MRTJ). First, let me give a brief sketch of the theory itself and its theoretical setting.[9]

If belief and judgement are conceived as two-place relations between a subject (or a mind) and a proposition then, given that some judgements are false, it becomes almost inescapable to admit *false propositions* as objective entities. Seeking to avoid this, Russell proposed (though only some years after the period we are dealing with) an alternative, according to which judging is not a two-place but rather a *multiple* relation, relating the judging subject and each of the constituents of (what would formerly be regarded as) the proposition. A judgement, which is itself a complex, is true when there is a fact *corresponding* to it, and false otherwise. This view relieves us of the commitment to false propositions as a means for accounting for false judgements – though all of what would have been, on the former view, those proposition's *constituents* are required just the same.

Both with correspondence and denoting we have an indefinable logical relation between two complex entities which precludes the possibility of one being a constituent of the other (which in the MRTJ's case, would bring back false propositions); both relations require the possibility of extending to levels higher than the elementary case (in the MRTJ, when it is judged that

---

8 I am indebted to Dummett (FPL: p. 267) for this perspective on the difficulty.

9 The theory appeared first as a tentative proposal in the final section (which was later suppressed) of Russell's 1906 *Aristotelian Society* paper 'The Nature of Truth', but it was not endorsed by him before 1910. Statements of it may be found in: 'The Nature of Truth and Falsehood' (in *Philosophical Essays* (New York: Simon & Schuster, 1966; originally published 1910) pp. 147–59); PM: pp. 43–4; KAKD: pp. 219–20 and *The Problems of Philosophy* (Oxford: Oxford University Press, 1974; first published 1912) pp. 72–5. In the posthumous manuscript from 1913, *Theory of Knowledge* (Part II Chapter 5), Russell developed a more elaborate version, but that undertaking was left incomplete. In the present discussion only the earlier, cruder, version is considered.

a judgement has occurred); and, most important of all, both relations are many–one: any given fact may have a host of *different* judgements it corresponds to (e.g. your judgement that the cat is on the mat and my judgement to the same effect, when true, will have the same fact corresponding to them). For this reason there can be, in the MRTJ, no more of a 'backward road' from facts to judgements than there is from denotations to meanings; and it does not provide any means for recovering a *particular* judgement from a given corresponding fact – only a characterization of the *class* of such judgements.[10] The two relations seem very much on a par from a logical point of view. I come now to where the analogy breaks down.

If we ask, with regard to some particular fact, 'what characterizes the judgements to which it corresponds?', the MRTJ can reply by saying that they are all complexes consisting of all of the fact's constituents related, together with a mind (or subject), by the multiple relation of judging. This constitutes a non-trivial characterization of any judgement a given fact corresponds to, or of pairs (i.e. judgement and fact) between which this relation obtains.

Whatever the MRTJ's defects are on other scores, this reply clearly meets the challenge embodied in the question, and it does so, significantly, without appealing to any ad hoc devices, as would have been the case if the notions of *a mind*, or *judging*, or that of a multiple relation, were not ones we could expect to meet elsewhere. The MRTJ's reply illustrates, I suggest, the *kind* of account which would have satisfied Russell in the case of denoting. This is what prevents 'correspond' from becoming 'wholly mysterious'.

Conversely, we might observe how useless the MRTJ would have been if, having posited a relation of correspondence, when asked *which* judgements a particular given fact corresponds to, its proponent could say no more than 'those it corresponds to'. Characterizing such judgements solely in terms of their relation to the fact is plainly circular. It tells us nothing more than was already contained in our question, and does nothing to explain why some judgements rather than others bear this peculiar relation to it. It leaves the relation of correspondence 'wholly mysterious'.

To sum up, the theory of denoting, when called upon to characterize the complexes denoting a particular C1, is unable to provide any real explanation. It is confined to negative characterizations ('a complex other than C1, which does not contain C1') and a condition ('which denotes C1'), whose circularity is the same as in the hypothetical version of the MRTJ, though perhaps less immediately apparent. Another important point the analogy

10 The comparison with the MRTJ brings up a point which might have been made sooner: since no denoting complex (of those denoting C1) is privileged above others, the quest must be for a characterization of *the class* of such complexes, and our talk of C2 as '*the* complex denoting C1' is strictly inappropriate, since there could be infinitely many. However, once this point is acknowledged, it is nonetheless convenient to continue speaking of C2 as a *single* complex.

with the MRTJ helps make plain is that the absence of any non-trivial characterization of pairs between which the relation obtains is *not* what one ought
to expect on account of denoting being an indefinable relation.

We can now explain the need, emphasized earlier, to focus on a *particular* example. To the *general* question 'how can a proposition be about a denoting complex?' the theory's answer, 'by containing a (second-level) complex
which denotes the first', is adequate as far as it goes. But when a similar question relates to a *particular* complex, a more specific answer is called for, i.e.
one which is sensitive to specific features of the first-level complex in question (as illustrated by the MRTJ). What Russell's objection 'but this cannot
be an explanation' calls for, in other words, is an explanation of what we
mean by '<C>' (in the sense of 'what does it stands for') – assuming we meant
something quite definite by 'C' – and it draws our attention to the fact that
saying 'a complex distinct from C1 which denotes it' is blatantly inadequate
as an explanation. It is vital that this point be seen clearly, whether or not
one believes that some *other* account of the matter can do the job.

This being the main thrust of Russell's case, it gives rise to a few further
matters which deserve consideration lest they be thought to undermine it.
Most of these I will leave until after we have discussed the symbolic round
(in section IV below), but one point may be dealt with immediately. Reflecting upon what has gone before one might wonder, given that it is *the very
same relation*, that of denoting, which is said to obtain both between C2 and
C1 and between first-level complexes and their denotations, why did we need
second-level denoting to bring the lack of explanation to a head? Surely at
the first level we have no more of an explanation as to why the relation obtains.
Moreover, given some denotation, we are equally unable to characterize the
class of first-level complexes denoting it. Did we simply fail to notice a glar-
ing fault at the first level? And if it is not a fault there, how could it not be?
The challenge of this question is perhaps the most difficult one confronting
an interpreter of the passage, and it goes to the heart of the problem. The
answer is encapsulated in Russell's saying: 'the meaning cannot be got at
except by means of denoting phrases'.

Indeed, we have no more of an explanation, or general account, of the
complexes denoting a given denotation, in the case of levels 1 and 0, than in
the overtly problematic case of levels 2 and 1, but the crucial difference between
the two cases is that only in the latter is such an explanation ever called for.
In the first case we can be content with recognizing the relation whenever a
given pair (of first-level complex and its denotation) is proposed: we are never
required to go from denotation to meaning. This is because at the first level
being given the denotation already puts us in a position where we can speak
or reason about it, and if we are given only the complex, then we can proceed from it to the denotation. What makes denoting complexes unlike anything else whatsoever is that even when they are 'given' to us in the way that
for anything else would suffice for understanding propositions about it, this

does not equip us to form or understand propositions about them. Doing so requires an impossible 'backward road'. While approaching an entity by means of a denoting complex ('from above', so to speak) is, in every other case, only optional, with a denoting complex this roundabout course becomes the *only* possible way of speaking or thinking about it, and since the route from denotation to meaning is not generally available, the theory has created an untenable situation. Russell's opening comment, that the theory raises 'rather curious difficulties, which seem in themselves to prove that the theory that leads to such difficulties must be wrong', is a reflection upon this anomalous situation. Russell's point is not that denoting complexes are inaccessible, but rather that the theory entails the absurd consequence that they can only be accessed via a route there is no systematic way of reaching. This he regards as an indication that the whole distinction has not been properly thought through.

Having discussed the first two, closely related, charges ('the relation remains wholly mysterious' and 'where are we to find the denoting complex "*C*" . . .?') it remains, before turning to the symbolic round, to discuss the third and last charge of the substantial round.

(iv) The third charge

The third and final charge Russell raises in the obscure passage reflects upon the conclusion stated at the beginning of (*G*). This, more independent, charge occupies the last portion of our passage (from 'Moreover' in (*G*) to the end). The theory, it is claimed, ends up giving two contradictory answers to the question of whether the *meaning* of a denoting phrase is relevant to the identity of a proposition in whose expression it occurs.

The case for an affirmative answer, articulated in paragraph (*H*), is straightforward enough. Harking back to the first of the three puzzles introduced earlier in OD, it is noted that George IV bears a certain relation to the proposition expressed by 'Scott = the author of *Waverley*' (namely that of wishing to know whether it is true) which he does not bear to the proposition expressed by 'Scott = Scott', and hence that the two must be distinct propositions. Since Scott and the author of *Waverley* are one and the same, the theory we are considering appeals to the *meaning* of 'the author of Waverley' to account for the difference. Hence the phrase's meaning is indeed relevant to the proposition's identity.

On the other hand, the result stated at the opening of (*G*) seems to dictate a negative answer to the same question. This is likely to emerge more clearly if we abandon the notational convention employed so far (i.e. '*C*' and '<*C*>') with its false suggestion of two entities related in a manner in which, as we have seen, they cannot possibly be, and replace '<*C*>' by, say, '*D*'. We can now say that the meaning has, in Russell's phrase, been 'wholly relegated' to D, because the original phrase 'C' (and hence the corresponding complex) is *excluded* from sentences about the meaning; while only *another*, structurally unrelated, phrase (namely 'D') effects talk about the meaning. So we end up with only denotations (both of 'C' and of 'D') being relevant. By 'relevant' I take Russell to mean here 'relevant to determining the truth value of propositions or sentences in which it occurs'. The assumption underlying the meaning/denotation distinction was that one entity was twofold, i.e. had two aspects, but now, as Russell puts it in OF, 'We have now not one complex with the two aspects of meaning and denotation, but two entities, "*C*", the complex, and *C* the denotation of "*C*".' (OF: § 39, p. 383).

Another way of bringing out this point might be by asking, how can we make out that 'the author of *Waverley*', when embedded in a 'George IV believes that . . . is Scott' context and in a 'plain' context, are *related*? Two avenues which might have secured this were found to be blocked, namely that they are one and the same entity in different modes of occurrence, and that the one entity contains the other as part. But in the absence of a theoretical account of this relatedness, two such occurrences of the phrase would have to be deemed akin to plain lexical ambiguity – the phrase standing for a completely different entity in each case but without this being immediately apparent. The contents expressed by 'P' and by 'A believes that P' (when 'P' contains a denoting phrase) end up having no common element, and a logically correct notation would thus require that in a 'believes that . . .' context some *other* symbol be used than the one used for the phrase in a plain occurrence. This conclusion is so absurd and counter-intuitive that it seems barely credible that it should follow. But it does, and it is this implausibility that makes Russell's complaint so elusive. We are inclined to think that the very fact that the same words occur in both contexts is itself a connection, but this, as Russell had made plain earlier in the passage, is not so. *That* relation (as with a lexical ambiguity) is merely linguistic. Unless our theory of such phrases can provide a logical grounding of the relatedness then, on that theory, there is none.

Russell came to notice this difficulty when, thinking of how to introduce the '< . . . >' notation, he stumbled on a peculiar phenomenon. The exposition of this phenomenon is the subject of the symbolic round, to which we turn next.

III The argument: the 'symbolic' round

I come now to the difficulty which Russell takes up first in the passage in OD, and which, on the evidence of OF, is also closer to the form in which the problem initially struck him. Since denoting phrases are said to have both meaning and denotation – the denotations being what is spoken of in their usual employment – Russell needed, for purposes which need not concern us here, a means for indicating in the symbolism (regarding particular denoting phrases) that their *meaning* is being spoken of.[11] This, it is natural to think, can be achieved by adding some specifically designated sign to the phrase *simpliciter*, hence the proposal which launches the discussion in the obscure passage: 'When we wish to speak about the *meaning* of a denoting phrase, as opposed to its *denotation*, the natural mode of doing so is by inverted commas' ((*B*)). Russell then gives two pairs of instances to illustrate this special use of inverted commas (which I will continue to replace with '<' and '>').

(i) The twin phenomena

Our understanding that '*C*' and '<*C*>' stand for logically related entities is reflected in our decision to make the one the result of a notational operation upon the other. But the matter cannot be left there: if the occurrence of '*C*' in '<*C*>' is a mark of genuine relatedness and not a mere notational accident (as, e.g. 'rat' in 'Socrates'), it should be possible to introduce '<*C*>' as equivalent to an expression containing '*C*'. Russell considers two proposals. The first and perhaps most natural one is 'the meaning of *C*'. This will not do because it effects speech about the meaning of *the denotation* of '*C*' (if any). 'The meaning of <*C*>', on the other hand (though it gives us what we want) is clearly unhelpful because it uses the symbol we have set out to introduce.

In the substantial round it was argued from first principles that a complex that denotes C1 cannot possibly contain it as a constituent. Here a cognate point is established by demonstrating that if the denoting phrase *is* made part of the phrase for speaking about its meaning (as in 'the meaning of C') the resulting phrase will give us (i.e. denote) a meaning other than the one intended, if anything. This paradoxical phenomenon (as well as a similar one with 'the denotation of C', to be discussed shortly) flows from nothing more than the following two innocuous principles governing the use of denoting phrases. First, that using a phrase *simpliciter* effects speech about its denotation; and second (what is effectively a special case of this), that when one phrase is embedded within another, only the first phrase's *denotation* is relevant to determining the denotation of the whole phrase.

Since verbal descriptions of the phenomenon are hard to follow because they tend to become entangled with use and mention, it is best to depict it graphically. Using boxes to represent phrases, triangles for meanings and circles for denotations, Figure 1 depicts the basic kind of configuration under consideration. A horizontal line indicates a phrase's relation to its meaning

11 The train of thought began when Russell became aware of the need to distinguish two kinds of *variables*. When (an expression for) a denoting complex is replaced by a variable, it might indicate variability of the meaning only (while the denotation remains fixed), or that *both* meaning and denotation may vary. The need to mark this distinction led Russell to the problem (see OF: p. 360 ff.).

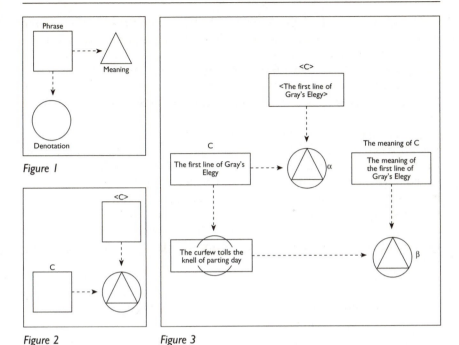

Figure 1

Figure 2

Figure 3

('express' or 'mean'), and a vertical line its relation to its denotation (i.e. 'denote'). The relation between a pair of phrases '*C*' and '*<C>*' is depicted in Figure 2: the meaning of the one is the denotation of the other (superimposition indicating coincidence). The example discussed in the first half of (*D*) is given in Figure 3. The meaning of '*C*' is α. But using the phrase 'the meaning of *C*' results in speaking about β.

So far we have dealt only with the first half of paragraph (*D*). In the second half (after 'Similarly') the discussion shifts to 'the **denotation** of *C*', which seems puzzling. If Russell's sole concern is to find an equivalent of '*<C>*', then 'the **denotation** of *C*' is a very unlikely candidate. Yet this is the phrase he goes on to consider in the passage. He observes that in this case a parallel phenomenon occurs: using 'the denotation of *C*' results in speaking not of the denotation of '*C*', but of the denotation of its denotation (if any). I shall refer to this and its 'the meaning of *C*' analogue as 'the twin phenomena'.[12]

Why does Russell bother with 'the denotation of *C*'? One thing which its consideration makes immediately clear is that the difficulty with 'the meaning

12 The details of the example Russell uses to illustrate this are of secondary importance. For completeness of exposition they are set out in Appendix B.

of *C*' cannot, as one is tempted to think, be blamed on the occurrence of the notion of meaning. On the account which the theory is proposing, 'the denotation of *C*' should have had the same effect as '*C*' by itself (just as 'the meaning of *C*' should have been the same as '<*C*>' by itself), but this is plainly not the case. The difficulty thus appears to have a more general source than the first instance alone would suggest. What precisely is Russell getting at?

The answer turns on what might at first seem a mere verbal peculiarity: Russell says that 'the denotation of *C*' does not *mean* the denotation we want. Later in the paragraph he speaks again of 'what we *meant* to have' when one would have expected 'wanted' or 'intended'. Surely, there could hardly be a more unlikely occasion to confuse 'mean' and 'denote' (in the first instance), or switch to a colloquial use of 'mean' (in the second). These are not verbal lapses, however, but alert us to the point that could only be properly made by reference to *both* of the twin phenomena, and which emerges most clearly in OF:

> These two facts show the indissolubility of meaning and denotation, and the impossibility of inventing a symbolism which will avoid the necessity of distinguishing the two sides in complexes. For 'the meaning of *C*' and 'the denotation of *C*' both have the two sides, and are therefore in no way less two-fold than '*C*' itself.
>
> (OF: p. 383)

'The denotation of *C*', Russell is pointing out, has meaning (as well as denotation) and similarly 'the meaning of *C*' has denotation (as well as meaning). Thus we do not overcome the duality in question by prefixing 'the meaning/denotation of . . .', because the same duality applies to these extended formulae as well. In the passage in OD, Russell sought the source of this phenomenon by turning to the level of propositions and denoting complexes (which I call the 'substantial' level), as opposed to the linguistic, or symbolic, level at which he began. But in a passage he wrote some years later, he seems to have found another, simpler means of bringing out the difficulty, which focuses on the second twin alone. Let us digress briefly to consider it.

In the passage in question Russell is responding to the proposal that 'Scott is the author of *Waverley*' be accounted for as asserting identity of denotations. After pointing out that 'the author of *Waverley*', unlike 'Scott', is not a mere name, and hence that talk of its denotation must be interpreted as talk of the denotation of what it means,[13] he proceeds,

---

13 This is a corollary of saying that the relation of meaning and denotation 'cannot be merely linguistic through the phrase', i.e. it is not the phrase, but rather the meaning it expresses, which denotes.

Let us call the meaning of 'the author of *Waverley*' M. Thus M is what 'the author of *Waverley*' means. Then we are to suppose that 'Scott is the author of *Waverley*' means 'Scott is the denotation of M'. But here we are explaining our proposition by another of the same form, and thus we have made no progress towards a real explanation. 'The denotation of M', like 'the author of *Waverley*', has both meaning and denotation, on the theory we are examining.

(KAKD: p. 227)

Since the theory is supposed to hold good of denoting phrases *in general*, it will apply to the phrases used as explanations as well, and this renders the explanation circular.[14] The problem with both 'the meaning of *C*' and 'the denotation of *C*' lies, then, not in their employing the notions of meaning and denotation, but rather in the very fact of their being denoting phrases at all.

(ii) Use and mention

Before concluding the discussion of the symbolic round we need to consider a purported solution which has suggested itself to some commentators so strongly that – helped by Russell's choice of inverted commas – they were tempted to read it into the text. Might not '<*C*>' be introduced thus:

$$<C> = \text{the meaning of `}C\text{' Df.}$$

i.e. by appeal to *mention*? A little reflection will reveal that this proposal is fundamentally misguided. When an expression containing mention quotes is being used – *something* must be used if we are to have a complete sentence – what is spoken of are shapes or sounds. Semantic properties do not enter into it. Bearing this in mind we no longer have – in any relevant sense – an occurrence of '*C*' on the right-hand side of the equation. So the purpose for which mention was brought in is defeated: its appeal rests on an illusion created by the notation. This observation, and its consequences for appeals to mention generally, though clear enough when considered in isolation, is easily lost sight of (as we shall see in our discussion of Frege).

---

14 Russell then proceeds to generate an infinite regress from this circularity. Speaking of 'the denotation of M', he continues, 'If we call its meaning M', our proposition becomes "Scott is the denotation of M'". But this leads at once to an infinite regress' (KAKD: p. 227). The regress is harmful because it implies that the process of analysis, translating into the explicit form, can never be completed. Note that Russell here simply waives the difficulty – so central to our passage – over 'the meaning of *C*' to facilitate the exposition of the difficulty.

IV 'But this cannot be an explanation', II

I come now to the second instalment of considerations relating to Russell's complaint 'but this cannot be an explanation'. While the first instalment was designed to expose the fault itself, the aim here is to deepen our understanding of it, first, by considering some possible responses and, second, by taking a more general vantage point which will help us to understand why denoting, unlike other logical relations, is doomed in this particular way.

(i) The burden of proof

One persistent obstacle to recognizing the full force of Russell's case is the thought that while his objections to those possibilities he examines (for what C2 might be) are valid, his case against the theory remains inconclusive so long as he has not proven that no *other* specification is possible. Such a view is a clear misplacement of the burden of proof. It seems to me plain (and it seems to be plain that it was Russell's view) that once the apparent plausibility of the theory's account of second-level denoting, namely that which is associated with the '<C>' notation, is undermined, then the onus is on the theory's proponent to offer an alternative.

As will be seen shortly, there are a host of theoretical possibilities for what C2 might be, possibilities which Russell's discussion does not mention. But the omission is justified precisely because they are mere theoretical possibilities – there is no substantial consideration to recommend them.

(ii) A survey of theoretical possibilities

Given that C2, as we saw, must be a denoting complex, the possibilities for what it might be can be arranged under three main headings according to whether *all, some,* or *none* of C1's constituents occur in it.[15]

In the absence of any guidance on what these other constituents might be, accepting the *none* option is accepting straight off that the relation between C1 and C2 is wholly mysterious (the symbolic expression of which is the 'D' mentioned earlier). *Some* can similarly be dismissed on essentially the same grounds. Both these options have no specific proposal to flesh them out, and Russell's ignoring them is justified.

Turning now to *all,* we need to distinguish the following sub-options:

15 Ultimately, the occurrence of C1's constituents may prove to be no useful guide at all to C2's identity. Nor can we exclude the possibility of C2 being *simple* (Russell recognizes the possibility of such denoting concepts in PoM § 72). But to assume either of these options is tantamount to conceding that C2's relation to C1 is wholly mysterious. Also, the mere determination of its constituents will not, in general, suffice to determine a unique denoting complex, though it would seem to be a necessary ingredient of such a determination.

(1) Whether the occurrence of all of C1's constituents in C2 implies the occurrence of C1 itself in C2.
(2) Whether C2 contains other constituents beside those of C1.

We thus obtain four sub-options.

The two where (1) gets a 'yes' were already discussed and dismissed: when combined with a 'yes' to (2) we get a sub-option dismissed earlier because of there being 'no backward road' from C1 to C2, while if (2) gets a 'no' then clearly C1 and C2 have become one and the same.

Of the two sub-options where (1) gets a 'no', and hence C1 is not a constituent of C2, the one where (2) gets a 'no' means that C2 differs from C1 in configuration only. But since no other configuration of exactly the same constituents suggests itself, we are inclined to conclude that C1 is the only possible complex comprising just these constituents (all we really need is the assumption that this will be the case for *some* complexes), in which case this sub-option too collapses into the thesis that C1 and C2 are one and the same.[16]

In the last of these sub-options ('no' to (1) and 'yes' to (2)), all C1's constituents occur in C2 without C1 itself occurring, but C2 contains additional constituents as well (such a relation obtains, for example, between 'Sam's brother' and 'the brother of Sam's son'). At first this seems to have no more to recommend it than other options we have just dismissed, but a specific proposal which comes under this heading does go some way towards the desired goal and deserves careful attention lest it be thought to undermine Russell's case.

(iii) C2 as a description of C1

Since denoting complexes are descriptions of their denotations, we might think of C2 as a *description of C1*. According to the surviving option from the previous sub-section this description would be of the form 'the denoting complex whose constituents are $a_1, a_2, a_3 \ldots$' where $a_1, a_2, a_3 \ldots$ are the constituents of C1.[17] Breaking C1 up into its constituents avoids the earlier dilemma that

---

16 Contrast this with our saying that the constituents of 'A kicked B' can form another, distinct proposition: 'B kicked A'. What justifies this is not merely the grammatical correctness of another combination of the same words – though this, no doubt, is ultimately related – but rather that we understand something different in each of them, can point to different implications, and so on. Can we think of anything similarly related to 'the centre of mass of the Solar System' (which, moreover, will denote the first complex)? I do not take Russell to be arguing that there cannot possibly be such an analogue complex, but rather to be drawing attention to the fact that the theory offers none.

17 I am indebted to John Campbell for drawing my attention to this possibility. For reasons which will become clear only in the following chapter, pursuing this route is a distinctly post-theory of descriptions move, and its application to the present problem situation is therefore, strictly speaking, an anachronism.

if C1 occurs in C2, C2 will fail to denote what we want, and if it does not, the relation will be wholly mysterious. But having broken up C1, can it now be reconstituted? That is to say, can such a description contain all that is required uniquely to determine C1?

Working out the details is far more difficult than would appear at first. First, a description of the form just mentioned leaves open which of the six kinds of denoting complexes C1 is (corresponding to 'the', 'a', 'some' and so on), and expressing this in a manner that is not merely linguistic (as I have just done in the last bracketed remark) is by no means straightforward. This difficulty can, I think, be overcome.[18] Second, to form such a description is to *produce* a second-level complex, when what we need is its *specification*, i.e. a description of C2, which requires us to produce (as opposed to describing) a *third*-level complex. (A moment's reflection on the analogous situation in the MRTJ makes it plain that it is a description of the complex, not the complex itself, that is needed.) What we need, in other words, is a *rule* for forming a second-level complex which denotes a given first-level one, not the second-level complex itself. This is why complexes arrived at in an ad hoc manner – though denoting the complex we want – were deemed an inadequate remedy. This, too, is not an insurmountable obstacle, since if we have a method for obtaining a second-level complex from a first-level one, reiteration should take us from the second-level to the third-level complex needed.

The difficulty seems to me to lie elsewhere. Though this kind of description will indeed determine a unique complex in some cases, it will not do so in all cases, and it therefore fails to provide the kind of general solution we need. The method will fail when the set of C1's constituents can combine into more than one denoting complex (as, e.g. '3^2' and '2^3').[19] In such cases the mere enumeration of constituents will not determine a unique complex. This possibility may strike one as rather remote, but further reflection reveals it to be crucial nonetheless.

First, it must be remembered that admissible permutations are here limited only by restrictions on *logical* category, not by intuitive plausibility. The constituents of 'the author of *Waverley*', for instance, would seem to have only one possible arrangement, but the implausibility of 'that which

18 The best course would be to characterize the *kind* of complex by the kind of combination it denotes (characterized with great subtlety by Russell in PoM § 59). Although this would be going from denotation to meaning the 'no backward road' difficulty is avoided because the relation between *type* of combination and *type* of denoting complex is one to one.

19 Russell had a long and hard struggle with the propositional analogue of this difficulty, which was required to illuminate the relation of correspondence between judgements and facts in a later and more elaborate version of the MRTJ developed (in his 1913 *Theory of Knowledge* Part II Chapter 5). A crucial feature of his solution to the permutation problem in that work depends upon the projected account of judgements of *molecular* facts. But since Russell abandoned the book before reaching that part, one cannot proclaim this solution a success.

was authored by *Waverley*' is owed to category restrictions which are not strictly logical and which must, therefore, be ignored in the present context. Moreover, it is natural to confine one's attention to complexes which have, or at least which it is thought might have, denotations, but any permutation which results in a complex – however obviously vacuous – is admissible in the present context. Secondly, even a single counter-example, however remote, suffices to undermine the adequacy of an account in logical theory. An account that cannot handle all cases, even if it can handle many, will not do.[20] I conclude, therefore, that the idea of specifying C2 by employing (or rather describing) a description of the kind proposed, though it goes some way towards the desired goal, cannot provide the kind of general solution needed, and it cannot therefore be counted as a satisfactory solution to the problem Russell finds in the theory of denoting.

(iv) Denoting and other logical relations

To conclude this second instalment of considerations regarding 'this cannot be an explanation', I will try to clarify why this problem arises with denoting by appealing to the contrast with two other logical relations: correspondence (in the MRTJ), and the relation of a class-member to its class.

Both correspondence and class membership (setting aside the problems which led to type theory) can be extended without difficulty to levels higher than the first: the very same relation may obtain both between entities of levels 1 and 0 (judgements and 'plain' facts; classes and individuals) and between entities of levels 2 and 1 (judgements concerning other judgements; classes containing classes as members). Why then should the situation differ in the case of denoting? From the very start the theory of denoting had to allow denotations which were completely simple,[21] and given that the very same relation must obtain both when one of the terms related is simple, and when both are complex, characterizing the relation by appeal to structural features of the denotation, or its parts, was never in question. All this contrasts markedly with correspondence which, since it can only possibly hold between complexes, gives room to a general characterization of the kind needed.

Class membership (unlike correspondence) is a relation which may hold *both* between complex and simple entities *and* between two complex entities. But here one of the entities forms *part* of the other. This is a straightforward guarantor of logical connectedness which has to be excluded in the case of

---

20 See, for example, Russell's criticism of the notion of assertion in PoM § 81–2; or the need to alter one's conception of a class to include the single case of the null class.

21 By 'simple' I mean 'has no parts'. In the present context I similarly speak of 'complex' in a sense which covers both what Russell calls unities (propositions and denoting complexes) and mere aggregates or classes.

denoting because it would undermine the epistemic role the relation was designed to play. If the denotation was, as a rule, part of the complex denoting it, then we would have gained nothing by placing it between us (or the phrases we use) and the denotation.

The upshot of this three-cornered comparison seems to be that constraints built into the relation of denoting, and which are essential to its theoretical utility, militate against the possibility of an explanation of the kind available with other logical relations.

This diagnosis cannot be found in Russell's text, but his deserting the distinction immediately upon discovering the fault, and his remark that it 'seems to prove that the whole distinction of meaning and denotation has been **wrongly conceived**' (Marsh: p. 50), strongly suggest he had at least an inkling that the fault had been written into the distinction from the very start.

This concludes the second instalment of considerations regarding 'this cannot be an explanation'. It remains now to complete the account of the remainder of the text.

V The transition

The difficulty with the twin phenomena brought to light in the symbolic round could not be left at that. Given Russell's theoretical framework, the move towards unravelling the root of the matter begins by asking, 'what state of affairs at the *propositional* level does this phenomenon reflect?' This brings Russell to the initial formulation of the problem in terms of denoting *complexes* which opens paragraph (*E*):

> The difficulty in speaking of the meaning of a denoting complex may be stated thus: The moment we put the complex in a proposition, the proposition is about the denotation; and if we make a proposition in which the subject is 'the meaning of *C*', then the subject is the meaning (if any) of the denotation, which was not intended.

This statement applies *mutatis mutandis* to the twin case. The meaning here is no longer the meaning of a *phrase*, but rather of a *complex*, and 'the meaning of *C*' and 'the denotation of *C*' are accordingly regarded as complexes, not as phrases. This is the first step in the transition between the two rounds, which takes place in paragraph (*E*).

The paragraph as a whole takes us from the model which underlay the symbolic round, where the distinction of meaning and denotation was applied to *phrases*, through the model which replaces talk of phrases with talk of complexes (in the first sentence of (*E*)) – while remaining neutral as to whether they are identical with their meanings – and it ends with a model comprising only two kinds of elements: denoting complexes which *are* meanings, and their denotations. This is the model underlying the substantial round.

One reason why the passage is so confusing is that the model which the transition leads up to is already assumed in the header. Having introduced '< >' as a means for effecting talk about meanings, to assert that '<the centre of mass of the solar system> **is a denoting complex**' is already to imply that the meaning and the complex are one and the same, as does saying that 'the meaning denotes the denotation', or speaking (earlier in OD, on p. 46) of 'the actual man **denoted by the meaning**'. The passage thus begins with an incidental identification of denoting complexes and meanings, continues (in (D)) in terms of phrases and then, after passing through a brief intermediate stage, arrives (by the end of (E)) back at the model it began with.

In broad outline, paragraph (E) consists of two steps. In the first, denoting *phrases* are dropped out of the account – this requires no argument. In the second, meanings and denoting complexes are collapsed into a single entity. The paragraph does not contain any new arguments against the theory of denoting. However, if we follow it we both see how Russell moved between the arguments we have discussed, and obtain a deeper understanding of the manner and terms in which he was thinking. Close reading of this paragraph is also required if our account of the text is to be complete. If we can make sense of every single sentence in it, then our reading of the passage as a whole is more likely to be on the right track.

When the twin phenomena are recast in the propositional model, they appear thus: the denoting complex <the meaning of C> gives us (i.e. a proposition in which it occurs will be about . . .) not the meaning of <C> but the meaning of what <C> denotes; similarly, <the denotation of C> gives us not the denotation of <C> but rather the denotation of what <C> denotes. In both cases we get the F of x's denotation instead of the F of x. This gives rise to the idea that it is not a twofold denoting complex that the distinction applies to, and that the meaning and denotation we are after are not of the complex but rather of what the complex *means* – i.e. the meaning. If we take C to *be* the meaning then, it would seem, 'the meaning of C' and 'the denotation of C' *would* give us what we want. This proposal coincides with the collapsing of the denoting complex and its meaning into a single entity. This is what I take Russell to mean when he says, 'This leads us to say that, when we distinguish meaning and denotation, we must be dealing with the meaning'.

Laying aside for the moment the grounds for this last step, let us first connect it with the response that follows (paragraph (F)): 'But this only makes our difficulty in speaking of meanings more evident'. This is so because, even if we assume that the *meaning* occurs in the proposition, there is no escape from conceding that propositions containing a first-level complex (or 'plain' occurrence of the corresponding phrase) are not about the meaning, but are rather about what the meaning denotes. This is borne out by the indisputable fact that the predication in such cases is held true only of the denotation. For a proposition to be *about* the meaning, something other than the meaning must occur, and this places us at the threshold of the substantial round –

which asks what this something is. The difficulty may be said to have become '**more** evident' because so long as the discussion was carried on in terms of phrases or complexes (the latter possibly distinct from their meanings), one could entertain the hope that a deeper level would reveal the sought-after common element connecting pairs like (1) and (2). But with a model stripped down to only the meaning and its denotation, it becomes patent that no further resort is available.

Having established the link to the substantial round, we can now return to the text which leads up to it. This brings us to the last two sentences of (E), which are arguably the most obscure in the whole passage. Let us begin with a question which we passed over earlier (in III(i) above), namely why is 'the meaning of $<C>$' thought to be the same as '$<C>$' by itself? More generally, why does Russell think of meanings as having meaning? It should be noted that in saying that a meaning has meaning, only one meaning is involved: there is no question of a meaning being, in this sense, the meaning of a different meaning, or (ultimately) of anything else whatsoever. The statement does not purport to be informative, it is merely an expression of the meaning's self-identity; it is not nonsensical, but tautological.[22]

The point of saying that 'the meaning has denotation and is a complex, and there is not something other than the meaning, which can be called the complex and be said to *have* both meaning and denotation', is therefore not to proclaim that the meaning has meaning (which was assumed throughout), but rather to bring out the fact that collapsing the denoting complex and (what was hitherto regarded as) its meaning into a single entity, makes the meaning the *only* entity which may be said to 'have' meaning as an intrinsic property, as opposed to the phrase, whose relation to the meaning is extra-logical, and is thus said to 'express' the meaning rather than 'have' it, or to the formerly distinct denoting complex, which might have been said to 'have' meaning had it not collapsed into the meaning itself.

About the collapsing of denoting complexes into their meanings, there is little to say. For no particular reason I am aware of, Russell (in OD, but not in OF) cautiously keeps these two objects apart – though it must be assumed that he supposed there to be a one-to-one correlation between them. Recasting the problem in terms of complexes (at the opening of (E)) leads to the observation that this separation is not fulfilling any role, and is consequently abolished: the denoting complex is declared to *be* the meaning.

---

22 That Russell had no qualms about predicating a concept of itself is evidenced in PoM § 95. On Russell's view, if the property of having (a particular) meaning truly holds of some entity, then the significance of applying it to any other entity cannot be denied – it will be either true or false to apply it in this way (ignoring for the moment restrictions due to the theory of types). Given this, it becomes necessary to assume that, if there is to be a difference in truth value between predicating it of itself and predicating it of anything else besides itself, each meaning is *truly* predicable of itself.

This move has an immediate corollary which, in conjunction with Russell's preceding discussion of complexes in OF, leads to a plausible reading of a phrase whose relevance to the discussion would otherwise have remained mysterious. Since denoting complexes are essentially propositional constituents, and propositions are also complexes (albeit of a distinct type) bearing a one-to-one correspondence with their meanings, the collapse of meanings and complexes in the case of denoting complexes leads to a similar collapse for propositional complexes, because a distinction between the latter and their meanings can fare no better. A way of summing this up – though perhaps not the most perspicuous – is to say, 'some meanings have denotations'. When we identify complexes (both denoting and propositional) with their meanings, we get two kinds of meanings, some of which denote, and others of which do not. (Frege, by contrast, might have said that *all* meanings have denotations.) This reading of 'some meanings' is suggested by Russell's frequent use, in the preceding discussion in OF (from which the OD passage derives), of 'complex' for both propositional and denoting complexes, and of 'meaning' as interchangeable with 'complex' (OF: §§ 23–34).

What would seem to be the only alternative reading of 'some meanings have denotations', namely as an allusion to the possibility of *empty* denoting complexes, suffers from the fatal defect of implying that this statement fails to engage with anything said elsewhere in the passage, either before it or after.

This concludes my account of the text of the obscure passage and of the argument it contains, which led Russell to abandon his PoM theory. This account leaves, undoubtedly, ample room for improvement. However, in relation to this exegetical task, too, I feel it apt to follow Russell in his ending remark in OD and

> beg the reader not to make up his mind against the view – as he might be tempted to do, on account of its apparently excessive complication – until he has attempted to construct a theory of his own on the subject . . . This attempt, I believe, will convince him that, whatever the true theory may be, it cannot have such a simplicity as one might have expected beforehand.

VI The discovery of the theory of descriptions

The final section of Richard Cartwright's 'On the origins of Russell's theory of descriptions', which deals with the same texts and problems as the present chapter, opens with a distinction between two tasks. Alluding to the 'inextricable tangle' discussed in the obscure passage, he comments that

> to unravel the tangle, if one can, is not yet to explain how Russell hit upon the theory of descriptions. And if 'On Fundamentals' provides

little light on the nature of the tangle, it provides even less on the process of discovery. The transition to something now recognizable as the theory of descriptions occupies no more than a manuscript page, and it is a page that raises more questions than it answers.[23]

While fully conceding the truth of the first quoted sentence, I maintain, contrary to Cartwright, that OF indeed does shed light on the process of discovery and that all his remark serves to show is that *without understanding the obscure passage*, no understanding of the transition to the theory of descriptions is possible either. Unravelling how Russell hit upon the theory of descriptions depends on making sense of the single manuscript page mentioned by Cartwright, which presents us with yet another obscure passage, § 40 of the posthumously published OF.

The difficulty this section presents us with is roughly this: while it is quite clear that immediately before it Russell is grappling with the same problem he discusses in the obscure passage in OD; and similarly clear that by the end of it he has effectively struck upon the theory of descriptions; it is not immediately clear what goes on in between, i.e. how the two are linked. In this final section I explore this passage and the transition it embodies. The passage follows immediately after Russell reaches the conclusion that '<C> and C are different entities' (as he put it in OD), and our task, therefore, boils down to one of clarifying the link between that negative conclusion and the emergence of the theory of descriptions.

Before going any further it needs to be said that this passage, too, is very far from self-explanatory, and I am aware of no simple way of making sense of it. First published only in 1994, there is hardly any body of exegesis relating to it, as there is for the obscure passage from OD, however lacking in consensus.[24] The following interpretation is thus offered as a tentative proposal.

Russell opens § 40 thus:

It might be supposed that the whole matter would be simplified by introducing a relation of denoting: instead of all the complications about '*C*' [i.e. our <C>] and *C*, we might try to put '*x* denotes *y*'.

But we want to be able to speak about what *x* denotes, and unfortunately 'what *x* denotes' is a denoting complex.

23 R. Cartwright, 'On the origins of Russell's theory of descriptions', in R. Cartwright, *Philosophical Essays* (Cambridge, MA: MIT Press, 1987) p. 128.

24 OF § 40 has been previously discussed in the final section of the above-mentioned paper by Cartwright, as well as in F. A. Rodriguez-Consuegra, 'A new angle on Russell's "inextricable tangle" over meaning and denotation', *Russell* n.s. 12 (1992–3) pp. 197–207. It must be added, in Russell's defence, that unlike the passage from OD, this passage, like OF generally, is part of a collection of rough notes which were clearly not intended for publication.

Russell's idea seems to be this: 'the meaning of *C*' fails because there is no 'backward road' from denotations to meanings. But the very *need* for a 'backward road' hinged on the assumption that using a denoting phrase *simpliciter* effects talk about its denotation, i.e. that what may be called the 'denotation-invoking' use is primary (this is what led to the attempt to derive a meaning-invoking use from it). But we might reverse this and take the *meaning-invoking* use as primary, so that using a denoting phrase will effect talk about its meaning. This, together with explicit mention of the relation of denoting – something we have a full right to in view of its status as a logical constant – offers a clear advantage. Instead of the impossible 'backward road' from denotation to meaning, we start with the meaning (the 'right', i.e. the 'many' side of the many–one relation) and use the relation of denoting as a 'forward road' to the denotation ('< . . . >' could then stand for 'the denotation of . . .'). However, only one line later Russell notices that if denoting phrases *simpliciter* effect talk about their meanings, this will apply to 'the denotation of C' (or 'what C denotes') as well, and thus effect speech about that phrase's *meaning*, not its denotation. This is why observing that it too is a denoting phrase undermines the proposal.

The failure of this rather radical manoeuvre makes it plain that there is no hope of avoiding the impasse so long as we regard denoting phrases as 'twofold' – as tools for speaking about both meanings and denotations. If we are to break out of this circle, speech about either must be effected by some other means.

But despite its being a failure, the moral of the advantage of using a 'forward' road has been learned, and Russell's focus shifts to attempts to speak about the *denotation* (or obtain an equivalent effect) by some other means, while settling on a single, meaning-invoking, use of denoting phrases. This, however, leads to a surprising result: it transpires that the relation of denoting has become redundant, and with it so has the denoting concept itself. Here is the remainder of the passage (the numbers are added for convenience):[25]

We might avoid this as follows: Let C be an unambiguously denoting complex (we may drop the inverted commas); then we have

[1] $(\exists y): C$ denotes $y : C$ denotes $z . \supset_z . z = y$
Thus what is commonly expressed by F'C will be replaced by

---

25 If we translate Russell's notation (which uses various numbers of dots for marking scope; as well as to express conjunction, and the subscript variable under the horseshoe for universal quantification) into present-day notation, formula [1] becomes $(\exists y)\,((C$ denotes $y) \wedge (\forall z)\,(C$ denotes $z \to z = y))$. The apostrophe of functional application in subsequent formulae (as in F'C and F'y) can be read as 'of', or else just ignored. Formula [5] would read as saying ' "the u is F" is equivalent to "there is exactly one u and it is F" ', an equivalence Russell immediately adopts as a *definition* of the former.

[2] (∃y): C denotes y : C denotes z. $\supset_z.z = y$: F`y

Thus e.g. F` (the author of *Waverley*) becomes

[3] (∃y): 'the author of *Waverley*' denotes y: 'the author of *Waverley*' denotes z. $\supset_z.z = y$: F`y

Thus 'Scott is the author of *Waverley*' becomes

[4] (∃y): 'the author of *Waverley*' denotes y: 'the author of *Waverley*' denotes z. $\supset_z.z = y$: Scott = y

This, then, is what surprised people, as well it might. On this view, we shall not introduce ɩ`u at all, but put

[5] F`ɩ`u = :(∃y): y ∈ u: z ∈ u. $\supset_z.z = y$: F`y

This defines all propositions about ɩ`u, which is all we need. But now F`ɩ`u is a bad symbol; we shall have to substitute (say)

(F`ɩ)`u.

On this view, 'the author of *Waverley*' has no significance at all by itself, but propositions in which it occurs have significance. Thus in regard to denoting phrases of this sort, the question of meaning and denotation ceases to exist.

(OF: pp. 383–4)

What 'we might avoid' is the detrimental effect of 'what x denotes' being a denoting phrase which gives us its meaning. The inverted commas can be dropped because, having given up on what they were trying to achieve, denoting phrases are only meaning-invoking.[26]

The decisive leap is, no doubt, to [1], from which the subsequent formulae follow without much difficulty. It will appear less abrupt if we bear in mind, first, that generality was already introduced by 'what x denotes' and 'x denotes y' at the start of the section and, second, that general propositions, such as [1]–[5], are on Russell's view assertions applying to propositional functions (more precisely, their values) – a conception laid down briefly at the beginning of OD, and more elaborately in PoM § 482. 'C denotes y' is a propositional function, and '(∃y) (C denotes y)' is the assertion that at least one of its values is true (or, in Russell's phrase, that it is 'sometimes true'). Accordingly, [4] is an assertion applying to the *whole* propositional function obtained by omitting the initial quantifier.[27] This gives a truer picture of what these formulae mean than some of their customary renditions (such as 'there exists an x (or something) such that . . . and it . . .') which carry the sugges-

---

26 This is neither revoked nor forgotten in [3] and [4], where the inverted commas are not in the '< . . . >' role, but indicate scope (in this case, of the relation 'denotes') – as they often do in Russell's writings.

27 On this point see PoM § 42.

tion of there being some entity, x, which is spoken of. On Russell's view, it is a *class of propositions* that is spoken of.

Since the denoting complex whose denotation we wish to speak of is said to be *un*ambiguous (i.e. denotes a single object), Russell builds the condition that *at most one* object is denoted by it into the propositional function itself; asserting that this function has *at least one* true value thus guarantees a *unique* denotation whenever the resultant proposition is true.

[2] brings out more clearly than before the effect of talk *about* the denotation (in those cases where there is one). [3] is an instance of [2], and [4] a special case of [3]. Why Russell was inclined to accept these formulae as expressing propositions *about* the denotation, laying aside earlier scruples,[28] is explained, I suggest, by the pressure of the earlier impasse: he had no alternative theory of denoting to resort to. Another crucial factor is his having a definite criterion for deciding whether this roundabout way of effecting talk 'about' the denotation will do (a matter I shall return to in the final section of the next chapter).

Russell indicates his recognition that [4] ('this, then, is what surprised people') provides a new solution to what in OD occurs as the first puzzle (George IV wanting to know whether Scott = the author of *Waverley*, but not whether Scott = Scott), and he seems to have all that is required for the crucial distinction of scope, which is also the key to his solutions to the other two puzzles in OD. (This ought *not* to be read as suggesting that the puzzles had any significant role in driving him to the theory of descriptions.) In short, even before [5] Russell seems to have found the solution to the problem he set out to solve, but has he reached the theory of descriptions? Clearly, not quite.

Though only a brief interlude, formulae [1]–[4] embody what may be regarded as a curious hybrid theory. It is natural, if not inevitable, to see the theory of descriptions as a 'package deal'. But if we pause before moving on to [5], we see that elements of the theory of descriptions which might be thought inseparable, not only could be, but *were* in fact separated. Inasmuch as the essence of the theory of descriptions is that what a proposition is about can be owed not to any one of its constituents in particular, but rather to the proposition as a whole, the theory of descriptions may be said to be 'in the bag' before [5]. But [1]–[4] still employ both denoting phrases and the relation of denoting, both standing 'for genuine constituents of the propositions

---

28 In PoM (§ 77) Russell objects to rendering 'all men are mortals' as '$(\forall x)(x$ is a man $\rightarrow x$ is mortal)' on the grounds that 'it is essential that x take *all* values, and not only such as are men. But when we say "all men are mortals," it seems plain that we are only speaking of men, and not of all other imaginable terms'. If this objection is sound, it applies to the present formulae as well, which are just as much about 'all imaginable terms' as the reading criticized.

in whose verbal expressions they occur' – which is Russell's own characterization of the theories he *contrasts* the theory of descriptions with. In this
respect, then, the hybrid theory is closer to Russell's first theory.

On the one hand, this hybrid theory embodies the crucial contextual move,
which resolves the problem Russell was grappling with in the obscure passage, which is why this move was introduced. We can now speak *both* about
the meaning – by inverting the 'normal' convention; and about the denotation – by means of the variable and the relation 'denotes'. On the other hand,
we are still left with denoting concepts and the relation of denoting (though
the former are no longer aboutness-shifters as in the original theory). This is
no mere residue, because essentials of the old theory remain intact; yet what
would appear to be the most essential feature of the new theory is also in
place.

It seems to follow that much of the achievement of the theory of descriptions comes only in [5], where Russell introduces the first formula which shuns
both denoting concepts and the relation of denoting. At this point there is
no more room for doubt: Russell has indeed arrived at the theory of descriptions. But if the hybrid theory solves the problem he set out to solve, why
did he ever proceed to [5]? What led him to abolish denoting concepts (except,
to be precise, for the variable itself) *after* he had in fact solved the problem?

A possible explanation points to C's having been specified as *un*ambigu-
ously denoting, and thus to the fact that Russell ends up securing the uniqueness of the denotation twice over throughout [1]–[4]. Since this initial
restriction disappears in [5], it is tempting to think that Russell may have
noticed this duplication only after [4], and that relaxing the initial restriction
leads him to [5].

This account seems to me less than compelling. First, because if it were
true one would expect some comment on uniqueness in the intervening text,
but there is none. Second, it does not explain the shift from propositional
functions of the form 'C denotes x' to the form 'x ∈ u', which is the chief
change between the preceding formulae and [5]. (Nonetheless, I believe the
observation that uniqueness was doubly secured before [5] is correct.)

More plausible, it seems to me, is an explanation that points us to the
broader setting in the course of which this whole discussion takes place, namely the logicist enterprise. Bearing this context in mind, it seems plausible that
having reached [3] Russell would consider the kind of formula in which an
unambiguously denoting phrase would actually be employed, and this brings
him to the symbol for a class concept, 'u'. It occurs on the left-hand side of
[5], as part of the form 'the u' would have in the notation if it had not been
for the discovery of the theory of descriptions.

From the very start, in PoM, denoting concepts were conceived of as derived
from class concepts. (As noted in Chapter 1, denoting concepts like 'some
man', and 'some dog' stand in the very same relation to the class concepts
'man' and 'dog' respectively, see PoM: § 72.) It is thus natural to expect that

the symbol for the class concept will occur in the symbol for the denoting concept. Since F῾ɪ̓u is just the kind of proposition for which the hybrid theory offers a novel equivalent, this equivalent calls for some occurrence of 'u' in it. But because the uniqueness of the denotation is already secured, and since the *only* role for which 'ɪ' is needed is to get us from the unit class concept to its sole member, finding a place for 'u' reveals that we do not need the denoting concept at all (nor, therefore, the relation of denoting), and that a 'usual' class concept will do.

'Will do' means that any context in which ɪ̓u occurs can be adequately expressed by the form on the right-hand side of [5]. The contexts and the adequacy here in mind – and this goes without saying – are those required for the needs in the *Principia*. This is to say, we should be able to replace each occurrence of an expression of the form on the left-hand side of [5] with the expression of the form on the right-hand side, without affecting derivations in which such expressions occur.

Instead of 'ɪ̓u denotes y' Russell can put 'y ∈ u' (which *may* be read 'y is-a u'; see PoM: § 57); and we then obtain the formula of the familiar theory merely by replacing 'y ∈ u' with the more general 'F῾y'. Having noted all this, one can hardly avoid the impression that the move to [5], with its substantial benefits, came as a stroke of luck, falling into Russell's lap with neither a struggle nor, so far as one can tell, any deliberate effort.

This does not purport to be an exhaustive account of the passage, and I have knowingly ignored some of the finer points. My aim has been merely to make Russell's transition from his first theory to the theory of descriptions, and his need to make use of contextual definition in particular, intelligible. It seems barely credible that anything approximating to this route would have been recoverable, or even imaginable, without the crucial text of § 40 of OF. I reserve comment on how the new theory accounts for the initial motivations requiring a theory of denoting until the final section of the next chapter.

The present chapter has aimed to provide a comprehensive account of the text of the obscure passage in OD, as well as a philosophical discussion of its argument. The final section showed how the discovery of the theory of descriptions was a direct outgrowth of Russell's attempts to circumvent the difficulty explored in that passage. Part of the point of this exercise has been to establish the theoretical framework within which the theory of descriptions was conceived. Doing so is particularly important in view of the contrasting tradition according to which the theory of descriptions marks the advent of a fundamentally new theoretical framework. This question of OD's place in Russell's philosophical development will be pursued in a more direct manner in the next chapter.

Chapter 3

The place of 'On Denoting' in Russell's development

In the last two chapters I have tried to give a full account of the theoretical background and problem situation which led Russell to propose the theory of descriptions in OD. This is not, however, the story one will find recounted in most presentations of the theory found in innumerable papers and introductory books in the philosophy of language, philosophical logic or Russell's philosophy. Although the differences do not affect what may be called the 'technical core' of the theory, the account that one finds of the problem situation, of Russell's *point* in so interpreting denoting phrases, is almost invariably along the following lines.

Take a statement like 'the present King of France does not exist' (taking any other statement with a similar subject will require only minor changes to what follows). It seems that there must be an interpretation which makes it true, and yet, unless there is, in some sense, a present King of France, then of what is existence being denied? How can the statement be meaningful? One possible response is to grant the present King of France some ontological status short of existence, which implies, more generally, recognizing a realm of entities which do not exist, but only subsist, or have being.

This line of reasoning has been associated with Meinong, and it will be convenient to label the resulting ontology 'Meinongian'. An innocent reader of a traditional presentation of the theory of descriptions would reasonably conclude, first, that prior to OD Russell subscribed to a Meinongian view, second, that its implausibility is what drove him to devise the theory of descriptions and third, accordingly, that the theory's most distinctive merit is its success in explaining such statements without incurring a commitment to non-existent entities.

Such a picture, it must be admitted, does seem fairly plausible in the light of OD alone (neglecting the obscure passage). Russell does indeed single out Meinong's view as an alternative he argues against, and devotes a substantial part of the discussion to three puzzles, two of which deal with empty denoting phrases. (Though a somewhat more discerning reader will observe that Russell neither says nor implies that no alternative theory can resolve these puzzles.) This view regarding the role of the Meinongian alternative is the centrepiece of a broader conception according to which OD marks a fundamental turning point in Russell's whole philosophical outlook. It is this conception which I will subject to critical scrutiny in the present chapter. And although the general thrust of the alternative view I will be recommending will, after the last two chapters, hardly come as a surprise, there is much detail, the careful examination of which is highly rewarding. If the previous chapters were concerned only with Russell's theory, the view taken here will be broader, encompassing both Russell's theory and aspects of its reception in subsequent analytic tradition.

Our subject divides naturally into two headings, each of which will occupy us in roughly equal measure. The first, more narrowly focused, concerns the place of the theory of descriptions in Russell's *ontological* development; the other broader issue concerns its place in his *methodological* development.

I 'On Denoting' and Russell's ontological development: some preliminaries

One of the most influential propagators of the traditional view of the kind sketched above has been Quine. His 'Russell's ontological development'[1] (henceforth 'ROD') is a particularly rich source in this respect, though the same view is evident in other writings of his where Russell is not the focus of attention (e.g. 'On what there is'[2]). I pick Quine not because his view of the theory of descriptions is singular, but rather because it is so characteristic of writers of that generation.[3] His merit lies in providing a clear and concise statement of it.

Early in that paper Quine writes, 'In *Principles of Mathematics*, 1903, Russell's ontology was unrestrained. Every word referred to something' (ROD: p. 291). By contrast, in OD, 'a reformed Russell emerges . . . fed up with Meinong's impossible objects' (p. 292).[4]

Clearly, such a view of the theory's achievement is tenable only if Russell did indeed subscribe to a Meinongian view immediately beforehand. But the evidence of EIP (cited in the introduction) makes it plain that *before* OD, and while subscribing to the theory of denoting concepts, Russell unequivocally *denied* the precise commitment Quine attributes to him.

---

1 In D. Pears (ed.), *Bertrand Russell: A Collection of Critical Essays* (New York: Doubleday (Anchor Books) 1972; first published in 1966) pp. 290–344.

2 In W. V. O. Quine, *From a Logical Point of View*, 2nd edn (New York: Harper and Row, 1961) pp. 1–19.

3 See also A. J. Ayer, *Russell* (London: Fontana/Collins, 1972) pp. 52–4.

4 Further remarks to the same effect occur elsewhere in passing: 'in 1905 Russell freed himself of Meinong's impossibles and the like by a doctrine of incomplete symbols' (p. 294) or 'after laying waste Meinong's realm of being in 1905, Russell trusted concepts less' (p. 295).

So it would seem to follow that by the time of EIP, Russell's view had changed. But now the question of *when* arises, and answering it is not just a question of fixing a date, because this question is inseparable from that which concerns *why* the change occurred. Peter Hylton, a more recent writer who is also more familiar with Russell's pre-OD writings, argues against Quine's view.[5] The change commonly associated with the theory of descriptions, he claims, as a matter of fact occurred beforehand: 'Russell's ontological views undergo an important change between *Principles* and OD, but the change is in fact independent of, and slightly earlier than, the change from the theory of denoting concepts to the OD theory' (p. 241).

Before asking about Hylton's grounds for supposing such a change to have occurred, we might first ask what Russell is supposed to have changed from. What was his view in PoM? Hylton portrays Russell as somewhat inconsistent. On the one hand,

> the theory of denoting concepts explains how we can meaningfully say 'the King of France is bald', and can truly say 'there is no present King of France', without presupposing that there is a present King of France subsisting (even if not existing) in the realm of being.
>
> (Hylton, *Russell*, p. 241)

But, Hylton maintains, on the other hand Russell had lost sight of this

> in those portions of *Principles* where more general metaphysical questions are under discussion. Even though the theory of denoting concepts would enable Russell, in *Principles*, to deny that the present King of France has being, there is no sign that he realizes this fact. More important, perhaps, there is no sign there that he sees reason to deny being to the present King of France. In that book he is, notoriously, willing to attribute being to any putative object we can name. In section 427 he argues quite generally that: '*A* is not' must always be either false or meaningless . . . This section is far from a grudging admission of the being of every putative entity. On the contrary, outside the context of mathematics, Russell willingly asserts that every expression that seems to refer to something does in fact refer to a real entity, which has being even if it does not exist in space and time.
>
> (p. 241)

There is much in this passage we will only attend to later, but let us first round up our account of Hylton's view. How, then, does he explain Russell's change of mind *before* OD? He suggests that it came in response to

5 Hylton, *Russell*.

Meinong's works which, as we know, Russell had reviewed at great length in the period leading up to OD.

> Meinong shared the ontological generosity of *Principles,* but had thought it through more rigorously, and was more aware of its potential problems. It is plausible to suppose, therefore, that reading and reflecting upon the ontological work of Meinong (and, later, his followers) made Russell realize the difficulties of his own ontological attitude, and led him to give it up.
>
> (p. 243)

Despite the somewhat tentative tone, Hylton offers no other explanation for what he takes to be a major ontological change in Russell's philosophy. Nor does he provide much further detail on the difficulties, presumably overlooked in PoM, which are supposed to have provoked it.[6]

Hylton's view, to sum up, is that in PoM Russell was committed, albeit unnecessarily, to putative denotations of empty phrases; a commitment which he later withdrew, but prior to and independently of his discovery of the theory of descriptions. So despite differing from Quine over when and why Russell abandoned a Meinongian ontology, he shares the view that in PoM, at least, Russell was indeed committed to it.

I submit that this shared view is mistaken. As for Hylton's version of the changes in Russell's view before OD, I find the evidence in its favour tenuous, and I think that a far simpler account of the matter is possible. The original sin of both writers is their mistaken assimilation of Russell's PoM view to Meinong's. This, I maintain, stems from a failure to take sufficient notice of two crucial features of Russell's PoM position: one is the distinction between two senses of 'exist' (and between one of them and 'being'); the other is his regarding denoting phrases as a different logical category from proper names.[7] I shall therefore begin by introducing the different senses of 'exist';

---

6 Hylton argues that the mistaken belief that the ontological change depended on the change from the theory of denoting concepts to the theory of descriptions is partly explained by the fact that Russell 'published almost nothing manifesting the new ontological attitude until he published OD'. This leads one to expect him to cite evidence from the intermediate posthumously published papers to support the claim that such a change did indeed occur. But the only evidence he cites (p. 244) is a passage from 'Meinong's Theory of Complexes and Assumptions' (Lackey: p. 62). This passage, in the first place, even as it stands in Hylton's text is far too weak to establish a claim of a complete ontological change; and second, even this limited effect is due, as closer inspection reveals, to Russell's words having been taken out of context. Russell is there merely listing points which might be raised *against* the view which, as he makes clear on the previous page, he wholeheartedly *endorses*.

7 In what follows I ignore Quine's claim that Russell posited denotations not only of (what would seem to be) empty phrases, but also of contradictory ones (or 'impossible objects' in Meinong's terminology). I find nothing in Russell's writings to support it.

and then proceed to disentangle Russell's view from Meinong's. Finally, I will examine the textual evidence that seems to have motivated views such as Hylton's and Quine's, and set forth my own view of the pre-OD developments.

'Being' (which Russell uses synonymously with 'subsist'[8]) is the weakest among the notions under consideration. It is considered to hold good of anything whatsoever, and to deny it of anything is always false. The last statement is not, as may seem at first, a symptom of an extravagant ontology, but plainly a tautology. This becomes apparent as soon as one remembers that it is propositions, not sentences, that are at stake. Unless *something* occupies the subject position in a proposition of the form 'x does not have being' (or, for that matter, in any subject–predicate proposition) then there is simply no proposition to begin with, and this holds good whether or not we allow *sentences* to contain empty names.

The reason a notion of being is called for in the first place is the need, which Russell thought mandatory for any plausible account of mathematics, to recognize abstract entities. Anyone who wishes to admit such entities (concepts, classes and propositions are paradigm cases) needs a categorical distinction to set them apart from entities which occupy particular regions of space and time – i.e. concrete ones. Only entities which are *not* abstract are said to exist in this restricted sense, for which, to avoid confusion, I will henceforth use the expression 'exist$_1$'.

This differs from the manner in which the abstract/concrete distinction is usually conceived, in regarding existents as a subclass of beings: everything has being, but only some beings have the additional property of existence$_1$. Existence$_1$ applies only to individuals, and since logic and mathematics are concerned with all beings regardless of whether or not they exist$_1$, from a logical point of view it is a property on a par with any other.

Exist$_2$, by contrast, is *not* applicable (i.e. its application does not even make sense) to individual things, and requires a class, or class concept, or propositional function for its meaningful application. To say of a class that it exists is to say that it has at least one member (or, of a class concept, that at least one entity falls under it, or, of a propositional function, that at least one of its values is true). It is in this sense that we speak of existence theorems in mathematics, and this sense is of course of special interest from a logical point of view. At the outset, then, these two meanings of 'exist' are, as Russell put it in EIP (p. 98) 'as distinct as stocks in the flower-garden and stocks in the stock exchange'. Both these distinctions are clearly observed throughout PoM,[9] and I am aware of no evidence suggesting that Russell might have abandoned

8 See note on p. 78 of Russell's 1905 review of *Untersuchungen zur Gegenstandstheorie und Psychologie* (in Lackey) though he rarely uses 'subsist' outside a Meinongian context.
9 Exist$_1$ and being are explicitly contrasted in § 72 and in greater detail in §§ 427. Existence$_2$ is discussed in §§ 25 and 93. All three are clearly distinguished in EIP in a manner which gives no reason to suppose that Russell's view had changed in this regard.

these distinctions after PoM, nor – contrary to common wisdom – that they were affected by the advent of the theory of descriptions. Being was still in use in 1912.[10]

Quine could not have been clear about these distinction when he wrote,

> take impossible numbers: prime numbers divisible by 6. It must in some sense be false that there are such; and this must be false in some sense in which it is true that there are prime numbers. In *this* sense are there chimeras? Are chimeras then as firm as the good prime numbers and firmer than the primes divisible by 6?
>
> (ROD: p. 292)

The sense in which it is maintained that there are prime numbers, but none divisible by 6 (given that both are class concepts) is exist$_2$. But this is precisely the sense in which Russell *denies* the existence of chimeras (though special complications regarding this case will be addressed later in this chapter). The same confusion occurs when, later in the same essay, Quine claims that Russell's 'bias towards the existential would explain his indiscriminate bestowal of subsistence in *Principles of Mathematics*'. But if there is anything Russell could be indifferent to it was existence$_1$, not subsistence – which is where his ontological commitment lies, since it is over all subsistents, not only existents$_1$, that the variable of quantification ranges. This confusion is again apparent when Quine writes, 'in *Principles* the classes occupied, however uneasily, the existential zone of being. To hold that classes, if there be any, must exist, while attributes at best subsist, does strike me as arbitrary; but such was Russell's attitude' (p. 297). Again, as explained earlier, classes are for Russell the primary reason for positing a notion of subsistence – he never held them to exist$_1$. (If, on the other hand, we take Quine to mean existence$_2$, then Russell would have said that not all classes do.) Clearly, Russell's ontology can be made to appear very arbitrary indeed when these distinctions are confused.

Hylton, though better informed than Quine on these matters, nonetheless gets things wrong with respect to a crucial point. He writes,

> Russell's account of mathematics demands that the notion of denoting must, from the outset, allow for the possibility of denoting concepts which do not denote anything. We must be able to say that there are no members of a given class, that there is no greatest number, and so on. Since the sort of putative entities that these statements deny are not spatio-temporal, this is not simply a denial of existence as distinguished from being. In terms of that distinction, it is a denial of being.
>
> (Hylton, *Russell*, p. 241)

---

10 See e.g. the last paragraph but one of Chapter 9 in Russell, *The Problems of Philosophy*.

The passage begins with what appears to be a clear notion of existence$_2$, but concludes, on the grounds that certain putative entities do not exist$_1$, that their denial is a denial of being. But this is clearly a false step. Existence$_2$, whether asserted or denied, does not concern individuals, and hence cannot concern any 'putative entities' (unless they be classes) either. On Russell's view there is simply no coherent way to deny being of anything. The grain of truth in Hylton's statement, though, is that a denial of existence$_2$ of a particular class concept, such as number, would indeed be incompatible with holding that individual numbers have being; but no denial of existence can strictly imply a denial of being. I mention exist$_2$ only to set it aside: henceforth 'exist' means exist$_1$.

II Russell's case against Meinong

I remarked earlier that the assimilation of Russell's PoM ontology to Meinong's is mistaken, and a first step towards a clear view of the former must therefore be its disentanglement from the latter. Since it is Russell's position I am concerned with, not Meinong's, I will simply avoid in what follows the question of whether Russell's presentation of Meinong is fair, and uncritically assume, for the sake of argument, that it is.

The most salient features of Meinong's position, as it emerges from Russell's discussions, is his admitting objects corresponding to empty descriptive phrases (e.g. 'the golden mountain') which are held to subsist but not to exist, and of objects corresponding to contradictory descriptions (e.g. 'the round square') which are held not even to subsist, and which are also called 'impossible objects'. Since Russell, too, recognizes non-existent objects, his repudiation of Meinong's position should, it would seem, depend solely on his objections to non-subsistent, or impossible, objects. This, however, is not borne out by the evidence.

Although Russell unquestionably argues against impossible objects as well, his case against Meinong does not depend on this feature of Meinong's position. His objections to Meinong's position occur in a number of places,[11] OD being the most familiar:

> This theory regards any grammatically correct denoting phrase as standing for an object. Thus 'the present King of France', 'the round square',

11 In the penultimate paragraph of his 1907 review of Meinong's *Über die Stellung der Gegenstandstheorie im System der Wissenschaften* (Lackey: pp. 92–3) and earlier in the review of *Untersuchungen zur Gegenstandstheorie und Psychologie* published in the same issue of *Mind* as OD (Lackey: pp. 80–1). Although the criticism in these places does indeed focus on impossible objects (in the first Russell is responding to Meinong's reply to his earlier criticism), it does not, as he points out in his letter to Meinong (see below) *depend* on this feature of Meinong's view.

etc. are supposed to be genuine objects. This is in itself a difficult view; but the chief objection is that such objects, admittedly, are apt to infringe the law of contradiction. It is contended, for example, that the existent present King of France exists, and also does not exist; that the round square is round, and also not round; etc.

(Marsh: p. 45)

This rather swift argument needs spelling out in greater detail: the contradiction is arrived at by considering the object corresponding to 'the *existent* present King of France'. Assuming the general principle that the object described as 'the FG' must be both an F and a G, we are led to conclude that the object in question exists. But on the other hand the theory's general position is that, since it does not occupy a position in space and time, it does not exist. The derivation of a contradiction from the case of the round square, which is an impossible object, takes a slightly different route, but the important thing to notice, for our present concern, is Russell's grouping (what on Meinong's theory would count as) merely possible objects together with impossible objects, and that his case against Meinong's non-subsistent objects would have held even if Meinong had not admitted impossible objects.[12]

It might be thought that this criticism depends in some way upon the position adopted only in OD, and this is precisely the impression Quine creates when he writes that 'Russell's long article on Meinong came out in *Mind* in instalments . . . In it he criticized details of Meinong's system, but still protested none against the exuberance of Meinong's realm of being' (ROD: p. 292). But this is grossly misleading.

In the first place a little attention to chronology will reveal that the tripartite review of 1904 relates (as Russell makes plain in a footnote on its first page) to earlier works of Meinong's than those referred to in OD and in the 1905 review. The relevant features of Meinong's system were simply not in place when Russell wrote in 1904. Thus Quine's intimation that in 1904 Russell had approved of the same views he protested against in OD is erroneous.

In arguing against Meinong's impossible objects in the 1905 review, Russell writes 'The difficulties of excluding such objects can be met, I think, by the theory of denoting' (Lackey: p. 81). What he means by 'theory of denoting' is explained in a footnote by reference both to Frege's 'On Sense and Reference' and to OD. So although the theory of descriptions offers a new account of the statements in question, as far as the problem of impossible

---

12 The same view occurs more explicitly in a later review from 1907, where Russell responds to Meinong's complaint that: 'my [i.e. Russell's] objections apply equally to such objects as "the golden mountain"', which are not impossible, but merely non-existent. This, of course, I admit; indeed the object I especially intended to abolish was 'the present King of France' who is on a level with the golden mountain' (Lackey: p. 93).

objects is concerned, Frege's distinction – which Russell regarded as essentially the same as his own earlier view – was, in Russell's view, a viable means of avoiding non-subsistent objects.

If all this still leaves room for doubt, we have a letter Russell wrote to Meinong *before* the theory of descriptions, in which he rejects Meinong's view and recommends Frege's theory as providing the right solution. He also groups the merely possible and impossible objects together. The letter, dated 15 December 1904, reads (I add Russell's original German in square brackets),

> I have always believed until now that every object must be [*sein muss*[13]] in some sense, and I find it difficult to recognize non-being objects [*nicht-seinde gegenstände*]. In a case such as the golden mountain or the round square one must distinguish between sense and reference (in accordance with Frege's distinction).[14]

Quine's picture is further undermined by the plain fact that, contrary to widespread belief, OD did *not* abolish Russell's commitment to non-existents. He employs the notion of being as distinct from existence in OD (first footnote on p. 54) and after, and when the distinction is properly understood there is just no reason why the theory of descriptions should be thought to affect it. Some changes as to *which* non-existents he was willing to admit did indeed occur shortly before OD (and will be explained momently), and others were implied by OD itself. But none of these changes challenged the need to recognize a category of non-existents, or the existence/being distinction in general.

As Russell points out in OD, Meinong's crucial assumption is that every grammatically correct denoting phrase stands for an object. But in Russell's first theory of denoting this is avoided. So before Meinong ever advocated his controversial view, Russell had the theory of denoting which fortified him (at least to his own satisfaction) against the kind of pressures which drove Meinong to admit non-subsistents.

Whether Russell's ontology in PoM deserves the epithets 'generous' and 'unrestrained' or not, it differs significantly from Meinong's, most strikingly in not admitting non-subsistent objects. It is not simply that Russell chose, perhaps in response to some 'sense of reality', to say 'no' where Meinong chose to say 'yes', but rather that Russell had devised a theoretical solution which enabled him to resist the pressures which led Meinong to say 'yes'. Let us now turn to examine Russell's ontology in its own right.

---

13 On the interchangeability of '*sein*' and '*bestehen*' see Russell's footnote in Lackey: p. 78.
14 J. F. Smith, 'The Russell–Meinong debate', *Philosophy and Phenomenological Research*, 45 (1985) pp. 305–50, 348. The original German can be found in A. Meinong, *Philosophenbriefe* (Graz: Akademische Druck- und Verlagsanstalt, 1965) p. 151. I have diverged from this translation with regard to '*nicht-seinde*'.

III Russell's ontology in PoM reconsidered

From what has been said so far it may seem that I maintain that there are not even *apparent* grounds for assimilating Russell's ontology in PoM to Meinong's. This is not so. Ignoring impossible objects – which, despite Quine, I find no reason to think Russell ever espoused – I finally come to what I propose is the correct view of Russell's PoM ontology. It emerges in the course of re-examining the evidence which has been thought to support the assimilation with Meinong. This evidence consists of one general argument, and four illustrative lists.

The general argument was already mentioned in an earlier quotation from Hylton. Russell held that 'A is not' (understood as a denial of being) must always be false.[15] Hylton concludes from this that Russell 'willingly asserts that every expression that seems to refer to something does in fact refer to a real entity, which has being even if it does not exist in space and time'. But what can be meant here by 'expression that seems to refer to something'? Does *Russell* recognize any category which fits this description? In other words, are we entitled to suppose that 'A' in this context stands *either* for a proper name *or* for a 'the' phrase? Such a supposition is surely required if we are to extract, as Hylton suggests, a commitment to a present King of France; but clearly, Russell's view is that sentences involving proper names and 'the'-phrases express very different kinds of propositions; and there is simply no general notion for Russell to make assertions about.[16] That 'A is not' is false for any *name* 'A', and that every proper name refers to an entity, may well be regarded as tautological. I find nothing to suggest that Russell would extend his claim to denoting phrases, and this evidence does nothing to support, therefore, the assimilation of his ontology with Meinong's.

Four places in PoM are almost invariably cited in support of the traditional view and seem to have inspired the assimilation of PoM and Meinong's view. In the first, Russell explains his use of 'entity' as synonymous with 'term': 'every term has being, i.e. *is* in some sense. A man, a moment, a number, a class, a relation, a chimaera, or anything else that can be mentioned, is sure to be a term; and to deny that such and such a thing is a term must always be false' (PoM: § 47).

Again, in explaining the notion of a *thing* (as opposed to a *concept*), he writes,

> Points, and instants, bits of matter, particular states of mind, and particular existents generally, are things in the above sense, and so are many

---

15 The inverted commas here indicate not mention, but scope (of 'is always false'), and Russell's statement concerns the proposition, not the sentence, 'A is not'.

16 He could, and occasionally did, join the two categories for the sake of a particular statement, but in view of his general position this cannot be presumed by default.

terms which do not exist, for example, the points in a non-Euclidean space and the pseudo-existents of a novel.

(§ 48)

But the remark which is probably the most often cited of all occurs when Russell explains the notion of being (as opposed to existence₁): 'Numbers, the Homeric gods, relations, chimeras and four-dimensional spaces all have being, for if they were not entities of a kind, we could make no propositions about them. Thus being is a general attribute of everything, and to mention anything is to show that it is' (§ 427).[17]

It is crucial to bear in mind that PoM does not contain any more explicit, theoretically self-conscious, statements on what the realm of being comprises, nor are these statements themselves part of such an explicit ontological discussion. The point being served by each of these lists, as becomes clear from their respective contexts, is chiefly negative, i.e. to controvert the supposition that the application of certain logical notions (and hence, by implication, of logic itself) is confined to existents. Russell's position is that anything that may be mentioned (a term he associates with naming, not denoting), counted or thought about (and hence that may be the subject of a proposition) must be something, i.e. must have being, and that logic and mathematics are concerned with all beings regardless of whether they exist.

Let us take a closer look at the items on these lists. They seem to fall naturally into two groups. One comprises those abstract entities which are, broadly speaking, mathematical objects, i.e. numbers, relations, classes, four-dimensional spaces and their points. These cases, as explained earlier, were Russell's primary motivation for recognizing non-existent entities in the first place. Though ultimately some of them may be reducible to others, it is not these that induce one to assimilate Russell's ontology to Meinong's. (Moreover, since Russell's admitting these entities was unaffected by the discovery of the theory of descriptions, if their inclusion renders one's ontology 'Meinongian' then Russell's ontology must have remained Meinongian even after the theory of descriptions.)

The other, more tendentious group includes chimeras, the Homeric gods and the pseudo-existents of a novel.[18] It is undeniable that in PoM Russell counted fictitious figures as beings. But why did he? Since we have clearly ruled out a need to make sense of empty denoting phrases, the answer, I propose, is that Russell felt compelled to account – in a manner somewhat reminiscent of Meinong – for the apparent intelligibility of sentences con-

---

17 A fourth list of similar character occurs in explaining what may be counted as a member of a class in PoM § 71.

18 An explicit discussion of particular fictional figures – which removes any lingering doubt one might have regarding the seriousness of Russell's commitment – occurs in the chapter on motion (PoM: § 444).

taining the *proper names* of what might count as fictitious entities (e.g. 'Hamlet was a Danish prince'). For those cases the theory of denoting (as yet) had nothing to offer. Nonetheless, the contrast with Meinong is here significant: Russell's 'ontological exuberance' in PoM regarding fictitious entities is name-driven, not description-driven, and this difference is crucial because names, being simple, do not, as descriptive phrases do, allow us to draw any conclusion regarding their bearers, and hence give no scope to the kind of arguments Russell directed against Meinong regarding 'the existent present King of France' infringing the law of contradiction in OD (p. 45). Russell *never* admitted, as Meinong did, objects which have no being, like the round square.

That this was indeed Russell's position is corroborated by two facts. First, it is precisely because he had a theory of denoting to handle empty and contradictory phrases (together with the crucial severing of names from denoting phrases) that fictional names presented Russell with a stark choice: either to deny that they were names (i.e. dismiss them as empty noises), or to find some ontological status for their putative bearers. The PoM framework allows no third option, and this flows directly from the principle that 'A is not' – now confined to proper names – must always be false.

Second, and perhaps even more importantly, we have the grounds which led Russell to withdraw this commitment later on (i.e. in EIP). After explaining 'there are no Centaurs' as meaning ' "x is a Centaur" is false whatever value we give x' he contrasts this case with another which seems superficially alike:

> The case of nectar and ambrosia is more difficult, since these seem to be individuals, not classes. But here we must presuppose definitions of nectar and ambrosia: they are substances having such and such properties, which, as a matter of fact, no substances do have. We have thus merely a defining concept for each, without any entity to which the concept applies.
> (EIP: p. 100)

Russell's change of position with regard to fictitious entities was the result, then, not of any relaxation of the principles which led him to admit them earlier, but rather of the discovery that their names could be replaced by definitions, i.e. by denoting phrases, which could then be accounted for as empty denoting phrases. This, given the theory of denoting, made the former problematic commitment no longer necessary.

If this view is correct, then, it was not the thought that 'everything goes' that led Russell to admit fictitious entities into his ontology, but rather a specific principle (i.e. that 'A is not' is always false) he was committed to, together with the reluctance to dismiss apparently intelligible talk of such entities as empty noise. As soon as the possibility of construing these expressions otherwise than as proper names emerged, without requiring any further change in his position, the commitment disappeared.

The idea of construing proper names as disguised descriptions has come to be known primarily in association with the theory of descriptions. But it originated, as evidenced by EIP, when Russell still held the theory of denoting concepts, and is quite independent of the theory of descriptions. The exercise achieves its point with either theory: it depends upon one's having an account of descriptive phrases which avoids the unwanted commitment – it matters not whether this is discharged by the theory of descriptions or by the former theory of denoting.

If the line of explanation suggested above is correct, then Russell's listing the Homeric gods among beings is on account of the intelligibility *not* of sentences containing the *phrase* 'the Homeric gods', but rather of those containing *proper names* of individual gods (and similarly for the pseudo-entities of a novel). Of the various items on Russell's lists this leaves chimeras as the only item which resists this line of explanation.

The difficulty is that 'chimera' is a class concept, not a proper name, and in the absence of known proper names for individual chimeras Russell's decision to count them as beings cannot, it would seem, be explained in the same manner as it was in relation to Homeric gods. Moreover, explaining Russell's listing by appeal to possible names seems to me untenable in the light of evidence to be produced shortly.

I noted earlier that considering the contexts of all of the above quotations mentioning chimeras makes it clear that they were *not* intended as deliberate statements about their ontological status. They do not occur in the course of an ontological discussion. However, elsewhere in PoM one can find a discussion which comes much closer to being precisely that: in it Russell focuses specifically on chimeras – though of course only as a representative case – not merely as an item on a list of disparate entities which are said to have being but not to exist, but rather in the course of a detailed discussion of empty denoting phrases. This discussion, however, proceeds on the assumption that chimeras do *not* have being.

In the course of his discussion of denoting phrases which do not denote anything (PoM: § 73), Russell singles out 'all chimeras' to exemplify an empty phrase, and tries to provide an account of the apparent truth of '(all) chimeras are animals'. Although in that section Russell considers a number of different proposals, none of which seems to satisfy him, the subject of the whole discussion (i.e. denoting concepts which fail to denote anything), as well as a specific remark occurring in it ('if there were chimeras . . .'), leave no room for doubt that Russell maintained that there is *nothing* falling under the concept *chimera*, and this clearly incompatible with the assumption that chimeras have being (though, for reasons explained in relation to Hylton, this is not quite the same as to deny their being). An account along the same lines as that found in EIP for 'there are no centaurs' not only *could* be given in PoM, it *was* in fact given in PoM (regarding chimeras), though, as noted earlier, Russell was not completely satisfied with it there.

Granted that the problem presented by centaurs and by chimeras is the same, and that Russell had not changed his views about setting this problem apart from the problem of fictitious individuals – and despite the new solution in EIP we have no reason to suppose he did – this gives further support to the idea that Russell's mention of chimeras on the above-mentioned lists in PoM is not strictly in order by his own lights, and to the idea that it may plausibly be regarded as a slip. It is easy to understand why he might be prone to making it, given that he does recognize fictitious entities on other grounds. It also meshes well with the figurative use of 'chimera' to mean 'creature of fantasy' generally, and with the fact that the point at stake is that logic is not confined to entities encountered in actual experience.

We can now take stock of the pros and cons of the present view of Russell's ontological development as against that proposed by Hylton. On Hylton's account Russell in PoM had overlooked a rather obvious consequence of a theory he devised in that same work, and subscribed to a Meinongian ontology. Then, shortly before OD and for reasons which are vaguely associated with Meinong but not specified, his ontology undergoes a major shift (of which he himself seems unaware), resulting in his rejecting non-subsistent objects. My contrasting proposal is that the only element of the PoM ontology which Russell was to reject later is the recognition of bearers of fictional names as beings – which was explained as flowing from a principle he explicitly endorses. This recognition was withdrawn shortly before OD on specific grounds which bring about a change in *which* entities are admitted into the ontology, but involve no change of ontological principle (nor, indeed any change in the range of admissible propositional constituent; it was merely a novel way of matching some proper names with formerly admitted constituents). As for the ontological significance of OD, I am in complete agreement with Hylton (as against Quine) that it abolishes no more than denoting concepts.

I conclude that the assimilation of Russell's PoM ontology to Meinong's does not bear scrutiny. Evidently not on Quine's crude account, nor yet on Hylton's more subtle one. Both pay insufficient attention to distinctions fundamental to Russell's outlook, and give undue weight to a single item recurring on illustrative lists which further evidence suggests is probably a slip. This view must, I maintain, be held even in the face of what would appear to be authoritative evidence to the contrary. Russell's retrospective testimony[19] portrays the very picture which I argue is a myth, but it was made

19 Most notably in his 1937 introduction to the second edition of PoM (p. x), and in *My Philosophical Development* (London: Allen and Unwin) in 1959. In the latter he describes the fallacy that unless the golden mountain subsisted it would have made no sense to deny its existence, and falsely remarks that 'I confess that, until I hit upon the theory of descriptions, this argument seemed to me convincing' (p. 64).

so long after the events in question, and contrasts so starkly with the contemporary evidence, that it must be dismissed outright. It is these statements which, most probably, nurtured the prevailing view I have argued against. These statements also concern the other department of Russell's development, to which we turn next.

IV Methodological developments: 'every word must have some meaning'

I move now to the second theme, mentioned at the opening of this chapter, of OD's place in Russell's methodological development. The questions facing us are, to what extent does OD embody or imply – as is often supposed – a renunciation of general tenets that Russell had adhered to until then, and to what extent does it introduce a novel analytic method? Here too I will appeal to views advanced by Quine and Hylton for contrast.

The transition from the ontological discussion in the previous sections can be made smooth by starting with a principle already alluded to in the first quotation from Quine: 'In PoM, 1903, Russell's ontology was unrestrained. Every word referred to something'. One immediately notices that Russell's wording in PoM is somewhat different; he does not speak of reference: 'every word occurring in a sentence must have *some* meaning: a perfectly meaningless sound could not be employed in the more or less fixed manner in which language employs words' (PoM: § 46). I will be returning to this point later.

This principle, and the associated ontology stand, on Quine's view, in blatant contrast to the stance adopted in OD. After characterizing the reform in Russell's view in OD as involving 'defining a term not by presenting a direct equivalent of it, but by what Bentham called *paraphrasis*: by providing equivalents of all desired sentences containing the term', he continues,

> The new freedom that paraphrasis confers is our reward for recognizing that the unit of communication is the sentence and not the word. This point in semantical theory was long obscured by the undeniable primacy, in one respect, of words . . . Bentham was perhaps the first to see the sentence thus as the primary vehicle of meaning. Frege took up the tale. But Russell, in his theory of singular description, was the first to put this insight to precise and effective use.
>
> (ROD: p. 293)

Leaving aside the issue of the unit of *communication* – a matter I find no evidence of Russell being in the least concerned with – Quine's view is fairly straightforward: in PoM Russell thought every word in a sentence had a meaning (which meshes well with our discussion of fictional names). By contrast, in OD, whose import is that denoting phrases do not have meaning, this principle was abandoned. But does PoM sanction this interpretation? Does

Russell's *practice* in PoM lend support to Quine's view of this principle? Consider the following instances.

In § 72 Russell considers the question (which incidentally concerns denoting phrases) 'if *u* be a class concept, is the concept "all *u*'s" analyzable into two constituents, *all* and *u*, or is it a new concept, defined by a certain relation to *u*, and no more complex than *u* itself?' He concludes that ' "all *u*'s" is not so analyzable', and that 'language, in this case as in some others, is a misleading guide. The same remark will apply to *every*, *any*, *some*, *a*, and *the*' (PoM: § 72). From this it follows that all these words are not considered to have a meaning of their own as the principle demands – only the whole phrase they are part of has meaning.

A similar conclusion emerges from Russell's discussion of the relation of a class-member to a class of which it is a member (PoM: § 76): language expresses this relation with two words ('is a' as in 'Socrates is a man'), but logic regards this as a simple and indefinable relation (indicated by the Greek epsilon). So in this case too, not *every* word has a meaning.

The supposition that Russell believed that there was a one-to-one correspondence between words and meanings is further upset by the case of single words having complex meanings. In § 53 he speaks of the proposition expressed by 'A is' (an equivalent of which we considered earlier), commenting that 'the *is* here is quite different from the *is* in "Socrates is human"; it may be regarded as complex and as really predicating Being of *A*' (§ 53).

These instances prompt us to take a closer look at the sentence immediately following Russell's statement of the principle that every word has some meaning. It reads, 'The correctness of our philosophical analysis of a proposition may therefore be usefully checked by the exercise of assigning the meaning of each word in the sentence expressing the proposition' (PoM: § 46).

It seems to me that the alleged tension between the principle and the theory of descriptions disappears as soon as we attend to the locution 'correctness of our philosophical analysis'. The principle does not imply that in language as we use it, every word has a meaning. What is meant, rather, is that this should hold good of the *final* stage of analysis (i.e. after 'is a' will have been replaced with an epsilon, 'is', in other contexts, with 'has being', and so on). It is to the *output* of the analytic process, not its input, that the test is supposed to apply (which suggests that 'symbol' might be more apt than 'word'). And even when this amendment has been made, the principle states only that every word has 'some meaning', not some reference, as in Quine's reformulation. In view of the legitimacy of empty denoting phrases in the PoM theory, this difference is crucial.

I conclude that despite the fact that the theory of descriptions presents, no doubt, a more striking case than ever before of a gap between pre- and post-analytic forms of sentences, it does not go against the principle that every word has meaning when that principle is properly understood. On the contrary, it provides a remarkable vindication of this principle because in the analytic form provided by the theory of descriptions each word (or rather symbol) *does* have a meaning. So the consideration of this principle does not, as has been supposed, lend support to the view that the theory of descriptions embodies a fundamental change in Russell's views.

V Contextual definition

I turn now to consider two allied notions which it is customary to regard as novelties of which the theory of descriptions is seen as a first clear embodiment, namely contextual definition and incomplete symbol. The theory of descriptions is rightly considered as the paradigmatic embodiment of both, but to what degree are they new? I begin with contextual definition.

There are at least two places in PoM which show Russell considering contextual definition as a perfectly legitimate procedure. First, we have a *general* endorsement when, in response to a possible objection against his *defining* negation by means of implication (though I do not wish to suggest this definition is contextual), Russell explains that 'when a purely formal aim is to be served, any equivalence in which a certain notion appears on one side but not on the other will do for a definition' (PoM: § 19).

That the phrasing of this last remark is no slip is evidenced by his discussion, later on, where the definition of denoting phrases (not including 'the'-phrases) by means of formal implications is considered:[20]

> Let us observe, to begin with, that the explicit mention of *any*, *some*, etc., need not occur in Mathematics: formal implication will express all that is required. Let us recur to an instance already discussed in connection with denoting, where *a* is a class and *b* a class of classes. We have
>
>> '*Any a* belongs to any *b*' is equivalent to '"*x* is an *a*" implies that "*u* is a *b*" implies "*x* is a *u*"';
>> '*Any a* belongs to a *b*' is equivalent to '"*x* is an *a*" implies "there is a *b*, say *u*, such that *x* is a *u*"';
>
> ... and so on for the remaining relations considered in Chapter V. The question arises: How far do these equivalences constitute definitions of *any*, *a*, *some*, and how far are these notions involved in the symbolism itself?
>
> (PoM: § 87)

---

20 Russell sometimes uses 'formal implication' to cover quantified statements generally. Thus in the theory of descriptions analysis of denoting phrases would come under this heading as well. The prominence of formal implication (and hence its being taken as a logical constant in the restricted sense indicated in Chapter 1) is explained by Russell's belief that all logical and mathematical truths have that form.

Russell's reply to the question ending this quotation is that *some* and *a* (though not *any*) 'may be legitimately replaced by their equivalents in terms of formal implications' (§ 89), a conclusion about which he expresses reservations in the following section. What is important for our present concern is not so much whether he actually adopted any of these equivalences as definitions, but rather the considerations he brings to bear, and in particular, the *absence* of any reservations concerning the legitimacy of the procedure. Thus the fundamental idea of contextual definition is clearly in place, and any scruples one might have about the theory of descriptions in this regard would apply to these proposals as well.

Russell's considerations are, first, that despite the equivalences holding good, the *definiens* and *definiendum* do not mean exactly the same – an obstacle he is willing to ignore for mathematical purposes (§ 89). Second – and this is the grounds for setting *any* apart from *some* and *a* – there is the question of whether the notions being defined are already 'involved in the symbolism'. The danger here is plainly that of circularity: i.e. we might define *any* in terms of formal implication and then find it presupposed in that rather complex notion itself. This is indeed the verdict, since *any* is found to be presupposed by formal implication (§ 89).[21]

To conclude, the notion of contextual definition in general and, more specifically, its use for defining denoting phrases in terms of formal implications, is firmly in place in PoM. The application to 'the'-phrases was of course new with the theory of descriptions (a very significant addition, as will be explained in the final section below), but there is no reason to suppose that there had been any change of principle with respect to this strategy between PoM and OD. So rather than a revolution, the theory of descriptions is, in this respect, no more than an application of a familiar technique to a fresh case which was not known to be amenable to it beforehand.

VI The notion of an incomplete symbol

Contextual definition is, undoubtedly, a crucial feature of the theory of descriptions, but focusing on it alone tends to obscure another, arguably even more important, aspect which emerges when reflecting upon this theory as an instance of the allied notion of an incomplete symbol. The remarks that follow aim not only to show, as might be expected, that this notion is not completely new with the theory of descriptions, but also to illuminate the

---

21 That this is indeed the danger in mind becomes apparent in Russell's use of this turn of phrase when he comments on the indefinability of propositional functions: 'Every relation which is many–one ... defines a function ... But where the function is a proposition, the notion involved is presupposed in the symbolism, and cannot be defined by means of it without a vicious circle: for in the above general definition of a function propositional functions already occur" (PoM: § 80).

notion of an incomplete symbol itself. The feature I have foremost in mind emerges when we observe that the transition from the theory of denoting concepts to the theory of descriptions may be described in the following manner. Instead of a complex entity occurring as a propositional constituent, the complex, to use Russell's phrase, is 'broken up'. It has not simply disappeared, because its constituents have been absorbed into the embedding complex, i.e. the proposition in which it occurred.

Russell attached the label 'incomplete symbol' to a number of distinct analytic moves he made in other cases (relating to classes, relations, matrices and propositions). In PM, where it is first given that label, Russell characterized an incomplete symbol as 'a symbol which is not supposed to have any meaning in isolation, but is only defined in certain contexts' (PM: p. 66).

The first thing to note about this characterization is that if we regard it as a sufficient condition, we are led to acknowledge some rather uninteresting cases as incomplete symbols (e.g. brackets, punctuation marks, 'etc.' and probably all the initial words in denoting phrases). I mention this not to suggest that something is amiss with the characterization, but rather to bring out the fact that the point of declaring something an incomplete symbol depends upon the *contrast* with a former view which regarded the symbol in question as *having* some meaning in isolation. We may characterize a complete symbol as one which is guaranteed to have some piece of non-symbolic reality corresponding to it in every case.[22] In view of this our subject is more appropriately described as *the exercise of declaring* something, formerly thought of as a complete symbol, to be an incomplete symbol. This is because something's merely *being* an incomplete symbol is not always an interesting logical fact. This is the kind of move I wish to consider, and I will be referring to it as 'the exercise' for short.

My contention regarding this exercise is that despite its 'symbolic' correlate being heuristically more convenient to focus on, its true essence is ontological. Such a view is suggested by observing the various cases of Russell arguing that something is an incomplete symbol. In each of them the import of the exercise is the withdrawal of a former ontological commitment to some kind of entity: classes, relations, propositions or, in the case of the theory of descriptions, *denoting concepts*.

Before explaining why I consider the symbolic aspect to be secondary, I will introduce a case not generally acknowledged as instantiating the exercise. This is intended to serve the dual purpose of showing that the idea is not completely new in OD, and of shedding light on the more general

---

22 I say 'guaranteed in *every* case' bearing in mind that in Russell's first theory of denoting, denoting phrases are *not* regarded as incomplete symbols. They can lack a denotation, but not a meaning (this is true of Frege's theory of sense as well).

question of the relation between the ontological and symbolic facets of the exercise.

In the appendix to PoM devoted to Frege, Russell criticizes Frege's notion of a function (correlative to his own 'assertion', as employed in PoM §§ 43–4). He first characterizes this notion as 'what remains of the said unity when one of its terms is simply removed' ('unity' may be here regarded as equivalent to 'proposition') and asserts squarely that

> confining ourselves to one variable, it was maintained in Chapter VII that, except where the proposition from which we start is predicative or else asserts a fixed relation to a fixed term, **there is no such entity**: the analysis into argument and assertion cannot be performed in the manner required. Thus what Frege calls a function, if our conclusion was sound, **is in general a non-entity**.
>
> (PoM: § 482)

Leaving aside the cogency of this argument as an objection to Frege, I propose that despite its pre-dating the introduction of the expression 'incomplete symbol', the case exemplifies most, if not all, of the essential ingredients of the exercise familiar from the 'canonical' cases.

Although the discussion is held directly at the ontological level, it is easily transformable into symbolic terms. We may then take Russell's case to be that a symbol Frege regards as being (in Russell's sense) complete *in general* has no meaning in isolation (though he admits it will have meaning in some cases). Although the manner in which such a symbol is formed guarantees that in at least some of the contexts in which it occurs it will have a meaning (or, loosely speaking, that *it* will have meaning in those contexts), what was supposed to be the symbol's meaning in general is declared a non-entity and a false abstraction.[23]

Recognizing this early case as embodying the essential characteristics of an incomplete symbol exercise depends on one's acknowledging the ontological facet of the exercise as primary. For that purpose I turn now to the case which I consider to provide the strongest evidence in favour of this view, namely propositions. That propositions are incomplete symbols is a facet of the multiple relation theory of judgement which had already entered our discussion in the previous chapter.

On the face of things there appears to be a mismatch: if propositions are not, as we have insisted all along, symbols, what sense can be made of a claim

---

23 For Russell's use of this expression see also his 1906 paper 'On the Substitutional Theory of Classes and Relations' (Lackey: p. 166). Such a claim raises a difficulty: how can being be meaningfully denied? – which we will address shortly.

that they are incomplete ones? I know of no way of reconciling *all* of Russell's statements relating to this discrepancy but,[24] bearing in mind the need to cater for the other cases of denoting concepts and classes as well, the following interpretation seems to me the most plausible. Russell's claim can be understood as follows: what were formerly regarded as propositions become (in the new theory) non-entities or false abstractions. Judgements take a role analogous to that taken by propositions in the former cases: they are the kind of entity which corresponds to the 'complete' symbol which is the result of supplementing the incomplete symbol with a suitable context.

Now the curious thing about the case of propositions is that despite Russell's conceiving of it as a clear instance of the very same strategy he applied in the former cases – I take the shared label as an indication of no mere 'family resemblance' – there is no analogous *symbolic* move: no paraphrasis, no contextual definition or the like. It is, indeed, difficult to see how any of these might apply. The symbols to which propositions were held to correspond are complete declarative sentences, but then so are the symbols corresponding to judgements. There seems to be no coherent way of construing the exercise with propositions as an instance of the same strategy that was used in the former cases unless we take the essential aspect of the move to be ontological. The symbolic facet of the exercise turns out not even to be a necessary ingredient.[25]

It has been suggested that making 'incomplete symbol' a technical term is a sign that language acquires a more important role in Russell's philosophy than before.[26] But although symbols do acquire *some* special role, when this role is examined carefully it does nothing to upset the primacy of the onto-

---

24 The relevant passages occur in the first few pages of Chapter III and, with respect to judgements and propositions, p. 44 of Chapter II, of the introduction to PM. In the latter, Russell seems to oscillate between talk of symbols and the non-linguistic entities they are supposed to stand for. He says, on the one hand, that 'the **phrase** which expresses a proposition is what we call an "incomplete" symbol; it does not have meaning in itself, but requires some supplementation in order to acquire a complete meaning'. But in the next sentence also that 'judgement in itself supplies a sufficient supplement,' and that 'when I judge "Socrates is human," the meaning is completed by the **act of judging**, and we no longer have an incomplete symbol'. Surely, an *act* of judgement cannot count as *symbolic* supplementation.

25 It might be thought that propositions could be brought into line with the other cases by contending that only sentences with two verbs (one of which expresses a propositional attitude) are complete symbols. But then we face the problem that such sentences might be *false*. To fulfil their role as complete symbols one must suppose there are entities they stand for, but conceding this defeats the whole purpose of the exercise, which was to do away with false propositions. If, however, we take the ontological perspective as primary, then there just is no complex unless a judgement actually occurs. This is consonant with what Russell says on this matter – with full awareness of the problematic situation – on p. 44 of PM.

26 See Hylton *Russell*, p. 269.

logical dimension of the exercise. In fact, this role is owed to the ontological nature of the exercise.

The 'incomplete symbol' exercise effects an ontological reduction. But strictly speaking, as he puts the matter in his 'On the Substitutional Theory of Classes and Relations' (1906), 'we do not deny that there are such entities, we merely abstain from affirming that there are' (Lackey: p. 188).[27] This leaves the exercise itself indescribable: how can we explain that something has been abolished if mentioning it commits us to its being? It is at this point that the appeal to symbols becomes helpful. The matter is explained most clearly in that same essay when, speaking of matrices by means of which assertions are made about classes and relations, Russell says,

> None of these are entities, and thus there are no such things as classes and relations.

> Since absolutely everything there is is an entity, it may be asked what is the meaning of saying that a matrix is not an entity. When we say 'so-and-so is not an entity', the meaning is, properly speaking, '**The phrase** 'so-and-so' is not a name of an entity'. Thus when we say a matrix is not an entity, we mean that a matrix is a set of symbols, or a phrase, which by itself has no meaning at all, but by the addition of other symbols becomes part of a symbol or phrase which has meaning.

> (Lackey: p. 170)

We may explain the appeal to symbols thus: if we regard symbols as serving to create a model of reality, then declaring something to be an incomplete symbol is to point out an artefact of the model – a feature of it which has nothing corresponding to it in what is being modelled. By appealing to the symbolism we can describe the exercise without committing ourselves to the kind of entity it abolishes. Its value is therefore purely heuristic, and does not signify that symbols have become part of our subject matter any more than they were before.

VII The role of language

The last point leads straight to the last issue I wish to pursue in this discussion of OD's place in Russell's methodological development, namely the role of language. I will again appeal to a particular strand of Peter Hylton's account

---

27 A similar remark occurs in PoM: 'In the above manner, it would seem, we can make use of propositional functions without having to introduce the objects which Frege calls functions.' (§ 482).

for contrast.[28] He contends that OD marks a turning point in the significance which Russell gave to language in his philosophy.

To put the following remarks in context, however, it is important to stress at the outset that I do not wish to cast doubt on the fact that the theory of descriptions was a more spectacular case than ever before of the gap between surface form and logical form,[29] and that its discovery inspired Russell to give an 'incomplete symbol' treatment, along the same lines, to other kinds of putative entities. *In the long run* this did indeed affect his more fundamental views, but these changes did not flow from OD as directly (or as rapidly) as the traditional view, or Hylton's for that matter, would suggest.

After OD, Hylton writes, 'language becomes a subject of philosophical interest', contrasting this with the PoM view, where

> propositions were not thought of as constructs, or as entities which were to be inferred from our use of language. They were held, rather, to be directly and immediately accessible to the mind. Propositions, on this view, were themselves the data for philosophy. Both Russell and Moore simply assumed this view, and did not even articulate it. From the outside, however, one can see that it depends on the further assumption that there is a congruence between sentences and the propositions that they express, so that language is a transparent medium through which propositions can be perceived. It is this very transparency of the medium, as they assume, which enables Russell and Moore to ignore it. The effect of the OD theory is to undermine these assumptions.
>
> (Hylton, *Russell*, p. 269)

This portrayal of the pre-OD position does not bear scrutiny. If one could count on propositions always being perceived through a transparent medium, what role could there possibly be for analysis? Analysis is the progression from something muddled or vague to something clear and precise. But if one has the end product from the start, what scope is there for analysis?

The grain of truth in this is that on Russell's view there is a presumption in favour of surface structure. But all this means is that *in the absence of any grounds to the contrary* grammatical structure may be taken as a guide to

---

28 Hylton, *Russell*, pp. 264–73, and in greater detail in an earlier paper, 'The Significance of "On Denoting"', in C. W. Savage and C. A. Anderson (eds), *Rereading Russell* (Minnesota Studies in the Philosophy of Science, Volume 12, Minneapolis: University of Minnesota Press, 1989). His views that OD marks a change in Russell's conception of analysis, in his regarding whole sentences, rather than their parts, as the units of analysis, has already been implicitly controverted by our discussion of contextual definition in PoM.

29 This, and the current discussion generally, employs a very rough and ultimately inaccurate 'translation' of the theory of descriptions into current nomenclature, which will suffice for bringing out the disagreement with Hylton.

logical structure. This is not the kind of substantive position Hylton leads one to believe it is and, as already noted, even in PoM Russell was perfectly able to admit, when he saw fit, that language was misleading. The matter is made very clear at the outset of Chapter IV in PoM (which is where the earlier quotation of the principle that every word has some meaning occurs): 'Although a grammatical distinction cannot be uncritically assumed to correspond to a genuine philosophical difference, yet the one is *prima facie* evidence of the other, and may often be most usefully employed as a source of discovery.' And after stating the said principle he continues, 'On the whole, grammar seems to me to bring us much nearer to a correct logic than the current opinions of philosophers; and in what follows, grammar, though not our master, will yet be taken as our guide' (PoM: § 46).

Such a view, surely, is far from a simple and uncritical assumption of a congruence between sentences and the propositions they express, i.e. the view that language is a completely transparent medium. And when this is acknowledged it becomes apparent that all OD had done in this respect was to bring to light yet another case of sentence/proposition discrepancy over and above those already acknowledged.[30] In short, OD can hardly be portrayed as Russell's first encounter with such discrepancies.

My complaint against Hylton's contrast between OD and Russell's former views is not confined to his portrayal of the pre-OD positions. By stating that before OD 'propositions were not thought of as constructs, or as entities which were to be inferred from our use of language', he intimates, though he does not expressly assert, that OD signifies a change in this respect. But is there anything in OD to lend credence to the idea that propositions might be constructs or inferred from language (any more than there was in PoM)? I find nothing to support this view, and every reason to suppose that in OD propositions are exactly the same as in PoM – except for the fact that denoting concepts are no longer counted as possible constituents.[31]

Talk of propositions as constructs, or as inferred from language, is more appropriate to Russell's position much later, certainly no earlier than 1910, and this provides an opportunity for me to explain why I have chosen 1910 as the cut-off point for the present study.

Russell's view did indeed move eventually in the direction Hylton indicates. A concise statement of the kind of view he was eventually to arrive at occurs in the introduction to the second (1937) edition of PoM: 'In the end, it seems to result that none of the raw material of the world has smooth

---

30 Similarly, maintaining, as Russell did *before* OD, that some proper names are descriptions in disguise is yet another case of recognizing such a discrepancy – despite the subject–predicate form remaining intact.

31 Russell's view on propositions from the time of OD is clearly put in the 1905 essay 'The Nature of Truth' (only recently published as paper 21 in CPR Volume 4).

logical properties, but that whatever appears to have such properties is constructed artificially in order to have them' (p. xi). But can we say that the journey in that direction began with OD in 1905? I have argued that this is not the case. In 1910, on the other hand, there appears to be a change which does, it seems to me, undermine something truly fundamental in Russell's view, and arguably set the train (whose direction was indicated by the last quotation) in motion. It is the multiple relation theory of judgement and the abolition of propositions.

Once there are no propositions in the sense that this term has in PoM, the kind of view Russell had of logic becomes untenable (the nature of this view will be discussed in Chapter 7), because neither facts nor judgements can take their place, so central to logic. Facts, because they do not have the duality of truth and falsehood; and judgements, because, despite having that duality, they are inherently dependent upon particular minds. The whole framework which underlay his philosophy until then was undermined, though it was only gradually that this became apparent (the failure, in *Theory of Knowledge* in 1913, to develop a tenable version of this theory was surely a major event in this respect). I am not suggesting that in 1910 Russell saw clearly where the abolition of propositions would lead him, even less that he was already there, but only that a decisive move in this regard occurred then, and not before.

Returning to Hylton, most of his comments on these changes speak of Russell's thought 'after OD' (which strictly indicates any post-1905 date) and are not as explicit as they might have been about OD's being the cause. But the whole context of his discussion makes it plain that he regards OD as the crucial turning point. I propose that all these developments are more accurately ascribed to the period after 1910 (and it may well be that a later date is ultimately more appropriate), and that attributing them to OD is to read history back to front. This is important not only for Russell's development, but because OD is often regarded as a founding event for a linguistic method in philosophy generally. The facts noted in the present chapter will not, however, warrant such claims.

VIII Some positive remarks

To conclude the present chapter I wish to put forth a few positive remarks on the role of OD in Russell's methodological development, though I must confess that they are only tentative and I cannot assert them as definitely as I would have wished. Looking at Russell's course at the beginning of OD – proceeding from the variable and propositional functions to general propositions and 'the'-phrases – one wonders what precisely is new. Surely, the account of 'the'-phrases is new, but does it not signify something more general? The answer seems to me to lie in what may be described as Russell's giving up, or at least loosening a certain kind of hang-up which characterized his thinking on such matters up until then.

In PoM Russell was clearly aware of the equivalence of 'all Fs are Gs' and $\forall x(Fx \rightarrow G\,x)$, and despite the absence of any direct evidence I am aware of, must also be assumed to have been aware of the related equivalences presented at the beginning of OD (for 'everything', 'nothing', 'something', 'a' and 'some'). But despite this awareness, before OD he was unwilling to regard these formulae as providing the ultimate accounts of these notions, because they all presuppose the variable, which in turn presupposes 'any'. It is for this reason that he regarded the account of such phrases in terms of denoting concepts as being more fundamental than the account in term of the variable. This had clearly changed in OD.

At one level this change is easily explained. The discovery of a formal implication equivalence of forms containing 'the' alters the picture because now *all* denoting phrases can be reduced to forms containing the variable; and it therefore becomes a viable course to accept the variable as indefinable since it encapsulates everything 'any' might have been required for. The reasoning underlying such a move – 'economizing with indefinables' – is a familiar feature of PoM and the writings leading to the *Principia* generally. But it also seems to have a more general significance, because the duality between the account in terms of the variable and formal implication on the one hand, and in terms of denoting concepts on the other, marks in PoM a more general duality.

In an earlier quotation from Russell, about *any* equivalence capable of serving as a definition, I ignored the opening remark, 'when a purely formal aim is to be served', and similarly his pointing out, when the specific definitions were at stake, that 'any' and 'some' 'need not occur in mathematics: formal implication will express all that is required'. These remarks are symptoms of the more general duality (already mentioned in Chapter 1) which led him to sometimes admit an analytic account was satisfactory for technical purposes, but then to expect a second philosophical stage of analysis to follow and settle what is ultimately fundamental. This bipartite vision acted in PoM as a persistent hindrance to accepting solutions which would later be regarded as satisfactory (the discussion of empty phrases in § 73 exemplifies this most clearly). The most typical manifestation of this tendency is Russell's admitting that some pairs of propositions are equivalent, but rejecting the idea that one might serve as an analysis of the other on the grounds that they do not *mean* quite the same (e.g. §§ 40, 73, 90).

Because the variable marked, before OD, the technical frontier, the decision to take it as fundamental, rather than expect it to be given an analysis at a deeper, non-technical level, has the effect (which theoretically it might not have had) of sweeping away many of these philosophical hang-ups. OD marks Russell's abandonment of such reservations.

One of Russell's first remarks (in OF) upon discovering the theory of descriptions was 'this is all we need', which, to anyone familiar with the context clearly means (as when saying that formal implication will express 'all that is required') that it is all we need *for the deductive enterprise of the Principia*, i.e. that it can serve all the purposes for which we need definite descriptions in this undertaking. But in OD there is no mention of such a restriction. The distinction between mathematical and philosophical definitions (which Russell stressed in PoM[32]) seems inapplicable to the theory of descriptions. It is surely a mathematical definition, but that seems no longer to exclude it from also counting as a philosophical one – in other words, as providing the ultimate account of the matter. More generally, the setting aside of philosophical worries for later treatment is no longer found, and Russell appears to think that an account which will do for technical purposes will do generally. This, I propose, is the more general significance of the theory of descriptions which emerges when set against the background of the pre-OD writings.

In the present chapter I have tried to show that many, perhaps most, of the more general features which the theory of descriptions has often been assumed to have introduced for the first time were anticipated in one form or another in PoM, and that the alleged contrast between the theory of descriptions and what had gone before it is grossly exaggerated. This is due to a relative neglect of PoM and of Russell's work, both published and unpublished, between it and OD, on the one hand, and to a hasty appropriation of OD to a more thoroughly linguistic mode of philosophizing which developed only later, on the other. In 1905 the theory of descriptions was a far more local affair than would appear in the light of later developments. One could without undue exaggeration describe it as a spin-off of the logicist enterprise. I am not claiming there was nothing new in the theory of descriptions, but merely that it involved much more bringing together of elements which were already at hand, and applying them to a new case, than is generally acknowledged.

It must be admitted that the opposing, more traditional, view which was sketched at the beginning of this chapter, with its focus on empty phrases and the contrast with the Meinongian alternative, and its sharp contrast between OD and what had gone before, has the undeniable merits of a 'good story'. It is simpler, clearer, and may appear to enjoy a greater prima facie plausibility than the alternative, more complex, story I have been telling. But while conceding these advantages, it must also be said that it suffers from a flaw, which some may regard as fatal, namely failing to fit the facts.

---

32 See §§ 16, 31 and primarily 108, where mathematical definition is explained thus: 'Given any set of notions, a term is definable by means of these notions when, and only when, it is the only term having to certain of these notions a certain relation which itself is one of the said notions. But philosophically, the word *definition* has not, as a rule, been employed in that sense; it has, in fact, been restricted to the analysis of an idea into its constituents'.

Part II

Frege

Chapter 4

From *Begriffsschrift* to sense and reference

I Introduction

In his seminal paper *Über Sinn und Bedeutung* (1892, henceforth 'SuB') Frege introduces the distinction between an expression's *denotation* or *reference*, and its *sense*. The distinction is made, in the first instance, with respect to proper names. Very crudely, though 'Plato's mentor' and 'Xanthippa's husband' have one and the same referent, namely (the man) Socrates, each corresponds to a different way in which this man is presented or determined. Corresponding to each of these modes of presentation is what Frege calls the name's *sense*.

Frege's discussion at the outset of SuB makes it plain that the distinction was occasioned by the discovery of a fault in a view he advocated earlier, in Bs. § 8, but, as with Russell's OD, in that paper he does little to impress upon the reader that this ancestry is indispensable for an understanding of his chief point. As in Russell's case, I maintain that ignoring this ancestry can lead a contemporary reader to gloss over fundamental misunderstandings regarding the theory propounded. My course with Frege's distinction will thus begin with a careful examination and reconstruction of the original problem (in section II), after which I move on to its earlier solution set forth in Bs. (section III) and to the fault, the discovery of which led Frege to abandon that solution (section IV), finally arriving at the new solution in SuB (section V). In view of the vast literature on the sense/reference distinction, it is surprising to discover how seldom this particular approach has been taken. After all, it is Frege himself who, at the beginning of SuB, puts us on the track to Bs.; reconstructing this route is therefore no sideways pursuit, but is to approach the distinction by the main entrance. Before launching into this discussion something needs to be said about the context in which the problem presented itself to Frege.

The problem arose, like Russell's concern with denoting, in the course of preparatory work for the logicist project. The concept-script (*Begriffsschrift*) was designed first and foremost to be the language in which this undertaking would be discharged.[1] Identity presented itself as an issue because identity-statements appear to be indispensable *in mathematics*, and hence a symbol for identity is indispensable *in the concept-script*. Whether or not this has implications for natural language, the original setting gives little reason to think that Frege is concerned with natural language. On the contrary, the original endeavour, as Frege explains in the preface, was 'to test how far one could get in arithmetic by means of logical deductions alone' (Bynum: p. 104). This, in turn, led to a further requirement:

> So that something intuitive [*etwas anschauliches*] could not squeeze in unnoticed here, it was most important to keep the chain of reasoning free of gaps. As I endeavoured to fulfil this requirement most rigorously, I found an obstacle in the inadequacy of language; despite all the unwieldiness of the expressions, the more complex the relations became, the less precision – which my purpose required – could be obtained. From this deficiency arose the idea of the 'conceptual notation' presented here. Thus, its chief purpose should be to test in the most reliable manner the validity of a chain of reasoning and expose each presupposition which tends to creep in unnoticed, so that its source can be investigated.
>
> (Bynum: p. 104)

Frege opens his discussion of identity in Bs. § 8 by introducing us straight away to the solution, leaving it for us to reconstruct the problem. This can indeed be done, first, by a careful examination of the manner in which he argues for his solution; second, by appeal to general features of his outlook in that work; and third, with the aid of his critical discussion of it at the beginning of SuB. Despite Bs. and SuB presenting different solutions, the *problem* they both confront is exactly the same. It is therefore essential to be clear about the problem if one is to understand both theories correctly.

II The problem

To understand why the sign for identity of content in the concept-script calls for special treatment, we must first know what the 'normal' treatment would be, and this hinges on the notion of content: 'symbols are usually only representatives of their contents – so that each combination of symbols usually only expresses a relation between their contents' (Bs.: § 8). Content, though

---

1 T. W. Bynum (in 'The evolution of Frege's logicism' in M. Schirn (ed.), *Studies on Frege* (Stuttgart and Bad-Cannstatt: Frommann-Holzboog, 1976)) has suggested that Frege's *commitment* to logicism may have dawned upon him only gradually, and was not firmly in place in Bs. This seems plausible, but does not affect my point since what is required of a conceptual notation is the same whether logicism is regarded as a mere hypothesis or is actually endorsed.

never characterized as carefully as were sense and reference later, is nonetheless a technical term in Frege. It is a fundamental notion which without change underlies his thinking from Bs. until SuB.[2]

Both simple and complex symbols are held to have contents, which divide into two basic kinds: those which can be asserted, that is, judgeable contents (*beurtheilbare Inhalt*), and others which cannot, i.e. unjudgeable contents. 'Content' throughout this discussion will always indicate *conceptual* content. Not everything concerning content is made perfectly clear, but this much is: that the content of a proper name is the object whose name it is, the content of a concept name is a concept (Gl. § 51), and the content of a complete indicative sentence is a judgeable content. Judgeable contents resemble Russellian propositions in many respects (while differing in others): they are the bearers of truth,[3] the entities which enter into inferential relations, and the kind of entity one's relation to which can constitute knowledge. In a nutshell, everything logically significant about a symbol is embodied in its content, and what is logically irrelevant is excluded from it.[4]

The content, as is clear from the quotation above, is what is spoken about, or expressed, when symbols of the concept-script are used. Although it is convenient to speak of a content as the content *of* a word, expression and so on – it is only by reference to such things that some types of contents can be specified – it would be a mistake to think of content as being *essentially* linked to linguistic entities, i.e. as being identity-dependent upon them, or upon language in general. Similarly, content is crucially independent of anything mental. (These matters will emerge more clearly when we come to Frege's attack on the Bs. theory.) In view of this, I will try to bring out the problem in terms of content rather than in terms of sentences or words, but it must be remembered that even when this policy, for the sake of brevity, is not strictly adhered to, it is the content-related rather than language-related formulation that is, as a rule, intended.

Returning now to identity: since identity is a relation held by every object only with itself, it would seem to follow that any *true* identity-content concerning an object *a*, would be the same. Put differently, if (the content expressed by) 'a = b' is true then, since the content of 'b' (the object) is *ex hypothesi* the same as the content of 'a', there could not possibly be any difference between it and the judgeable content expressed by 'a = a'. In the absence

2 In the present discussion I regard SuB as the place where the distinction was first introduced, despite its having been anticipated in the slightly earlier 'Function and Concept' (1891), where it occurs only as a side issue.
3 This is implicit in Bs. § 2 despite Frege's use of 'affirmed', rather than 'true', throughout Bs. Part I. See also Gl. § 36.
4 Frege makes this point in the preface to Bs. (Bynum: p. 104): 'I have omitted everything which is without importance for the chain of inference. In § 3, [where he dismisses the subject/predicate distinction] I have designated by *conceptual content* that which is of sole importance to me'.

of any special reason to the contrary, Frege's conception of content would prescribe a dismissal of the feeling we have in some cases of a significant difference between 'a = a' and 'a = b', leading him to conclude that since any difference between the two does not belong to the content, it cannot be logically significant. Like the difference between the active and passive voices, or pairs such as 'and' and 'but' (Bs.: §§ 3 and 7), it would seem to be a difference of a kind that the concept-script is designed to filter out, and there should therefore be no need for a sign for identity of content in a concept-script.

In Bs. Frege singles out two reasons which seem to compel us to admit a sign for identity of content nonetheless. First, identities in mathematics often require proof and embody knowledge which was not available at the outset. It is therefore implausible to suppose that they express the same content as that expressed by the corresponding 'a = a'. This is illustrated by a geometrical example in Bs. § 8 (and similarly on p. 57 of SuB), where identity-statements involving different names for the same point in a geometrical construction seem to express something mathematical, not merely linguistic. The other point he mentions (while remarking that it is more superficial) is the need to introduce abbreviations of lengthy expressions; the sign for identity of content is needed here as well. So we must somehow reconcile the view of content and identity which prescribes the contrary, with the brute fact that there can be a striking difference between 'a = a' and a true 'a = b'. These two cases, it is worth noting, raise essentially the same questions which, as we saw in Chapter 1, Russell thought were answered by the theory of denoting: how can it be worthwhile to assert an identity, and how can a mathematical definition be both a discovery and a mere notational abbreviation.

Now that we have an initial account of the puzzle before us, and before moving on to Frege's first solution, I wish to bring it into sharper focus, by disentangling it from some elements which are often mistakenly thought to be essential to it and then by emphasizing other elements which I think are essential, but whose role is not made sufficiently clear in most presentations – not even in Frege's.

The first point may be a stumbling block only for beginners. One of Frege's examples appeals to the contrast between the empirical nature of 'the evening star = the morning start', and the apparent a-priori nature of 'the evening star = the evening star'. Now though this contrast is indeed useful in bringing out the distinctness of 'a = a' and 'a = b' *in those cases where the latter is empirical,* it is by no means necessary for generating the puzzle. If that were the case the puzzle would not be relevant to arithmetical contents, which it is essential that it should be.

Another, more significant, point which needs clarifying is the absence of any assumption of compositionality. By compositionality, in this context, I mean the tenet that a judgeable content, the content of a complete indicative sentence, is composed of a definite set of constituent contents which are its *parts*. Deciding whether this assumption is essential to the puzzle is important for at least two reasons. First, because it has been thought to be essential even by writers who have striven to delineate its exact nature with the utmost care;[5] and second, compositionality cannot be ascribed to the Bs. position with any confidence and my claim that it is precisely the same problem in Bs. and in SuB. therefore hinges on the possibility of generating the puzzle without it. It is natural (though not strictly necessary) to construe compositionality as implying that the content of each word or phrase in the sentence (or each symbol in a formula) forms a discrete *part* of the content expressed by that sentence. I take Frege's talk of parts quite literally. It is no mere metaphor.[6] Although Frege clearly endorsed this tenet later, with regard to senses – the complex sense corresponding to a complete declarative sentence, a 'thought' is constituted of the senses of its constituent expressions – Bs. contains no clear evidence of his commitment to it. It contains, instead, a rather strong, though indirect, piece of evidence to the contrary.[7] We are thus faced with certain questions. Does the puzzle arise on a noncompositional view of judgeable contents as well? Would it arise if we regarded judgeable contents as unstructured?

On a non-compositional view, a judgeable content is still the *value* of a function for some given argument, but neither function nor argument are considered to be its *parts*. On such a view it is at least possible that the value of the function for an argument will be a simple entity, which is excluded on the compositional view. Now consider, on such a view, the judgeable content expressed by 'a = a'. Among the various pairs of function and argument it is the value of, one must surely be the contents of '( ) = a' and of 'a' as function and argument respectively.[8] If we then assume that 'b' has the same content as 'a', the value of the said function for *b* (the content of 'b') as argument cannot differ from its value for *a,* since we are supplying the very same argument in both cases. Hence the judgeable content expressed by 'a = a' must be the same as that expressed by 'a = b', and the puzzle does

---

5 See N. Salmon, *Frege's Puzzle* (Cambridge, MA: MIT Press, 1896) p. 55, and W. W. Taschek, 'Frege's puzzle, sense, and information content', *Mind*, 101 (1992) pp. 76–91.

6 There is ample evidence for this. See, for example, his letter to Russell of 20 October 1902, where he writes, 'the sense of "3", the sense of "+", and the sense of "5" are **parts** of the sense of "3 + 5" ' (PMC: p. 149).

7 Speaking of the distinction between function and argument, Frege says in Bs. § 9 that it 'has nothing to do with the conceptual content; it concerns only our way of looking at it'. Now this *could* be interpreted as going beyond the mere admission that a given content can be 'carved' or analysed in different ways. If the carving into function and argument does *not* reflect any internal structure of the content, then this opens the way to a non-compositional view which would allow the judgeable content to be *simple*.

8 I take function and argument to be entities, not symbols. Frege's rather linguistic presentation of the distinction in Bs. should, I think, be regarded as mere carelessness and not as the expression of a considered view of the kind he was to criticize so strongly in later writings.

not, therefore, require the assumption of compositionality. Having shown this, I will continue, for the sake of brevity, as if the thesis of compositionality held good.

Another thing we must take account of is the idea that the puzzle concerns *language* in some essential way.[9] This idea is so deeply rooted in most presentations that it is no easy task to disentangle the puzzle from it. Since this issue will come to the fore in section IV below in relation to Frege's criticism of the Bs. theory, I confine myself here to a few preliminaries.

I use 'word', 'symbol' and 'sentence' (or more generally 'linguistic entity') exclusively to indicate entities which, though *used* to express meanings (in some loose sense of the term), have their identities fixed quite independently of those meanings. In short, they are syntactic elements. The common way for making assertions about such entities is by *mentioning* them. The question is whether such entities play any essential role in the puzzle (there can be no question about their *practical* indispensability in explaining it[10]).

On the conception of content I attribute to Frege, when we speak of 'a = b' being informative, true and so on, it is not the sentence, the linguistic entity, but rather the judgeable content it expresses that is at stake. Accordingly, what is understood and known is, properly speaking, not a sentence, but rather its content. After presenting my account of the puzzle it will become clear why observing this distinction is crucial.

Coming now to what I wish to argue *is* essential to the puzzle, my contention is that the heart of the matter lies not in the consideration of identity-statements alone; it concerns, rather, the relation between *subject* and content; and only by bringing a subject (a knower, believer and so on) into consideration does the puzzle emerge. This is not as immediately clear from Frege's presentations as it might have been.

The traditional presentations of the puzzle emphasize, justly, that (in the appropriate cases) 'a = b', unlike 'a = a', is a discovery or a surprise, or something of the sort. This feature is surely a crucial element in the puzzle-generating situation, but what precisely is its role? Clearly, these claims aim to establish that there is a *difference* between a true 'a = b' and 'a = a' or, more precisely, that they convey distinct *contents* – in the specific sense of that term introduced above. But it is precisely here that the usual presentations (including Frege's own in SuB) seem to me to stop short of their target: how do we establish that the difference is indeed a *difference in conceptual content*? We might simply point it out and hope for some intuitive recogni-

---

9 This is encouraged by the English translation of SuB – where *Satz* is translated sometimes as 'statement' (e.g. G&B: p. 56) and sometimes as 'sentence' (p. 57). While 'sign' carries an explicit linguistic sense, *Satz* has the kind of ambiguity between expression and its content which 'proposition' has in English (e.g. 'Euclid's propositions').

10 Frege says, 'we still distinguish between the symbols themselves and their content, even though it may be that the content can only be grasped by their aid' (Gl.: § 16).

tion: one just *sees* in the chosen kind of case that they are obviously different. The need to say more at this point may be brought out by considering the following challenge: How do we know the difference is indeed one of conceptual content rather than just seemingly so as, for example, with the difference between 'and' and 'but'? I am *not* proposing that the difference is indeed like that between 'and' and 'but'; what I wish to point out is the need for an *argument* to that effect which, as things stand, is missing.

So long as whether the difference belongs to the conceptual content is left to intuitive recognition, something crucial about the precise nature of the puzzle has been left out. Such an argument *is* indeed implicit in characterizing 'a = b' (by contrast to 'a = a') as being informative, a surprise, a discovery and the like, but it needs spelling out fully. Here is my proposal for what this implicit argument is.

To maintain that 'a = b' is a discovery, or has a different cognitive value from 'a = a', is to consider, in effect, not only these two contents themselves, but rather the broader contents 'S knows (or believes) that A' and 'S knows (or believes) that B' (where 'A' and 'B' abbreviate 'a = a' and 'a = b' respectively). If A and B were one and the same content – as the 'normal', unmodified, view of Bs. prescribes – then, by applying the same principle to these broader contents, S's knowledge of the one would just *be* his knowledge of the other. There could be no discrepancy between these two (broader) contents. By saying that B is a discovery we imply that, since we can assume that the subject knew that 'a = a' all along, before the discovery, the two broader contents had *different truth values*, and here we have a property which, unlike being a surprise, is unquestionably objective and belongs to contents in a primary sense. If the embedded contents A and B *were* identical then, so the argument goes, the two broader contents could not possibly have had distinct truth values. If they did, then we would have had contents which consisted in the same subject bearing the same relation to the same conceptual content being both true and false. So from the distinctness of the broader epistemic contents it follows that the embedded contents A and B must be distinct.

This roundabout manner of generating the puzzle is essential. As long as we confine our gaze to the identity-contents themselves, we lack an argument for their distinctness, and hence our understanding of the puzzle remains incomplete. If we wish to found the puzzle on something more substantial than the mere intuitive 'feeling' that the two identities are distinct, we must turn to the *epistemic* contents 'S knows that a = a' and 'S knows that a = b'.

The puzzle does not require that the statements under consideration be identity-statements. It can be generated with any other pair of statements produced by substituting 'b' for an embedded 'a', where 'a = b' is true. So although *occasioned* by the consideration of identity-statements, the puzzle's essence has to do rather with the substitution of co-referential terms in epistemic contexts, and it thus embodies the very same difficulties as Russell's puzzles about George IV wanting to know whether Scott is the author of *Waverley* (in OD), and why identities are ever worth stating (in PoM). Similarly, it is not essential that the epistemic relation involved be knowledge (rather than, say, belief) though it has some advantages as an example.

The role of pairs (like 'a = a' and 'a = b') characteristically employed to bring out the difficulty can now be explained more precisely as follows. The Bs. theory of content, unamended, prescribes a *numerical* identity between the contents expressed by 'a = a' and 'a = b'. What the familiar examples (like that of the identity of the morning star and the evening star) serve to establish is their numerical distinctness. The route to this starts from the *qualitative* diversity of the associated epistemic contents (their having distinct truth values), from which it follows that the two *embedded* contents are qualitatively distinct (one has a property, the other does not), and this, in turn, implies that the two contents are *numerically* distinct. It is noteworthy that the mere numerical diversity is what gives rise to the puzzle, and that the qualitative diversity is only a means to that end. This line of thought is also suggested in a letter Frege wrote to Russell where, in the course of arguing for the distinction, he points out with respect to the pair '$2^3 > 7$' and '$3^2-1 > 7$',

> The thoughts contained in those *Sätze* are evidently different; for after having recognized the first as true, we still need a special act to recognize the second as true. If we had the same thought, there would be no need for two acts of recognition but only for a single one.
>
> (PMC: pp. 157–8)

The exception I take to the linguistic mode of presenting the puzzle can now be explained more fully. On the one hand it involves us in difficulties which are quite irrelevant to Frege's puzzle, and on the other, when followed strictly and literally, ends up not generating the puzzle. It invokes an experiment-like situation where a subject is confronted with a pair of identity *sentences*, only one of which he assents to. A typical expression of the approach I have in mind occurs in Gareth Evans's formulation of what he calls 'the Intuitive Criterion of Difference' for senses (which he thinks is the only constraint Frege puts on that notion): 'the thought associated with one sentence S as its sense must be different from the thought associated with another sentence S′ as *its* sense, if it is possible for someone to understand both sentences at a given time while coherently taking different attitudes towards them, i.e. accepting (rejecting) one while rejecting (accepting), or being agnostic about, the other'.[11] The difficulty is that the attempt to spell out precisely the conditions of this experiment leads to a host of considerations which would be quite superfluous for Frege. Unpacking the notions of possibility, acceptance,

11 Evans, *Varieties*, pp. 18–19.

understanding and coherence (as well as others Evans does not mention, like that the speaker should have perfect command of the language, be sincere in his or her response and so on) to which one appeals is a major undertaking. This language-dependent mode of the puzzle tries to wrap up the specification of the contents at stake (under some typically behaviouristic constraints) in the course of stating the puzzle. For Frege all this would be quite unnecessary because he regards the notion of content as already given, which enables stating the puzzle directly in terms of it and a subject's (epistemic) relation to it.

Not only does this mode of presenting the puzzle divert attention to irrelevant problems, if taken strictly and literally it is also questionable whether it even gives rise to the puzzle. Having noted that it is the *numerical* diversity of the object of belief or knowledge that needs to be argued for, by taking *sentences* to be what is believed or known then we have settled the question in advance. If we regard sentences as the objects of belief and knowledge then there is just no temptation to identify understanding, knowing or believing 'a = a' with having the same attitudes to 'a = b', simply because they are two distinct sentences. This is too obvious to require any demonstration, since only the latter involves any relation between the *subject* and the constituent *symbol* 'b'. The question we are confronted with in the puzzle, whether or not understanding or knowing the one sentence is the same as understanding the other, only makes sense on the assumption that it is *not* the sentence that is known or understood. Of course no reasonable reader will take the puzzle in this way, but all this shows is that proponents of the linguistic version do not strictly mean what they say.

Before concluding the account of the puzzle it may be worth reminding ourselves of the possibility of simply dismissing the difference between 'a = a' and a true, informative, 'a = b' as something which, though in some sense imparted by the expressions, does not pertain to their conceptual content (Frege's favoured term for this was 'colouring'; an exemplary expression of its contrast with content occurs in a letter to Husserl. PMC: p. 67). Bearing in mind Frege's attitude to other formerly respected logical distinctions, such a response is not as far-fetched as one would suppose at first. The tension between such a response, and the need to account for the difference between the two statements in terms of content, is reminiscent of that facing Russell when he needed to decide whether the concept occurring as subject was strictly the same as when it occurs as predicate. We need *both* difference (to prevent the contents from collapsing into each other) *and* (logical) relatedness.

In Frege's case, if one regards the difference as logically significant, one must recognize that the contents of the two statements in question (and hence of the constituent 'a' and 'b') are distinct. This, if the fundamental framework is to remain intact, entails modifying the conception of content. And modifying the conception of content is, as we shall see, precisely what Frege did.

III Frege's solution in Bs.

In Bs. § 8 Frege says,

> The need for a symbol for equality thus rests on the following fact: the same content can be fully determined in different ways; and *that*, in a particular case, *the same* content is actually given by *two ways of determining* [*Bestimmungsweisen*] *it*, is the content of a *judgement* . . . It is clear from this that different names for the same content are not always a trivial matter of formulation; if they go along with different ways of determining the content, they are relevant to the essential nature of the case.

With the hindsight of the later solution of SuB, one wonders why it was not already adopted in Bs., since Frege is already employing what would appear to be the most salient feature of the notion of sense – as far, at least, as proper names are concerned. That the notion of a 'way of determining' (*Bestimmungsweise*, which I abbreviate to 'BW') used here, and that of 'way of being given' (*Art des Gegebenseins*, abbreviated 'AdG') used in SuB are effectively the same is made plain by the role they play in relation to two (for our purposes, identical) illustrations employed in Bs. and SuB. In both places Frege describes a situation where, to different names for a certain point in a geometrical construction, there correspond different ways in which the point is determined.[12]

It seems, therefore, rather perplexing that he should have opened the same section by stating that

> Elsewhere, signs are mere proxies for their content . . . but names at once appear *in propria persona* so soon as they are joined together by a symbol for equality of content; for this signifies the circumstance of the two names' having the same content. Thus along with the introduction of a symbol for equality of content, all symbols are necessarily given a double meaning – the same symbols stand now for their own content, now for themselves.

> (Bs.: § 8)

Let us first try and clarify what precisely this account of identity (henceforth 'the Bs. theory') is. Frege is proposing that in the content of '$a \equiv b$' it is the

---

12 Sluga, in *Gottlob Frege* (London, Boston and Henley: Routledge and Kegan Paul, 1980) p. 153, goes so far as to render both these expressions by the same English phrase 'mode of determination'. Though I agree that in Frege's use they are effectively equivalent, I am uneasy about obscuring the fact that the original German phrases are not quite the same.

symbols themselves that are related,[13] and the relation asserted to hold between them is that of 'designating the same (thing)'. On this reading neither 'a' nor 'b' is being mentioned – Frege regards the case rather as one of ambiguity – but the effect is the same as if they had been. The symbols are being spoken of, and the relation of 'designating the same' would seem to apply (that is, non-trivially) only to entities which designate, i.e. to symbols. It follows that the symbol's content when it occurs in other contexts is no part of its content in identity contexts – though it is obliquely associated via the said relation. This theory, it must be admitted, seems to get the truth conditions right: 'a ≡ b' is indeed true when and only when 'a' and 'b' designate the same thing and, most crucially for our purpose, it makes the contents expressed by 'a ≡ b' and by 'a ≡ a' distinct. But how exactly does it work as a solution to the problem discussed in the previous section?

Since clearly not *all* true identities of the form 'a ≡ b' are informative – some cases will indeed impart no more than verbal knowledge – how does this theory draw the line between those cases where the difference of symbols is significant and the explanatory device is therefore needed, and those where it is not? (The question would not have arisen if different symbols were *sufficient* for a cognitive difference.) The answer appeals to the notion of BW: 'different names for the same content are not always just a trivial matter of formulation; **if they go along with different ways of determining the content**, they are relevant to the essential nature of the case' (Bs.: § 8). So the problem of accounting for a significant difference between 'a = a' and 'a = b' arises only when 'a' and 'b' 'go along' with different BWs; and it is precisely in those cases that distinct BWs explain the cognitive difference. One is led to presume that when an identity is *not* informative, the distinct symbols 'go along' with the *same* BW.

The tension inherent in this solution is quite obvious, and does not require the hindsight of SuB to be discerned. The ingredient that actually explains the difference between 'a' and 'b', the BW, makes only a shadowy appearance via the rather vague relation of 'going along' with the different symbols. 'Shadowy' because the BW is clearly *not* regarded as the content, nor as part thereof. On the other hand the distinct symbols, which are recognized as the contents, do not in themselves suffice to make the difference significant (and, indeed, Frege needs to retain the option that it might not be). The difference between them is significant when, and only when, it 'goes along' with different BWs. It appears then that it is the BWs that do the explanatory work of accounting for the difference, while the symbols are only serving as a peg to hang them on.

13 I switch here to the notation Frege used in Bs. where the question of whether this relation is to be identified with equality as used in mathematical equations seems to be left open. Both occur when demonstrating an application of the Bs. (Bynum: pp. 204 ff.).

Bs. § 8 wraps together what are really two different accounts of identity-statements: an 'official' account stated at the opening in terms of content, which is identified with the symbol, and alongside it an *effective* account in terms of BWs. At one point, quoted at the opening of this section, Frege does seem to be implying that BW are part of the content ('*that*, in a particular case, *the same* content is actually given by *two ways of determining it*, **is the content of a *judgement*'**), but the section as a whole suggests otherwise. Clearly, elevating the effective explanation to an 'official' status would require that BW be made part of the content (or somehow contribute to its identity).

This inner tension in the Bs. solution is completely absent from Frege's recapitulation of it at the beginning of SuB. He recounts the story as if the identification of symbols with contents exhausted the Bs. theory, and omits any mention of BWs. Upon reflection, this is not as unfair to his former self as it might appear at first, because the appeal to BWs would clearly not affect the criticism levelled at that solution in SuB. Nonetheless, it remains misleading, because it creates the impression that the earlier solution has nothing in common with the new one. It is not until we come to SuB's solution that the fate of BWs is revealed.

To understand why Frege was driven to such a convoluted account – why he admitted symbols, rather than BWs, into the content – we must turn to some of the fundamental features of the Bs. outlook. One of the most important guiding principles of that work is that a clear distinction ought to be observed between what is logically relevant and belongs to the (conceptual) content, and what is not relevant and does not belong. The first step in this line is the separation of the act from the content of a judgement. This, in turn, is followed by the exclusion of a host of hitherto respectable logical distinctions from the conceptual content, and thus to their dismissal as irrelevant to logic: subject and predicate; active and passive (Bs.: § 3); and categorical, hypothetical, disjunctive and apodictic (i.e. necessary and possible) judgements (Bs.: § 4).[14] As already mentioned, even the distinction between function and argument, except where quantification is involved, was claimed not to belong to the content.

This was the backdrop against which Frege needed to decide whether BWs were to be recognized as belonging to the content. His refusal to do so – probably guided by worries about their objectivity[15] – when combined with

---

14 Bs. § 4. In relation to necessity he is most explicit: 'If I term a proposition "necessary", then I am giving a hint as to my grounds for judgement. *But this does not affect the conceptual content of the judgement; and therefore the apodictic form of judgement has not for our purpose any significance*' (Bs.: § 4).

15 The attitude I have in mind is manifest in Frege's remark, cited earlier, that the distinction between function and argument has 'nothing to do with the conceptual content; it concerns only our way of looking at it' (which, as noted, does not apply to contents involving generality). In Bs. BWs are clearly *not* the same as the distinctly subjective 'ways of looking', but are still not sufficiently objective to be given a place in the content.

the desire to avoid an implausible view of identities (i.e. that their apparent informativeness was *always* illusory), seems to have landed him in this half-way house regarding BW. If admitting something into the content may be compared to placing it 'on the pitch' of logic, and explaining something away (as Frege did in other cases) to banishing it from the stadium altogether, BWs in Bs. acquire an odd status, comparable to that of being placed on the sideline. They feature in the explanation, and are clearly not dismissed, but are not allowed onto the pitch either. (I will return to this simile in the next chapter.)

This theory of identity cannot be dismissed as a youthful aberration. Frege adhered to it after Bs., and most probably up until the eve of SuB thirteen years later. This is evidenced in Gl. § 57, where, reinterpreting 'Jupiter has four moons' as stating an identity, he adds (which is hardly called for by the context), 'So what we have is an identity, stating that the **expression** "the number of Jupiter's moons" signifies [*bezeichne*] the same object as the **word** "four" '.

Despite its obvious defects, we ought not to judge this theory too harshly. It is usually considered solely for the purpose of contrast with the position advanced in SuB, i.e. as a solution to the problem of informative identities. But this is to forget that it is also a theory of definition, and as such it is perfectly plausible. Definitions do concern two symbols serving to designate the same thing, and they are indeed ultimately about symbols, not about the thing symbolized. The odd thing is that Frege, while saying all the right things about definitions being merely notational abbreviations and not expressing judgements (Bs.: § 24), failed to separate them in his mind from identities, and '≡' in Bs. serves both purposes.[16] The temptation to conflate the two was poignantly explained in Russell's remark about identities acquiring a 'merely symbolic' nature once they are adopted as definitions (PoM: § 63, quoted in Chapter 1 above). But Frege seems to have lacked, on this issue, the kind of ruthless clarity with which Russell kept definition and identity apart.[17]

16 I say this despite Frege's employing the ' ⊩ ' sign to distinguish definitions in Bs., because '≡' remains a significant part of the notation; as is also made plain by his appeal (in Bs. § 8) to definitions as a ground, albeit a secondary one, justifying the need for the latter symbol.

17 The conflation seems to be a persistent theme in Frege. In Gl. § 67 (as in Bs. § 24) he seems to recognize that adopting an equation as a definition involves a 'gestalt switch' along the lines described by Russell in PoM (§ 63), but seems to think of it as moving in the opposite direction to that described by Russell: from being 'merely symbolic' to being a significant assertion. The issue comes up in their correspondence, when Frege objects to a definition of identity on the grounds that identity is presupposed in the sign for a definition, to which Russell replies: ' "= . . . Df" counts for me as one symbol which does not express the same thing as "=". Definitions are not really part of the theory, but typographical stipulations. "= . . . Df" is not one of the primitive ideas of mathematics, but merely an expression of my will' (PMC: p. 169). The final remark might strike one as having a distinctly Wittgensteinian flavour; but it dates from 1904, when Wittgenstein was still a schoolboy.

The pre-SuB theory of identity is admittedly a bad one, but it at least addresses, however crudely, the challenge that it came as a response to. It explains identities as concerned with symbols, and by doing so provides the sought-after objective difference between pairs of contents which otherwise would be forced, implausibly, to count as one and the same. The *difference* was thus accounted for, and made logically respectable. The theory's fatal fault lay, as we shall see, in its account of the *relatedness*.

IV 'Sinn und Bedeutung': the collapse of the first theory

Because the Bs. theory is so obviously inadequate, it is tempting to dismiss it without much ado and, in particular, without bothering to carefully delineate Frege's grounds against it. Such an attitude seems to me mistaken. However many compelling arguments against the theory may spring to mind, it remains significant to settle what Frege's own grounds for dismissing it were. As is often the case in philosophy, one's *grounds* for accepting or rejecting a view may be just as important – possibly even more important – than the verdict itself. Moreover, in this particular case the grounds point to very fundamental issues, and are therefore an important guide to the general outlook underlying the distinction. SuB is, after all, the *principal* discussion in which Frege draws the distinction between sense and reference and argues for it.

Frege's case against the Bs. theory is condensed into a mere five sentences in the first paragraph of SuB. He comments upon the Bs. view that identity-statements assert a relation between symbols as follows:

> But this relation would hold between the names or signs only in so far as they named or designated something. It would be mediated by the connexion of each of the two signs with the same designated thing. But this is arbitrary. Nobody can be forbidden to use any arbitrarily producible event or object as a sign for something. In that case the *Satz* a = b would no longer refer to the subject matter, but only to its mode of designation; we would express no proper knowledge by its means.
>
> (SuB: pp. 56–7[18])

Before attending to the argument itself, it is worth noting that despite the central position of this passage in the argument of SuB, one is hard pressed to find any detailed discussion of it in the immense secondary literature on the distinction. For instance, in the whole of Michael Dummett's voluminous writings on Frege, where the sense/reference distinction occupies a very central position, I was unable to find any detailed account of this passage. Dummett questions the importance of the discussion of identity-statements

---

18 I will comment on Black's translation of this passage shortly.

in motivating the sense/reference distinction[19] and, of course, one needs to keep an open mind about the apparent grounds not being the real ones (though for my part I remain unconvinced that any alternative is nearly as plausible as taking Frege at face value). But one would expect Frege's apparent reasons, at the very least, to be given a hearing.

Similarly dismissive attitudes are shared by two other writers, who can hardly be suspected of doing so out of conformity with Dummett. Hans Sluga, after discussing *other* arguments which he thinks are more effective against the Bs. theory, gives Frege's own argument short shrift: 'This argument is peculiar because it contains nothing that Frege had not been fully aware of at the time of the *Begriffsschrift*; it merely repudiates what the *Begriffsschrift* account asserts' (Sluga, *Gottlob Frege*, p. 153). Baker and Hacker devote to it no more than half a paragraph, beginning 'this argument is opaque' and ending with the rhetorical question 'is that knowledge [i.e. that Molière is the same man as Jean-Baptiste Poquelin] *really* any different from what is expressed by " 'Moliere' and 'Jean-Baptiste Poquelin' " name one and the same man?'.[20] David Wiggins's paper 'Frege's Puzzle of the Morning Star and the Evening Star' contains only one brief comment on Frege's own criticism of the Bs. theory, which reads, 'This criticism was that any linguistic or conceptual account of the content of a statement of identity is mismatched with the essentially astronomical and objectual character of the Babylonian discovery that Hesperus was Phosphorus'.[21] This is true as far as it goes, but it

---

19 In 'Which end of the telescope', he writes,

> 'It is frequently asserted . . . that Frege's original motive for introducing the [sense/ reference] distinction was to obtain a better explanation of identity-statements, but there is no evidence for this: all we know is that he rightly believed that they provide the excellent first means for persuading others of the need for it. It would be more plausible to say that his original concern was to explain the general notion of the cognitive value of a statement'.
>
> (FOP: p. 234)

Inasmuch as Dummett's point is that the difficulty is not essentially about identity-statements but rather one about conceptual content (which must serve *inter alia* as cognitive content) which was *occasioned* by the discovery of fault in his former theory of identity-statements, I wholeheartedly agree. But inasmuch as he presents Frege's distinction as deriving simply from a general interest in cognitive content, which has little or nothing to do with the need to account for identity-statements, I think the picture he draws is misleading. (My view on the essential role of the logicist project in this regard is set out in the two final sections of Chapter 7.) His suggestion that for the sake of rhetorical effectiveness Frege might have presented a route to the distinction which was not really *his*, strikes me as grossly implausible and completely at odds with Frege's intellectual character – as well as with Dummett's own assessment of that character elsewhere in his writings.

20 G. Baker and P. Hacker, *Frege – Logical Excavations* (New York: Oxford University Press and Oxford: Blackwell, 1984) p. 285.

21 David Wiggins, 'Frege's puzzle of the morning star and the evening star', in M. Schirn (ed.) *Studies on Frege* (Stuttgart and Bad-Cannstatt: Frommann-Holzboog, 1976) Volume 2, p. 226.

does nothing to explain the precise nature of the mismatch.[22] If all one wanted to know was whether the theory succeeds or fails, then perhaps this statement would suffice, but in order to properly follow Frege's line of reasoning one needs to understand the precise nature of this mismatch, which to my mind is highly instructive.

None of the writers just mentioned offers anything approximating a detailed explanation of Frege's argument. What one typically does find, instead, is attention being diverted to some *other* argument against the Bs. theory which does *not* occur in Frege's text. The situation is strikingly similar to that encountered earlier in relation to Russell's obscure passage from OD. In both cases the author spells out his grounds for rejecting his former theory on the subject, which leads him, in turn, to a new theory designed to overcome those defects. In Frege's case, however, the omission in the secondary literature seems to me far less understandable, because Frege's text is not nearly as obscure as Russell's. I will attempt to elucidate the argument of this passage even at the risk of stating the obvious.

If identity-contents are about the names themselves, then the relation involved in such contents cannot be identity, because in that case *any* identity of a form 'a = b' would be false. The relation, rather, must be that of 'designates the same as'. But on this view we have smuggled in, unnoticed, the relation of each of the names to what it designates, and the truth of the identity-content thus comes to depend upon these two relations obtaining. But since a name's relation to what it designates – between each name and its (normal) content – is arbitrary, this cannot be a correct account of the content at stake. Frege regards this as a *reductio ad absurdum* of the theory, on the grounds that in that case knowledge that a = b could not be genuine knowledge. Clearly, not everything relevant to this conclusion has been spelled out – possibly because Frege regarded it as too obvious. Why, then, should knowledge that the names 'a' and 'b' designate the same thing not be proper knowledge? After all, is it not an objective fact like any other?

One might take Frege's point to be that on the Bs. theory the identity fails to convey the *appropriate item* of knowledge, not that it fails to convey any knowledge at all. This fits in with Wiggins's line and, indeed, one could argue for such a reading on the grounds that 'proper' here means 'proper for the case at hand' (a sense which the original German '*eigentliche*' has as well).

---

22 Besides, Wiggins's far too brief characterization of the mismatch lacks focus. On the one hand it suggests a contrast between 'conceptual' and 'objectual' which, though a fundamental Fregean dichotomy, seems to have nothing to do with what Frege says in the passage. On the other hand, he mentions quite a different contrast with a 'linguistic' content, which, though closer to the mark, he explains no further; nor does he relate it to Frege's saying that it is not 'proper knowledge' – which strikes me as the heart of the matter. My reasons for discontent with Wiggins's account will emerge more clearly as my own reading unfolds, below.

On the reading I propose, on the other hand, Frege's saying that on the theory in question 'a = b' would not be 'proper knowledge' is intended to deny that it is *real* knowledge, i.e. that it is knowledge at all. I agree that if that sentence of Frege's was all he said against the theory then perhaps both readings would have roughly the same plausibility. But the difficulty for the narrower reading of 'proper' is that if that was indeed Frege's point, why then should he have spent the two previous sentences – out of a total of five in which his whole argument is contained – elaborating upon the *arbitrariness* of the relation of designation? What would be the point of insisting on this if all he wished to establish was that on the Bs. theory the identity amounted to a *different* item of knowledge from that intended? It seems clear to me that something more fundamental is at stake.

It is at this point that the standard English translation (by Max Black) may well have played an important role in fixing readers' ideas. Frege's words are rendered 'in that case the sentence *a = b* would no longer refer to the subject matter, but only to its mode of designation'. In the first place, what has been translated as 'no longer refer to the subject matter' (*'nicht mehr die Sache selbst . . . betreffen'*) would be more faithfully rendered 'would no longer concern the things themselves', a difference which on its own might have been of only minor importance. But in the translation of the latter half of the same sentence, where Frege explains what he thinks the identity *would* concern (if the Bs. account were right), a far more serious mistranslation has occurred. Frege's '. . . but only to **our** mode of designation' (*'**unsere Bezeichnungsweise**'*) has been translated '. . . but only to **its** mode of designation' ('it' supposedly harking back either to 'the sentence' or to the constituent names). In the present context, the difference is profound.

Frege's original invokes the contrast between what is *objective* ('things themselves') and *our*, subjective, mode of designation.[23] His whole point in the previous sentences has been that designating is not properly a property *of the signs*, but rather something *our* subjective, arbitrary mode of designation invests them with. Speaking, as Black's translation does, of the *sign's* mode of designation is to reintroduce the very misconception Frege is arguing against, namely the thought that the sign in itself objectively designates. Both these points in the 'standard' translation into English point in the same direction: they serve to obscure Frege's invocation of the objective/subjective dichotomy and enhance the suggestion of a mere mismatch of two states of affairs (i.e. relation among signs instead of designations) which are otherwise on a par. The reading I propose, by contrast, is not only more faithful to the words of that key sentence, but also fits in better with the emphasis Frege lays, in the preceding sentences, on the arbitrariness of the designation relation,

---

23   The use of 'our' is a clear mark of subjectivity in Frege. He never speaks of BW or AdG as being *our* mode of determination or presentation.

which in turn lends credence to the stronger reading of (his denial of) 'proper knowledge'.[24]

Since the relation, the subjectivity of which Frege insists upon in the passage, is often regarded as objective,[25] it is a matter worth pausing for. In considering this matter we must guard against the temptation to conflate the questions 'what *is* Frege's view?' and 'is it cogent?' My chief interest here is in the first question, though I will also advance some preliminary considerations regarding the second. Even if Frege's view is untenable, it is no less his view for that, and the very gravity of the issue suggests that it is important for understanding his overall view.

The adjective 'arbitrary', typically combined with 'way of looking' (*Auffassung*), is in Frege's writings consistently contrasted with what is objective.[26] I take Frege's underlying assumption to be that what is not fully objective cannot be an object of knowledge in the sense in which he employs the word – which is the only sense relevant to his undertaking as a whole. Moreover, whatever has so much as a subjective *ingredient* cannot be counted an object of knowledge, and since the relation of designation is arbitrary, whatever depends upon it cannot be an item of knowledge.[27] It must be remembered that the question at stake is not whether the knowledge

24 Lest attributing this view to Frege appear to rest on too narrow a textual basis, I refer the reader to Frege's discussion of the objective/subjective dichotomy in his 1897 work *Logic* (PW: p. 132), where almost all the remarks he makes on the property 'beautiful' (there contrasted with 'true') can be maintained, in view of what he says on it in SuB, regarding the property 'designates'. The opposition is between what is independent of our recognizing it as such and what holds only for him who experiences it as such; between what is the same for all and that which its being the case for one does not necessarily imply that it is the same for any other; between where the very fact that I consider it to be so makes it so for me, and something having a property in itself. And although these questions are not directly addressed in that context, the discussion seems to me clearly to suggest, first, that on Frege's view there could be no such thing as aesthetic *knowledge*, and second, that in terms of this dichotomy it matters little whether the (aesthetic or linguistic) convention is community-wide or idiosyncratic. This also emerges from the remarks in SuB beginning 'nobody can be forbidden . . .'.

25 See e.g. Evans, *Varieties*, p. 22 for a casual expression; and J. R. Searle, 'How to derive "ought" from "is" ', *Philosophical Review*, 73 (1964) pp. 43–58 for a more substantive appeal to the said assumption of objectivity.

26 In Gl. § 60, speaking of ideas, Frege writes, 'Even if, as seems to be the case, it is impossible for men such as we are to think without ideas, it is still possible for their connection with what we are thinking of to be entirely superficial, arbitrary, and conventional'. My contention is that in this respect words or symbols, on Frege's view, have precisely the same status. A rich source for Frege's use of 'arbitrary' and its typical association with '(our) way of looking' (*Auffassung*) can be found in Gl. §§ 30, 33 and 45.

27 If we assume that the relation between a sign and what it signifies is *not* arbitrary, but somehow intrinsic to the symbol (as, for example, its shape is), this would undermine Frege's objection, because such a relation – though it leaves the mismatch with the intended content – would not infringe the objectivity of what is known.

of a convention, when the convention is the subject matter, is true knowledge, but rather, since the theory is supposed to hold of identity *in general,* whether there are *any* identities which are *in*dependent of convention. Frege's claim against his former position is that it carries the implication that no identity-content can be the object of true knowledge. The fundamental stance which Frege is taking here is by no means new, but its effect on the theory of identity is. The same contrast is brought out clearly in Gl. as follows:

> The objectivity of the North Sea is not affected by the fact that it is a matter of our arbitrary choice which part of all the water on the earth's surface we mark off and elect to call the 'North Sea.' . . . If we say 'The North Sea is 10,000 square miles in extent' . . . we assert something quite objective, which is independent of our ideas and everything of the sort. If we would happen to wish, on another occasion, to draw the boundaries of the North Sea differently or to understand something different by '10,000', that would not make false the same content that was previously true: what we should perhaps rather say is, that a false content had now taken the place of a true, without in any way depriving its predecessor of its truth.
>
> (Gl.: § 26)

Despite the fact that the principal target in these remarks is psychologism, the criticism against the Bs. theory would, I suggest, place our mode of designation, i.e. the matching of signs and contents, with what Frege calls here 'everything of the sort';[28] and the fundamental viewpoint underlying the criticism in SuB is here manifest. Expressions, in short, cannot be allowed (at least in general) to be involved in the identity of the contents they serve to express.

The divide which Frege seems to be pointing to is that between what is independent of any element of convention – facts which are 'out there' regardless of our beliefs, attitudes, conventions and what is dependent upon them. That snow is white has nothing to do with our beliefs or attitudes. That 'snow' means snow is, by contrast, *constituted* by our beliefs and agreement in regarding this sound in some particular ways. Mere agreement suffices to *make* any 'arbitrarily producible event or object' mean snow; but no agreement is involved in snow *being* white.[29]

---

28 This is why the omission of the word 'our' from Black's translation encourages a misunderstanding of Frege's point by suggesting that the mode of designation belongs to the symbol itself.

29 There are, of course, facts concerning symbols (like the fact that 'Boston' consists of two syllables) which *are* objective, and hence knowable in the strict sense. But Frege's objection relates only to the involvement of properties which depend upon the symbol's conventional, meaning-giving, relation to extra-linguistic entities.

Without attempting to settle the issue of whether this distinction is as fundamental as Frege takes it to be, there is one attempt to establish the objectivity of 'semantic facts' which it would be useful to respond to. Since it seems relevant to Frege's position that such facts can change, might have been otherwise, and vary between one language and another, one might wish to defend the objectivity of 'semantic facts' by emphasizing a restriction to a particular language. Just as Frege admits that the concept 'inhabitants of Germany' must be supplemented with a definite time indication to obtain a proper concept with definite cardinality (Gl.: § 46), so a specification of the language in question, saying that 'snow' means snow *in English*, might seems to yield us an objective fact.

Further scrutiny, however, reveals that such an attempt to 'anchor' semantic facts is circular, because the identity of the entity indicated by 'English' is not completely independent of the fact that 'snow' means snow. It is as if, trying to fix the content of 'inhabitants of Germany' by specifying a definite time, it turned out that what time it was depended on whether someone was an inhabitant of Germany. This circularity is obscured by a vagueness inherent to our common-sense notion of a language (which preserves its identity despite some words changing their meaning), but it becomes apparent if we regard a language's identity as consisting (*inter alia*) in a pairing of words and non-linguistic entities.

It is no use to insist at this point that the designation of *complex* expressions – as some Fregean names would seem to be – is *not* arbitrary because it is a function of the designation of the parts. While it must be conceded that this relation is not as *purely* arbitrary as the case of a simple, unanalysable expression, the relation is still dependent upon the arbitrary relations of the parts, and thus would fail the objectivity test I take Frege to be demanding for knowledge.[30] It might also be thought that the fact that we speak of *knowing*, for example, someone's name might tell against this view, but I think Frege would not be moved by such considerations. He is clearly not in the business of recording ordinary discourse, and would be happy to admit that the notion of knowledge he appeals to is stricter and narrower than that used for everyday purposes.

A full discussion of this issue would take us too far afield, and cannot be pursued here. My chief aim has been to establish that Frege's *sole* charge against his Bs. theory derives from a fundamental principle according to which knowledge must be of things objective in a sense in which 'linguistic facts' are clearly not, and that 'linguistic facts' fail this test because the relation of

---

30 Sluga (*Frege*, p. 153) reproaches Frege for overlooking this very point in his criticism of the Bs. solution in SuB, which, in turn, hinges on his view of the Bs. theory as applying (it would appear, exclusively) to *complex* names (see p. 152). But not only could I find no hint of such a restriction either in Bs. or in SuB, it also seems to be belied by Frege's own example in Bs. § 8, where 'directly in experience' is proposed as one of the ways a point A in a geometrical construction is determined, without there being any *complex* name involved.

the signs and the extra-linguistic entities they stand for is (or at least could be) arbitrary. This point seems to me absolutely fundamental to the whole of Frege's outlook, and is integral to the line of reasoning which prescribes the need to postulate objective judgeable contents (and later thoughts) as distinct from sentences, in the first place. It is crucial that we observe that *Frege* held these views regardless of whether we find them appealing.

Acknowledging this as Frege's point is particularly important because nothing about it appeals to any specific feature of identity, and it therefore immediately generalizes to what may be counted as an object of proper knowledge in general. If we recognize the occurrence of *mentioned* expressions in the expression of an item of putative knowledge as sufficient to render that item *im*proper in this sense (as is natural to suppose), then Frege's charge implies that any content whose expression involves mentioned expressions (except where typographic or phonetic features are at stake) would not be an object of true knowledge and, more generally, that language plays no constitutive role in what can be known – in other words, in what there (objectively) is. In view of its fundamental nature, this point can constrain or guide us in interpreting Frege's words elsewhere as well.

This Fregean dichotomy is essentially the same – despite the difference in context – as the one we encountered underlying Russell's remarks on the contrast between the logical and the linguistic: 'both designating and expressing have to do with language: the logically important matter is the relation between what is expressed and what is designated'; and when he emphasizes denoting's being 'a fact that concerns logic, not the theory of language or naming' (OMD: pp. 317–18). The very same dichotomy is what underlay Russell's exclusion of the possibility that the relation between the meaning and the denotation might be 'merely linguistic through the phrase', and his avoiding any appeal to mention when considering putative equivalents of '<C>'.

Returning now to the route from Bs. to SuB, the precise nature of the defect pointed out in SuB is also important because it effectively constrains plausible interpretations of the new theory it prompted. If anything resembling the present account is correct, then it is hardly credible that Frege would proceed from this objection to propose a notion of content in which language or mind have a constitutive role. Any plausible candidate for the notion of content should therefore have at least these two properties: that it *be* a strictly objective entity (though this requirement was satisfied by the 'official' Bs. theory), and that its *relation* to whatever further entity might be involved (in the sense in which the designation was involved in the Bs. theory) must also be objective and clear of any element of convention.

V 'Sinn und Bedeutung': the new solution

The criticism considered in the last section occurs in SuB as a preamble to the new solution. It is therefore apt to ask how the new theory handles the initial problem, and how it compares with its predecessor. The fact that the changes to the notion of content proposed in the Bs. theory proved inadequate does not alter the fact that we still need an account both of the difference and of the relatedness of the respective contents of 'a' and 'b' in true informative identities, and that such an account cannot be given without introducing some change to the 'simple' notion of content as it is known in the Bs. Before we knew that the problem facing both the new and the old theories was the same, and that AdG (mode of presentation) was effectively recognized in Bs., the point of such a comparative approach may justly have seemed moot. But in the light of these facts it becomes apt to ask what precisely had changed and, if possible, to try to construe the second theory as resulting from *specific* changes in the first (rather than coming out of the blue). SuB may be the turning of a new leaf, but it is clearly part of the same tale that began in Bs. § 8.

In rough outline, the strategy of the SuB solution might be explained in the following way: the problem that Bs. § 8 was grappling with was how the two sides of a true identity could have distinct contents which are nonetheless related (a fact of which, as we saw, Bs. § 8 failed to provide an adequate account). SuB resolves this by putting forth a *bipartite* notion of content. This allows us to say that the contents are the same with respect to one part and different with respect to the other – it is *parts*, not aspects of a single entity, that are in question.

Confining our attention to the original problem, we may briefly enumerate the changes embodied in the SuB solution as follows: first, symbols are dropped from the account of content altogether. Second, a new bipartite notion of content is introduced, consisting of the erstwhile content (what the judgeable content is about) and an AdG. Third, the bifurcation of the content of names between identity-contexts and all others is abandoned. These are unquestionably major changes, but the elements involved are all familiar from Bs. To what extent does the new solution only reshuffle familiar elements, and to what extent does it alter their natures?

Just to illustrate how answering these questions is not as trivial as it may seem, consider Frege's first positive remark (at the end of the first paragraph of SuB) after completing his demolition of the Bs. theory. He says that contrary to the account which left 'a = b' expressing no proper knowledge, a cognitive difference 'can arise only if the difference between the signs corresponds to a difference in the AdG' (SuB: p. 57). This as yet does not go beyond what he had already conceded in Bs. But by the end of that sentence he speaks of two different names of the same geometrical point as indicating (*deuten . . . auf*) their respective AdGs – which he would not have said in Bs., where their Bs. counterparts merely 'go along' with the names.

Let us first spell out how the familiar ingredients from Bs. are pieced together in the new solution. The new, bipartite, notion of content takes the erstwhile notion of content, clearly enough, to be that part of their respective contents which the two names in an informative identity share. This is crucial in freeing us from the need to separate identity-contexts from other contexts. The other part of the content is the AdG.[31] But is that all that SuB is doing?

R. L. Mendelsohn,[32] one of the very few writers to underline the connection between the Bs. theory and SuB, regards the distinction between senses and referents of complete sentences as the chief novelty of SuB. Though I share his view on the importance of the Bs. theory, I profoundly disagree with this conclusion. It rests on the view that Frege had effectively recognized the sense/reference distinction in Bs. – though only for proper names. But BW, or AdG – which I agree are effectively the same – are only *one ingredient* in the notion of sense. Without the crucial step of elevating this notion to the status of an objective entity, enabling its relation to the referents, in turn, to become logical and objective, the distinction would not be the sense/reference distinction – not even for proper names. The latter view has the prima facie advantage of making Frege's change to the sense/reference distinction relate directly to his grounds for rejecting his former theory as explained in SuB, i.e. to its being inconsistent with the view that knowledge of identities could be genuine, objective knowledge. In Mendelsohn's account, by contrast – and in this he resembles most, if not all, other writers – the decisive change relates to grounds against the Bs. theory which Frege could, or should, have had – not to the ones he actually put forth.

To take stock, there seems little reason to suspect that Frege's notion of the referent, the ingredient which corresponds to the erstwhile (unjudgeable) content, has changed in SuB, nor that his notion of a symbol has; it would seem that our only hope is to enquire whether any change has occurred in the notion of an AdG. Clearly, it has now become part of the content, which it was not before, but does that have any further consequences?

A way of bringing out the essential change between Bs. and SuB is to consider a hybrid theory which was never advocated (nor, as far as we know, even contemplated) by Frege, which stands midway between the Bs. theory and SuB. Consider a theory which was like that of SuB in advocating a bi-partite notion of content, but instead of a sense, or AdG, picks the *symbol* as the part of the content other than the referent. AdGs will still have the role they had in the Bs., i.e. they will 'go along' with the different names. (This is indeed awkward, but this awkwardness, it must be remembered, was not, after all, what brought down the Bs. theory for Frege – and it may therefore be regarded as tolerable.) The hybrid theory's account of true and informative identities differs from the Bs. theory in *not* requiring the problematic relation 'designates the same thing': this is because the referent is now part

31 As I will explain in section III of the following chapter, I do not think that the notion of sense can be *identified in general* with that of AdG, but that senses have a one-to-one correspondence with AdGs *in those cases where there is a referent*. Nonetheless, since it is convenient for fixing one's mind on, I will proceed as if this identity held good.

32 In 'Frege's *Begriffsschrift* theory of identity', *Journal of the History of Philosophy*, 20 (1982) pp. 279–99.

of the content. Would such a theory survive the criticism in SuB? I think it is clear that it would not, and this helps us discern what is essential to the SuB solution.

The hybrid theory gets rid of the involvement of the relation of designation, whose inappropriateness rendered the former solution inapt, but it fails to put anything in its place. So although the objectivity of both parts of the content is secured (as indeed it was in the Bs. solution too), the relation between them has not been accounted for and it remains, in the absence of any special explanation, as arbitrary as the former co-designating relation. So if the new solution in SuB is to avoid the faults Frege points out in the Bs. theory – which seems to me a mandatory assumption for any plausible account – two features of the AdG emerge as crucial. In contrast to the role the AdG played in Bs., where it was not part of the content, making it an element of the content implies first, that it be recognized as an objective entity and second, that its relation to the referent must be logical, in the sense explained in Chapter 2 above in relation to denoting. (Without intending it as a definition, we might say that having the referent it has is an essential property of the sense.) It is these two changes that constitute the crux of the difference between Bs. and SuB – at least as far as the account of identity is concerned. I am not claiming that this sums up *all* that is essential to the notion of sense, but only that these features clearly are, and that no account of sense which neglects them can be even roughly adequate.

It is also useful to review the status of the symbol on this new view, and to compare its account of identity-statements to that of Bs. The Bs. theory's appeal to the relation I dubbed 'designation' was implicit, and its unearthing may be illustrated as follows. An identity content consists of two symbols, related by the relation of co-designation. This relation breaks down, in turn, to each symbol's relation to what it designates, and identity. It was recognizing the arbitrariness of the first of these relations that brought down that theory. In the SuB theory we surely still have symbols somewhere, and hence, inevitably, also the arbitrary relation of designation, but now it is no longer even relevant to the identity-content. Although Frege does not spell this out as explicitly as he might have, a remark he makes in SuB suggests that a relation which is essentially similar to designation now relates the name and its *sense*. In the sentence ending the first paragraph of the paper he speaks of the names' *indicating* the AdG; thus it is the sum of this arbitrary relation, and the very different, logical, relation of 'determining' holding between the sense and the referent, that constitutes the name's relation to the referent. The relation has now become mediated. As Frege puts it, 'to the sign there corresponds a definite sense and to that **in turn** a definite reference' (SuB.: p. 58).[33]

---

33 The point is made even more clearly in *Comments on Sense and Meaning*, where he writes, 'it is *via* a sense, and only *via* a sense that a proper name is related to an object' (PW: p. 124).

The content of an identity can now be explained without appealing to names: it contains two senses which, despite their distinctness, determine, via the relation 'the referent of', one and the same referent. The role of this relation is analogous to that of 'the designation of' in the Bs. theory, where its obtaining between each of the distinct signs – which were taken to be the contents – and the same entity, constituted the content's truth. It now becomes clear how crucial it is to distinguish the relation of 'being the sense of', as applied to names, from the relation of 'being the referent of', as applied to senses. One is arbitrary and is not strictly part of the theory, while the other is objective and is what the theory is trying to single out. This is also very much in harmony with Russell's comments, quoted in Chapter 1 above, contrasting the theory of language with logic. It is for this reason that wrapping both these relations together in speaking of 'the way from the name to the referent' is grossly misleading, which is one of the topics to be dealt with in the following chapter.

Chapter 5

Further considerations regarding sense and reference

The present chapter relates to our discussion in the last chapter in roughly the same way as did Chapter 3 to the discussion of Russell's theory of descriptions in Chapter 2. It combines a further development and amplification of matters which could only be hinted at in the preceding chapter, with a critical discussion of some widely held views of the sense/reference distinction which, as I shall try to show, falsify Frege's notions in important respects. The sections that follow are not centred on a single theme, but rather take up in succession a number of disparate, though ultimately related, issues.

I The priority of the distinction for proper names

The theory of sense and reference is a far more elaborate matter than our discussion so far has revealed. At least three important features, which for Frege were part and parcel of the same theory, spring to mind. First, complete sentences – though ultimately regarded as a special case of proper names – are held to have senses, with truth values as their referents. Second, concept- and function-words are also held to have senses and referents. Third, the thesis of compositionality, i.e. the tenet that the senses of the words composing a sentence are *parts* of the sense of that sentence, is clearly endorsed – a matter which was moot or absent from the Bs. conception of content. Important though these features are to Frege's position as a whole, the fact remains, or so at any rate I wish to argue, that the distinction for the case of proper names has a more fundamental role than it has for any other kind of expression, because in it lies Frege's chief rationale for drawing the distinction.

Before seeing how the distinction applies to expressions other than names (by which I mean proper names in the narrow sense, and thus will not be employing Frege's terminology), we might begin by noting that in relation to neither complete sentences nor functional expressions do we find anything approximating to the kind of ancestry in Frege's thinking that we discovered in relation to names. Not only is there, for names, a credible and perfectly rational course leading from Bs. to SuB, but by recounting it in SuB Frege makes it plain that he considered it to be the relevant background for a correct understanding of the distinction. This alone strikes me as strong prima facie grounds for regarding the case of names as his chief reason for drawing the distinction and, since no substantial evidence, so far as I am aware, suggests otherwise, it should be allowed to prevail. The chief consideration in favour of the priority of names does not, however, depend on such 'circumstantial' evidence, but rather on the examination of the relation between the distinction for names and for other kinds of expressions.

As far as the distinction for names is concerned, I think it is fairly clear that since the referent can be identified with what was formerly regarded as the name's content, it is primarily in the introduction of the notion of *sense* that the theory's novelty lies. This novel notion is introduced to account for a phenomenon which would be inexplicable without it, so although what is argued for is a *distinction*, only one of the elements being distinguished is new and needs arguing for (which is indeed Frege's course). We did not need to read Frege to discover that names have bearers, nor that this is what matters for determination of the sentence's content as true or otherwise, but the matter is different with regard to the tenet that they have senses as well. Moreover, with regard to proper names there is no plausibility whatsoever in saying, as Frege does in relation to other kinds of expressions, that the former notion of content was a *conflation* of the two elements distinguished. It was quite clearly one of them and not the other. Let us look now at the distinction in relation to other kinds of expressions.

Regarding complete sentences, neither the notion of content (i.e. judgeable content) nor the notions of truth or falsity, which apply primarily to such contents, are notions newly introduced in SuB, and hence the tenet that they are *distinct* can hardly be regarded as new either. So although Frege's view of the precise nature of this content had undergone an important change, the very idea of there being such an objective content and of its having a truth value are not new. What is new in this regard, however, is, first, that this content is now conceived of as being composed of constituent senses (which requires, of course, that the notion of such part-senses be previously established); and second – which is no immediate corollary – that this content is *itself* taken to be a sense, which is to say that it is capable of having a referent, which Frege identifies with its truth value. It must be borne in mind that this identification is no inevitable consequence of the point just mentioned. It is at least conceivable, as far as this application is concerned, that, for example, *facts* might have served as referents of thoughts. The novelty of SuB's view of the contents of complete indicative sentences thus resides not, as it does in the case of names, in its introducing a new element, but rather in regarding the *relation* between two elements, which are already familiar, as an instance of the same relation, i.e. the relation between sense and reference, which was formerly introduced by the example of proper names. It is precisely in relation to this point that the priority of the distinction for proper names emerges most clearly.

Imagine being told that a declarative sentence had a sense, and that its truth value was its referent, *without* having any prior notion of the sense/reference distinction in relation to proper names. It seems clear to me that despite one's familiarity with the notions of the content of a judgement and of a truth value, in such circumstances the claim would not even be intelligible. What we would fail to understand is not what a content or a truth value are, but what saying that one is a sense and the other its referent amounts to. Without a prior understanding of these notions from the case of proper names, I contend that the claim is not merely bizarre, but that we would not even *understand* what it means – it would be devoid of content. If the distinction between sense and reference of sentences is not even comprehensible except as an extension of, or by analogy with, the distinction for proper names, then it seems to follow that Frege's argument for the distinction in general did not just *happen* to begin with proper names, but that it *had* to begin from proper names, because their case serves as the foundation on which the distinction for other kinds of expressions depends.

So far we have only considered the relation between the distinction regarding complete sentences and that regarding proper names, but how does the thesis of the priority of names fare from the comparison with the distinction for concept- and function-expressions? (For brevity, I speak in the present chapter only of concepts, intending what is said to apply, *mutatis mutandis*, to other functional expressions as well). Regarding these kinds of expressions the priority of the distinction for names seems to me to hold, ultimately, with equal force. However, establishing it in this case is a more complex matter, for two reasons. First, because after the advent of the sense/reference distinction Frege shifted to a non-standard use of the word 'concept' (*Begriff*), a move which complicates and obscures the scene. This necessitates some preparation before we get a clear view of what the distinction for concept-words actually amounts to. The other, deeper, reason will become clear only later, because it has to do with my contention that despite the substantial respect in which the sense/reference distinction for names is prior, it nonetheless bears a special relation to another distinction familiar from the case concepts. Since that will be spelled out only in section V, the judgement on whether the distinction for names is prior to that for concept-words will have to be postponed until then. However, it can be noted at this point that since proper names, complete sentences and concept-expressions exhaust, on Frege's view, all the kinds of expressions there are, this is the only category where clarification is pending.

Another angle on the priority of names is provided by the observation that Frege might have drawn the distinction for proper names and taken it no further – Russell, as we shall see, may be construed as having done just that. Such a course would be quite impossible with the distinction for other kinds of expressions. Even if one could begin by distinguishing judgeable content from truth value, and then proceed to argue that an analogous or identical distinction applies to proper names, it is hard to see how this would amount to the same distinction as the one we are concerned with. It thus seems plausible to conclude in the light of both these considerations, and of the textual evidence mentioned earlier, that if it had not been for the case of proper names, Frege would never have found the need to draw the distinction in the first place; and that the particular route which led him to it, as delineated in the previous chapter, is not a mere matter of presentation, but arguably the most reliable guide to the essence of the notions distinguished. This is not to say that the case of names is necessarily where the distinction's greatest theoretical value lies – though I would not wish to exclude this either – but only that their case is more fundamental in Frege's rationale for the distinction than those for other kinds of expressions. Our next section might also be regarded as illustrating this.

II Sense and indirect speech

After submitting that Frege's notion of reference coincides with the current notion of an interpretation for formulas of predicate logic, Dummett raises the question 'why, then, do we need a notion of sense as well as a notion of reference?', at which point he writes,

> A very bad answer, sometimes given to this question, would be that the notion of sense is needed by Frege to explain operators which, in Quine's terminology, create opaque contexts – expressions such as 'necessarily' and '. . . believes that . . .'. It is true enough that Frege does deploy his notion of sense in treating of such expressions: he says that, within opaque contexts, a term stands for what, in ordinary contexts, constitutes its sense. But, obviously, it would be useless to offer any such explanation unless it had first been established that there is something which, in ordinary contexts, constitutes the sense of a term: so we must be satisfied that there is a prior need for a notion of sense, as possessed by expressions occurring in ordinary contexts, before we can invoke this notion to explain opaque contexts.
>
> (FPL: p. 90)

Plausible as this view may seem at first, what is here proclaimed as being 'a very bad answer' strikes me as by and large the right one (though 'necessarily . . .' was, of course, none of Frege's concern), and the precise converse of Dummett's statement seems to be the case. If the puzzle with identity-statements is construed, as it was in the previous chapter, as already involving epistemic contexts, then Frege's course is *not* first to establish, on independent grounds, the need for a notion of sense and only then apply it, as a kind of afterthought, to epistemic contexts. On the contrary, he establishes the need for a notion of sense by appealing to considerations regarding epistemic contexts, and its place in ordinary contexts flows from that.

Just how it flows becomes clear if we view the distinction from the vantage point of a fundamental assumption which underlies Frege's whole line of reasoning, namely that belief, understanding and knowledge consist in a *relation* between a subject and some objective entity, which for the moment need not be more finely specified than simply as the 'epistemic object'.[1] Frege's conception of what precisely this object was had indeed undergone change, but the assumption that there must always be such an object had not. Viewed from this angle, the chief moral drawn from the puzzle discussed in the previous chapter was that since identity-contents can be the objects of genuine knowledge, the identity of the epistemic object the subject is related to cannot be determined solely by the *referents* of the names flanking the identity sign, and that what the subject is related to must therefore be *something other than the referent*. The principal role of these 'other things' is to provide *distinct* entities (corresponding to the occurrences of 'a' and 'b' respectively) so that the relata of the epistemic relation in each case will be distinct as well. I have deliberately phrased this statement in a way that captures the Bs. solution to the puzzle as well, where the (distinct) *symbols* play this role of 'something other than the referent', i.e. of the epistemic object. The failure of that solution was due to the particular kind of 'other object' chosen – not to any doubt over the principle that *some* such object is required.[2]

The thesis therefore is that the occurrences of 'a' and 'b' in the sentence reflect the occurrences of *distinct* such 'things' in the epistemic object, which may be called 'senses' (if we guard against taking this to mean any more than is strictly implied by the present considerations). But this thesis will constitute a solution to the puzzle *only if* it is also maintained that *it is the subject's relation to these things, rather than to the referent, that is asserted in 'S believes*

---

1 This assumption becomes explicit in a letter to Russell, where Frege says (of 'Copernicus thought that the planetary orbits are circular') that in it 'Copernicus' designates a man and 'that the planetary orbits are circular' designates a thought, 'and what is said is that there is a relation between this man and that thought, namely that the man took the thought to be true' (PMC: p. 164). Similarly in *Thoughts*: 'by grasping a thought I come into a relation to it and it to me' (CP: p. 371).

2 Even if speaking strictly, the knower's relation to the epistemic objects as a whole need not imply relations to its constituent parts (if any), the very procedure of considering (as in the puzzle) the result of substituting *part* of the expression of the item of knowledge only makes sense on the assumption that the part's occurrence in the sentence corresponds to a discrete part of the epistemic object – or, at any rate, to a determinant of its identity (the 'functional model' of judgeable content in the last chapter has determinants which are not parts). Unless this is granted, the exercise becomes as senseless as considering a substitution for 'rat' in 'Socrates'.

that a = b'. The mere positing of such entities will not do, they must be assumed to be the kind of entity to which the subject relates.[3] It follows that when *we* make an assertion of the form 'S believes that a = b', the referents of *our* words, what we speak about, are the *senses* of 'a' and 'b', rather than their referents. But if someone else's belief is (as this account of the report of his belief implies) a relation between him and the *senses* of his words, then what constitutes *our* believing, knowing and so on must also be a relation to the senses of *our* words. This is not to deny any relation whatsoever to the referent. On the contrary, such a relation is implied, but it now becomes mediated. This line of reasoning assumes, which seems inevitable, that there is a parity, in this respect, both between our subject's judgements and our own, and – which the Bs. theory clearly got wrong – between identity-contents and other contents. So though this may seem paradoxical at first, the consideration of indirect speech ends up prescribing how direct speech is to be construed, rather than the other way around.

Since the role of sense in the account of '. . . believes that . . .' contexts flows from the mere assumption that it provides a prima facie solution to the problem this notion was designed to solve, it ought to be regarded as a *constitutive* feature of sense. Given that the features of many–oneness and aboutness-shifting (to the referent) are already incorporated in this role, it may be said that no other feature of sense is quite as essential. This view receives some support from a remark Frege makes when concluding his very brief account of the sense/reference distinction in the introduction to Gg. He writes,

> I have justified this more thoroughly in my essay on sense and denotation, mentioned above; here it may merely be mentioned that only in this way can indirect discourse be correctly understood. That is, the thought, which otherwise is the sense of the sentence, in indirect discourse becomes its denotation.
>
> (Gg: p. 7)

Before turning to the subject of our next section, we might consider the following reflection on what has just been said, taken from the vantage point of our previous discussion about the priority of the distinction for names: nothing in our latest discussion required that either complete sentences or concept-words have senses.

---

3 This fact is illustrated by the Bs. view which, despite its associating 'a' and 'b' with distinct BW, stopped short of allowing this association to affect the content's, i.e. the epistemic object's, very identity.

III Sense as a route and empty senses

It is of course crucial to recognize the essential features of the notion of sense, but it is just as important to guard against mistaking *in*essential features for essential ones. In the present section I examine the conception according to which the notion of 'mode of presentation', or 'way of being given' (of the referent) which invariably occur in presentations of the distinction – indeed, in most of the passages in which Frege introduces the notion – are essential to the notion of sense. On the evidence of SuB alone it is natural to take these characterizations in that manner – as telling us *what sense is* in the first place. However, when *all* Frege says about sense is taken into account they cannot, I submit, be so regarded.[4]

The conception of sense to be examined regards sense as a route: either from the word or expression to the referent or, in its non-linguistic version, from a *subject*, to the referent. The latter is suggested by the phrases 'mode of presentation' and 'way of thinking', which bring out more clearly the assumption of there being a *subject* to whom the referent is presented. Let it be clear from the start that I do not wish to discard this view of sense completely. My point is, rather, that despite what is often alleged (e.g. by Dummett), it cannot serve as a *general* characterization of sense. The chief difficulty for the route model is very straightforward. Frege recognizes the possibility that a proper name might lack a referent and yet have a sense, which is tantamount to admitting that some senses have no corresponding referent. Gareth Evans, who construes sense as a way of thinking about a referent, puts the matter thus:

> It is really not clear how there can be a mode of presentation associated with some term when there is no object to be presented. On my interpretation of the metaphor the difficulty remains acute: it certainly does not appear that there can be a way of thinking about something unless there is something to be thought about in that way.
>
> (Evans, *Varieties*, p. 22)

Dummett makes a similar point when he writes that

> as has been observed by Gareth Evans, if we say that what a name primarily does is to pick out an object, and characterize its sense as the way in which it does so, then an empty name lacks a sense: there *is* no 'way in which it picks up an object', since it fails to pick one out. *Before* he drew the distinction between sense and reference, Frege seemed to

---

4 It may be noted at the outset that Frege never quite says that sense *is* a mode of presentation of the referent, but only that it is *contained* in the sense (SuB: p. 57). Though I do not know what precisely this difference amounts to, it seems significant that even what is arguably the clearest piece of evidence in favour of the identification of sense with mode of presentation is not quite as unequivocal as one would expect.

have favoured just such a conclusion ... But, as soon as he had the senses/reference distinction, Frege allowed that a name lacking reference might still possess a sense, and hence that a sentence containing such a name might express a thought; so we cannot explain the sense of a proper name by means of the metaphor of a route, if a 'route' is understood as the path by which a particular goal was reached.

(IFP: pp. 45–6)

At this point Dummett goes on to suggest a way of resolving the difficulty. Elaborating upon the phrase 'particular goal' at the end of this paragraph, he invokes the distinction between the speaker's intended reference and the reference of the words he uses, and sums up by declaring that 'we may continue to use the metaphor of a route, but we must not think of the route as the route to a pre-assigned goal' (IFP: p. 46).

But for anyone who has not by that point lost sight of the fact that the question at stake is not whether the goal is preassigned, but rather whether it makes sense to speak of a route in the absence of any goal at all, this digression is really beside the point, and it cannot support Dummett's conclusion, to wit:

> We may then say that what the expression primarily does is to determine a route, and that the route of itself determines its terminus, which may then by transference be associated with the expression; and we may add, with no suspicion of inconsistency, that the route may sometimes be found to lead nowhere.

(p. 46)

But does 'a route that leads nowhere' really make sense? A route might lead elsewhere than expected or intended, and we might speak loosely of a path leading 'nowhere' to indicate that its terminus is a point of no interest, or irrelevant to the task at hand. But unless there *is* a terminus, interesting or not, talk of a route strikes me as plainly incoherent, and Dummett's 'solution' does not alleviate the difficulty. If being a route to a referent was essential to the notion of sense, then a sense without a referent should have been an outright impossibility.[5]

---

5 An anonymous referee suggested that one way a route can lead nowhere is if it goes on forever, pointing out that this seems to be what is at issue in two of Frege's examples ('the celestial body most distant from the earth' and 'the least rapidly converging series'). In both these cases the sense may be seen as prescribing a procedure for rejecting a potentially infinite series of unsuccessful candidates for being the referent. Though an interesting way of cashing 'a route that leads nowhere' in those cases, it will not save the route model. It fails to apply to other cases where the number of candidates is finite (e.g. 'the Apostle whose name begins with a "C"'), and seems plainly irrelevant to names in works of fiction – where neither candidates nor procedures are involved.

Another course in the attempt to mitigate this clash between the route model and the possibility of empty senses is taken by Evans, who argues that Frege's admission that names which lack a referent may yet possess a sense is not what it seems.[6] Fastening on a single passage where Frege associates such names, as he usually does, with fiction, and where he speaks of their senses as 'mock senses', Evans proposes that we read Frege's statements on this matter as follows:

> The unqualified passages ascribing sense to empty singular terms and sentences containing them do induce an inconsistency. But when they are interpreted in the light of Frege's views on fiction the inconsistency disappears, for we may gloss the passages in which Frege says that sentence containing an empty singular term may express a thought as follows. Yes: a sentence containing an empty singular term may have a sense, in that it does not necessarily have to be likened to a sentence containing a nonsense-word. But no: it does not *really* have a sense of the kind possessed by ordinary atomic sentences, because it does not function properly, it is only *as if* it functions properly.
>
> (Evans, *Varieties*, p. 30)

Close inspection of the passage Evans cites (from Frege's 1897 work 'Logic', in PW: p. 130) does not, so far as I can tell, warrant his conclusion. In the passage Frege does indeed say many things about empty names and what is expressed by their means: he speaks of 'mock proper names' which he says do not fulfil the usual role of proper names; he speaks accordingly of 'mock thoughts' (which he also labels 'fictitious') and says that they are neither true nor false and should not be taken seriously as thoughts in science are; he also says that such mock thoughts are no concern of the logician's. However, in all this catalogue I do *not* find him saying that they are not *real* thoughts – a step Evans takes on his behalf. One could take Evans's point here to be merely that referenceless senses are not *ordinary* senses (a claim which is of course true, but trivially so); but since Frege seems to allow no halfway house, the question of whether they *are* senses cannot be evaded. If they are, then this reading will *not* resolve the alleged inconsistency Evans points out.

But the chief difficulty for Evans is that the very contrary of what he says seems to be implied by Frege's saying (in the very passage Evans cites) that although 'William Tell' is a mock proper name **'we cannot deny it a sense'**, or that 'if the sense of an assertoric sentence is not true, it is either false or

---

6 This, though, is not Evans's only reason for discontent with Frege's admitting empty but senseful proper names. It also goes against his reading of Frege's notion of reference as semantic value (see Evans, *Varieties*, pp. 22–4) and also allegedly poses a threat (according to Dummett in IFP: pp. 129 ff.) to Frege's realism.

fictitious, and it will generally be the latter if it contains a mock proper name', and even that the thoughts in fiction 'ought not to be taken seriously'. These comments suggest quite clearly that there *are* such senses, for otherwise what is it that we are advised not to take seriously? Evans takes 'fictitious sense' to mean 'unreal sense', i.e. not a sense at all (which may well have been a feasible reading if that phrase was all we had to go by); but when the passage is considered as a whole, I think it is far more plausible to read 'fictitious sense' as meaning simply a sense as in fiction, i.e. one lacking a referent.

The implausibility of Evans's reading becomes even more apparent when we contrast Frege's comments on empty senses with comments made in other contexts where he *did* wish to rule out some theoretical possibility. Before he drew the sense/reference distinction, Frege made it plain in his pre-1884 'Dialogue with Pünjer on Existence' that if what appears to be a personal name does not actually designate, then it is merely an empty sound and not a name at all (PW: p. 60). Similarly he discarded, as not being concepts at all, (what would appear to be) concepts whose boundaries are not sharply defined (Gl. § 74; PW: pp. 195 and 229; and Gg.: p. 38n). With the senses of empty names his manner is very different. Their status as senses is never explicitly challenged, nor is the meaningfulness of the expressions in which the associated names occur ever denied – as it should have been if he held the view Evans maintained he did. Frege does, though, make it clear that such expressions have no place in scientific language. Elsewhere Frege makes this far more clear, as when he writes in the posthumous *Comments on Sense and Meaning*: 'Of course in fiction words only have a sense, but in science and wherever we are concerned about truth, we are not prepared to rest content with the sense, we also attach a meaning [i.e. reference] to proper names' (PW: p. 118).

A few pages later he comments on the name 'Nausicca' that it 'probably does not mean or name anything . . . But it behaves as if it names a girl, and it is thus assured of a sense. And for fiction a sense is enough. The thought, though it is devoid of meaning, of truth-value, is enough, but not for science' (p. 122).[7]

To conclude, whether or not Frege was right to admit empty senses, I find Evans's reading, according to which he did not think they were real senses, unconvincing. There are a great many places where Frege explains the possibility of empty names and associates them with fiction – this is, in fact, part of his 'standard presentation' from SuB on – without the slightest hint that they are any the less real senses for that. This would have been very unlikely, indeed grossly misleading, if he thought they were not senses.

---

7 Later in the same work he writes, 'A proper name must at least have a sense (as I use the word); otherwise it would be an empty sequence of sounds and it would be wrong to call it a name. But if it is to have a use in science we must require that it have a meaning too, that it designates or names an object' (PW: p. 124).

Dummett, too, seems to have remained unconvinced by Evans's interpretation, and he takes Frege to be committed to empty names' possessing a sense. But he also believes that there remains a way of conceding the essence of Evans's position nonetheless. After construing Frege's admission of empty senses as confined to *natural* language, he writes, 'To maintain, as do McDowell and Evans, that the account [i.e. Frege's] is not fully coherent is not, therefore, to criticize Frege but to agree with him: if the account were coherent, the feature so explained would not be a *defect*' (IFP: p. 134).

Despite its initial appeal, the idea will not bear scrutiny. Frege regarded senses as timeless and eternal entities which are 'out there', regardless of whether there are linguistic means of expressing them and, accordingly, that their relation to their referents, if any, is not a matter that linguistic reality can influence in any way (unless, of course, one's subject matter is language). In view of this, the real question confronting us is not whether there are any *expressions* which have sense but lack reference; this can only be secondary to the more fundamental question of whether there are *senses* which lack a referent. The matter is a *metaphysical*, not a linguistic, one: if there were no such senses, no linguistic misbehaviour could bring them into being. If, on the other hand, there *are* such senses, then there is room for the further question of whether they are expressible in language. Frege's view was that language can only *reflect* what is provided by the metaphysical framework, and cannot create, or even affect, what stands to be reflected. Calling such names 'defective' – which in an obvious way is correct – cannot undo the metaphysical situation which made them possible. For this reason Dummett's suggested compromise will not work. It does, however, illustrate the manner in which regarding senses as primarily a feature of one's account of language can lead one astray.

Frege's dismissive attitude to language is not only fundamental in a general way, but it also played a decisive role (as we saw in the previous chapter) in bringing him to realize that the Bs. theory was flawed – which realization pointed him, in turn, to the sense/reference distinction. The view there taken of what language *does* create, i.e. the relation of designation, was that it is not sufficiently objective to be a constitutive part of an object of knowledge. The grounds which tell against Dummett's proposal are thus at the very root of the notion of sense.

I conclude that the attempt to explain away empty senses as a defect of language is unsuccessful, just as were the attempts considered earlier to save the route model from being undermined by Frege's recognition of empty senses. In the section V, below, I will try to shed some light on the question of *why* Frege might have found it necessary to admit empty senses. Here my concern has been only to establish that he did.

It is time to take stock and ask where the repudiation of these attempts to reconcile the route model with Frege's recognition of empty senses leaves us. Something, it would seem, must give way: either the route model, or empty senses, or Frege's consistency. Evans maintains that it is empty senses, but also considers (though he does not clearly endorse) the possibility that Frege might have been inconsistent. Dummett seems to believe that they all can live in harmony, but his talk of a route which leads nowhere, and of empty names as a mere defect of natural language, is incoherent and makes nonsense of fundamentals of Frege's outlook. My own view is that the route model must give way to empty senses, and that the characterization of sense as 'a way (the referent) is given' holds good only when there *is* a referent, and not generally.

The situation facing us resembles the one brought about by the need to recognize the null class. It would be almost impossible to introduce the uninitiated to the notion of a class without some appeal to the idea of a group of elements, and this is not incorrect so long as we confine attention to non-empty classes. But such a characterization fails *in general* because we wish to admit that this special case is a class as well. I see no grave consequences for Frege's position ensuing from admitting that conceiving of sense as 'mode of presentation', though heuristically valuable, and true whenever there is a referent, cannot serve as a general characterization.

IV Sense determines reference, I: the question of relativization

The notion of sense was required first and foremost to make room for a difference between two contents (qua epistemic objects) which otherwise would have collapsed, very implausibly, into one. The intuitive difference between such contents is exemplified by pairs of sentences resulting from the intersubstitution of expressions like 'the morning star' and 'the evening star'. But why can we not say, then, that the expressions under consideration have the same reference and distinct senses and leave it at that? Why does sense need to *determine* reference, and what precisely does this dictum mean? The slogan 'sense determines reference' is by now established as a fundamental and unchallenged truth which most writers on Frege would subscribe to – and I am no exception. But its precise meaning, as I will show, is controversial and in need of careful delineation. My course in dealing with this matter will consist, first, of a negative move intended to purge the relation indicated by 'determine' from additions which are often attached to it. Then, in the next section, I will attempt to illuminate this relation by appeal to another, more familiar, relation. But before entering into these more special issues, let us recall, briefly, why *some* form of 'determination' is mandatory.

The most fundamental meaning of 'sense determines reference' is embodied in the requirement that the relation of senses to referents be many–one. Without this, the notion of sense would not have been any help in resolving the puzzle. However, leaving it at that strikes me as leaving the relation more mysterious and open to misunderstanding than is absolutely necessary. We may observe, to begin with, that were the requirement that sense determines referents dropped, the relation between sense and reference would become, to use Russell's phrase, 'merely linguistic through the phrase', and this would be as intolerable on Frege's view as it was on Russell's. If the pairing of senses and referents was a matter of linguistic convention, rather than of the intrinsic natures of the terms related, then the notion of sense would offer not a better, but a worse solution to the puzzle about identity-statements than did the line taken in Bs. Instead of the content depending on one arbitrary relation (that of designation) we get it depending on two (i.e. on the name's relation to the sense as well). On such a view there would be no reason why different expressions might not pair the same sense with different referents, in which case the grasping of a sense would be only arbitrarily linked with what one was thinking *about*. The first thing to be understood in 'sense determines reference' therefore (once the many–oneness is acknowledged), is that the relation between sense and referent is *intrinsic* to the related entities and holds independently of anything beside them. (If there is no referent, then that, too, must be intrinsic to the sense; it cannot acquire one 'later'.) In other words, that a given sense determines the particular referent it does (if any) is an *essential* feature of its identity – it cannot fail to do so while being the sense it is.[8]

The above description of the sense–reference relation may seem out of step with one's intuitive conception of statements commonly expressed in natural language. Surely, 'the president of the United States' refers to a different person now than it did ten years ago; does it not follow that the *sense* of this expression determined a different person then than it does now? Given the immutability of senses, there are two possible lines of response which suggest themselves here. The first is to maintain that the sense of such an expression, though constant, determines a referent only relative to some additional parameter to be specified (such as a time or a place). The other is to insist that the sense *alone* determines a referent, and deny that 'the president of the U.S.' expresses a complete sense. The latter line of response implies, more generally, that only when *everything* required to determine a referent is incorporated do we really have a sense. On this view the supplementation (such as of a time or a place) will not be something the determination is relative to, but rather an integral part of the sense itself. Practically, the difference between these two lines may seem insignificant, but theoretically, sense turns out to be quite a different thing depending on which we adopt.

8 The reason for regarding an internal relation as the only alternative to an arbitrary one in the present context may be this: relations between abstract entities seem either to derive from their intrinsic natures (as, e.g. inferential relations among propositions), or to be completely arbitrary (as, e.g. numerals, qua two-dimensional forms, and the numbers they stand for). Given that we are dealing with the very same relation, both when the reference is abstract and when it is not, it seems to follow that it will conform to constraints which hold good of relations between abstract entities.

(The former view is closer to our intuitive common-sense conception of linguistic meaning.)

By way of comparison, saying that a conclusion only follows from a set of premises given some additional assumption, is effectively to admit that it does *not* follow. In the same way, taking the first line mentioned above and relativizing the 'determine' amounts, in effect, to admitting that sense does *not* determine reference, and to say that it does is to imply that it suffices for such a determination *on its own*. There is absolutely nothing in Frege's writings to suggest that he might have permitted any relativization of the 'determines' in 'sense determines reference', and there is ample evidence – some only indirect – to the contrary. Of these two lines of response just mentioned only the latter, I contend, is consistent with Frege's fundamental conception of senses as eternal and immutable, and with his insistence upon a thought's truth being absolute. Frege's choice between the two lines is made plain in the following passage from the 1897 work 'Logic':

> If someone wished to cite, say, 'the total number of inhabitants of the German Empire is 52 000 000', as a counter-example to the timelessness of thoughts, I should reply: This sentence is not a complete expression of a thought at all, since it lacks a time-determination. If we add such a determination, for example, 'at noon on 1 January 1897 by central European time', then **the thought is either true, in which case it is always, or better, timelessly, true, or it is false and in that case it is false without qualification** . . . It is no objection that a sentence may acquire a different sense in the course of time, for what changes in such a case is of course the language, not the thought.
>
> (PW: p. 135)

If sense determined reference only relative to some additional factor, then a thought's truth (or falsity, or lack of truth value, as the case may be) could not be absolute either. This follows not only on account of the thought itself being a sense whose referent is its truth value, but also on account of its identity being determined by constituent senses. If a constituent sense could have different referents in different contexts, what would prevent a thought in which it occurs from acquiring different truth values? At what may be regarded as a more fundamental level, because it relies on a more general feature of conceptual content, Frege's conception of truth as absolute is also made plain in the contrast he expressly draws between a thought's being true, and the truth of a picture or an idea – which can only be relative to this or that external object (namely the object of which it is a picture or an idea).[9]

9 See the 1897 work 'Logic' (PW: p. 131).

Some writers on Frege[10] seem to think that relativization to a possible world fares better, and that however complete Frege's attempt to secure the absolute nature of a thought's truth value, he could not have considered such a relativization, and hence that we remain within the confines of a broadly Fregean view if we take sense to determine reference (and, accordingly, thought to determine truth value) only relative to a possible world. But this idea seems to me to go against the grain of Frege's notion of sense. In the first place, since Frege did not recognize a notion of possible world (or anything even remotely like it) there can be no grounds for supposing he would have found the appeal to such a notion acceptable. We do know, however, that he dismissed necessity – the account of which possible worlds are designed to facilitate – as a feature which does not belong to content, and is thus irrelevant to logic. But even if we ignore this and consider the grafting of possible worlds onto Frege's ontology, his response to such a relativization is almost certain to have been in line with his response to proposed relativizations to time (which, from a formal point of view, is essentially the same). The deeper point implied by the above quotation about 'inhabitants of the German Empire', as I understand it, is not merely that *time* indication needs to be included, but rather that *whatever is required for determining a unique referent* must be included. On this reading it is irrelevant whether Frege had in fact succeeded in considering all possible parameters on which truth might depend. We are therefore entitled to suppose that Frege's line of response would have been – in the possible world where Frege recognizes possible worlds – that if a specification of possible world is indeed required for a thought to have a definite truth value, then any purported sense lacking such a specification is no sense at all. Even if Frege could have been said to have 'forgotten' about possible worlds, his fundamental thesis is that the truth of a thought, and hence the relation of determining, are absolute. It follows that whatever is necessary for such determination must be regarded as part of the sense.

Another, apparently innocuous, relativization of the determination in 'sense determines reference' takes the form of appending to it such phrases as 'given the way the world is' or 'given the way things are'. Such additions are slipped in so casually, and doing so appears to make such good sense, that they are almost irresistible. It is for just these reasons that this relativization is particularly deceptive. Not only is there not a trace of evidence to suggest that this crucial addition might have been licensed by Frege, but it also goes against fundamental features of his position. If we ask what precisely is meant by 'the way the world is' (is the *whole* world relevant to the truth of the thought that I am presently sitting at my desk?) it transpires that we have effectively smuggled in *facts*, a category conspicuous by its absence from Frege's

10 E.g. David Kaplan, 'How to Russell a Frege-Church', *Journal of Philosophy* 72 (1975) section III.

ontology.[11] And since truth values are referents of thoughts, we will also have smuggled in a correspondence (or at least a relational) conception of truth – which, as is well known, Frege expressly rejected. That adding such phrases seems so plausible and natural is due to the tendency to conflate Frege's notion of sense with the intuitive notion of linguistic meaning. If one takes (every-day) *sentence meanings* as the primary bearers of truth then, surely, it is these meanings, together with the way the world is, that jointly determine whether these meanings are true. But this, quite clearly, is not Frege's conception of sense. On his conception, what thoughts are true just *is* the way the world is – their truth or otherwise is not a reflection of some other, independent segment of reality.

V Sense determines reference, II: the conceptual model

Having elaborated what I consider to be the essential features of 'determine' and, hopefully, staved off some common misinterpretations, I turn now to another angle on the 'determine' in 'sense determines reference', which I pro-pose as a means to illuminate it. Even when the essential features of the rela-tion mentioned above have been acknowledged, it remains something of a mystery *how* precisely sense determines reference, to put it crudely. Looking at the relation between a concept (considered intensionally) and its exten-sion, seems to me to be helpful in addressing this question.

Consider the two expressions 'equilateral triangle' and 'equiangular tri-angle' (here it is crucial to read inverted commas as indicating *mention*). On a familiar view, which was well established long before Frege, they are regarded not just as two names of the same class of objects, but rather as expressing, or standing for, two distinct *concepts*, each of which, *in turn*, deter-mine one and the same class. 'In turn' is here vital because the whole point of positing concepts is for the sake of their role in *determining* classes: if this role could have been assigned to the *expressions*, we could have done with-out concepts. Now the relation between the concepts and their extension is clearly intrinsic: any given concept could not determine a class other than the one it does in fact determine and, as this example makes plain, the relation is many–one.[12] Viewing the relation between concept and extension as intrinsic may controvert some intuitive, everyday, notion of a concept (for example, the extension of *man* might have been different if x had not been born), but according to Frege's more rigorous notion the earlier considerations with

---

11 Nominally, one might equate, as Frege suggests, facts with true thoughts. But then saying that they are that which *together with the thought* determines the truth value becomes non-sensical.
12 The same relation, essentially if not precisely, relates a definition and the object defined (in the sense, common in Frege and Russell, whereby it is objects, concepts or classes, not linguistic items, that are defined).

regard to the relativization of 'determine' to a time or a possible world apply to concepts just as they did to senses. It follows that if extensions are distinct, then concepts determining them must be distinct.

It may well be doubted whether this analogy goes any way towards *explaining* the 'determine' between sense and reference, because the relation to which we appeal may ultimately be just as mysterious as the one we seek to illuminate. But the merit I claim for the relation in the conceptual case which makes it valuable for our purposes lies in its being far more familiar and firmly established than the relation in the sense/reference case. Moreover, even if the relation is just as mysterious in the conceptual case, I would still regard it as helpful to learn that they were *the same mystery* (or at least closely related ones). We will have traded two mysteries for one. For one thing, the conceptual case strikes me as the true home of the talk of one and the same thing being determined, or given, 'in distinct ways'.

I am not at this point arguing that the senses of proper names *are* concepts, but only that their *relation to their referents* is at least analogous to that between concepts and their extensions. Whether, and to what extent, the two are ultimately more than just analogues is a matter we might throw some light on by considering the sense/reference distinction for concept- and function-expressions – a matter the discussion of which has also been pending since the first section, when arguing for the priority of the distinction for proper names.

In the case of the senses of a concept- and function-words the relation of concept and its extension[13] seems to me not just a model of, but (barring some reservations) close to *coinciding* with, that between a sense and its referent. I have not forgotten that for Frege it is not the extension that is the referent, but if, as I maintain, it is the *sense* of the concept-word that has taken over the role of the former notion of a concept (which is what the analogy appealed to), then the difference is not as significant as it at first seems. This view of things is somewhat obscured by Frege's adopting, after SuB, a deviant use of the word 'concept' (*Begriff*), but setting nomenclature aside, I think it is clear that it is the *sense* of a concept-word (and not its referent) which takes the role of the former, more familiar, notion of a concept. (To avoid confusion, I will indicate Frege's post-SuB use by 'F-concept'.)

The decisive fact I rest this claim on is that on Frege's view it is *senses, not F-concepts, which are correlated many–one with extensions,* and although the referent is on Frege's view the F-concept, not the extension, the fact that the relation between F-concepts and extensions is one to one permits us to say that the sense determines *both* the F-concept and its extension simulta-

---

13 For the sake of brevity I continue to amalgamate concepts and functions under the label of 'concepts'. Similarly, I will avoid complication due to Frege's regarding extensions as a special case of value-ranges, since it does not affect the point at stake.

neously (more precisely, that they are both equally determined by it). We surely do not need the F-concept to determine the extension, since it no more determines the extension than the extension determines it. Put differently, if for each extension there was only a single 'way of determining' it, then that notion could not fulfil the role concepts are required for. It would be idling, and we could just as well *identify* it with the extension.

To sum up, it is senses, rather than the F-concepts, that are the legitimate heirs of Frege's pre-SuB notion of a concept (and virtually everyone else's), and this is vividly testified to by the almost identical manner in which Frege argues in the passage cited in the last section (regarding the number of inhabitants of the German Empire) for the immutability of senses, and for the immutability of concepts in Gl. § 46 (which is all the more striking because it appeals to an almost identical example). It is for this reason that when, in the first section of this chapter, I considered how novel the distinction was for the different kinds of expressions, I regarded the distinction for concept-words as relatively insignificant. We already *had*, effectively, a notion of a concept-word sense before reading a word of Frege. What we did not have beforehand is a notion of an entity distinct from both concept and its extension, which is correlated one-to-one with extensions. But admitting such an entity is not a substantial matter, not nearly as substantial, at any rate, as the thesis that proper names have senses.

The determining of reference by the sense of a functional expression can thus be seen not only as modelled upon, but as actually an instance of, the relation between a concept and its extension. To be sure, F-concepts have a distinct role as well (namely mapping objects onto objects, among which are truth values), but with respect to the slogan 'sense determines reference' they serve merely to complicate and obscure the scene, rather than illuminate it. So far I have not considered the 'determine' with respect to complete thoughts and their truth value. I have left this case to the end because, although this relation is assumed to conform, on Frege's view, to the same model as the other cases – and ultimately to be an instance of the proper name case – I fail to see how it might serve to illuminate this relation in any way.

We are now in a position to take a synoptic view of the distinction for the various kinds of expressions, which brings us back to the question, discussed earlier, of the priority of names. While for proper names Frege's introduction of senses introduces a new, hitherto unacknowledged entity between the name and its bearer, with regard to complete sentences the distinction only modifies and refines views concerning previously establish entities. With concept-words the distinction *does* introduce a new kind of entity, what I have called an F-concept, but since it is correlated one to one with extensions, it can hardly be claimed to embody any new insight as does the introduction of senses for names. The more interesting feature in this case concerns the *relation* between sense and reference. It was suggested that our understanding of this relation in the case of names may derive from our understanding of the similar relation in the case of concepts.

It remains for us to bring out some of the implications regarding 'determination' as modelled on the relation between concept and extension. One clear advantage of construing 'sense determines reference' in this way (both for proper names and for concept-words) is that it steers us away from the temptation to conflate the linguistic and logical relations involved. Although there might also be *some* sense in which the *phrase* 'equilateral triangles' can be said to 'determine' a particular concept, the *concept*'s 'determining' its extension is clearly of a very different kind. It involves no element of convention, and is independent of language – features which are fundamental to the relation between sense and reference. This contrasts sharply with the relation between the linguistic item and its sense (or, whatever one takes to be the extra-linguistic item a word is *directly* related to), a relation which is arbitrary – as becomes most clear in relation to simple, unanalysable expressions. This arbitrariness is no defect of language, but rather a constitutive feature of it – without it, it would not *be* a language.[14]

If my repeated insistence on the need to keep the word–content relation clearly apart from the sense–reference relation seems to be labouring the obvious, consider the following characterizations of the notion of sense. The task of the theory of sense is said to be to show 'in what the association of **an expression and its referent** consists' (IFP: p. 246); the sense of a word is said to consist 'in some means by which a referent of an appropriate kind is determined **for that word**' (FPL: p. 93); or 'the particular manner in which someone associates a reference **with an expression**' (FPL: p. 103); 'the sense of a **word** . . . constitutes the contribution it makes to determining the truth-conditions of sentences in which it occurs precisely by **associating a certain reference with it**' (FPL: p. 93). The fundamental error embodied in these statements is their scrambling together these two relations – or rather regarding their sum as a single relation. Frege does indeed speak loosely of senses and references as being 'of' a word or expression, but he takes care to set the two relations apart, and is clear about the reference attaching in the first instance to the sense, and only derivatively to the expression, as when, in SuB, he says that 'to each sign there corresponds a definite sense **and to that in turn** a reference'. Similarly, when he speaks of empty names he says that every well-formed name may be granted a sense, 'but this is not to say that **to the sense** there also corresponds a reference' (SuB: p. 58).

If sense were, essentially, what establishes the relation between an expression and its referent, then that would make the expression itself an *essential*

---

14 To see this, try to imagine this relation somehow becoming logical; we notice that the linguistic nature of our symbols slips through our fingers, and they end up resembling Fregean senses.

ingredient of its identity, but Frege repeatedly insists that this is not the case, and that the sense's association with the expression is incidental to it. Since the sense is what we grasp when we know, it would also follow on the above view that the correct association of a *word* with a referent was an integral part of every item of knowledge. This is the very opposite of Frege's view. Even if awareness of this association was in practice necessary for our grasp, it would still have no part in the object of knowledge. The view of sense we have been considering is not just mistaken, it is ironic, because it was the observation that it was a grave *mistake* to allow the expression any role in the epistemic object, it may be remembered, that led Frege to repudiate the Bs. account of identity-statements, which in turn led him to the notion of sense.

Having set out my view of the conceptual nature of the senses of proper names, I wish, to conclude this section, to recommend what strikes me as another indirect advantage of it, by returning to the topic of empty names. But while earlier my concern was only to establish Frege's commitment to such names having senses, here my aim is to shed some light on *why* he might have done so. I think it is fairly clear that, other things being equal, Frege would have preferred, for the sake of the overall cohesion of his system, *not* to admit empty names. His earlier pre-SuB position indeed was, as we saw, to deny them. Their admission came to him at a considerable cost, and the question is, what induced him to pay it? In relation to this question, acknowledging the conceptual nature of senses, even for proper names, comes to our assistance.

In Gl. § 51 Frege explains what is distinctive about concepts: 'with a concept the question is always whether anything, and if so what, falls under it'. He also explains, when defending his appeal to a contradictory, and hence empty, concept to define the number 0, that a negative answer to this question casts no shadow on the concept's legitimacy. If senses, and those of proper names in particular, are conceived of as having a conceptual character, then the analogous question with regard to any given sense, namely whether anything is determined by it, can always arise, and the possibility of its failing to determine anything at all is thus essential to its very nature qua sense. This, in turn, makes the admission of senses without referents inevitable.

I am not suggesting that Frege had a clear or explicit conception of the conceptual nature of proper-name senses. As I will be suggesting in the next chapter, such a clear vision was critically missing, and there is far more in his general outlook that tells against such a possibility than there is telling in its favour. What I do wish to suggest, however, is the possibility that his conception of sense may have been *guided* by such a conceptual view – which he may have been only dimly aware of. All (or almost all) of Frege's illustrations of the senses of proper names are in line with such an underlying conception. If the sense of a name like 'Aristotle' is something like 'the pupil of Plato and teacher of Alexander', then surely there are other equally intelligible descriptions of the same form which lack a referent. This, rather than a relaxation of his earlier uncompromising attitude to empty names, may, I suggest, have contributed to Frege's admitting that empty names have senses. But I do not wish to suggest this was the only reason.

The recognition of senses without referents is, of course, guided at least in part by the considerations which tell *against* the alternative course. Problematic as the consequences of Frege's line on this matter may be, those of denying sense to all expressions which lack a referent are even worse. Here we must bear in mind that for the uncompromising Frege, unlike later writers who have more lenient attitudes towards empty names, the consequences would be radically implausible. Since sense's chief role, as we saw, is that of the epistemic object (i.e. that to which we relate when believing, knowing and so on – Frege's view makes them, in fact, the sole kind of epistemic object), denying sense to empty names would imply that when such names are involved *nothing is believed* (and not merely, as is often the case, that the apparent belief needs some, possibly radical, reconstrual). Let us illustrate this with a particular example.

At the time Frege wrote, physicists thought that there was a substance surrounding the Earth, called 'ether', which was supposed to be the medium through which electromagnetic waves were propagated. As a result of subsequent scientific developments, this belief was abandoned. If there is no such thing as ether then the name 'ether' lacks a referent, but to deny it a *sense* is to imply that the apparent beliefs of those past physicists were not beliefs at all, and hence that their talk about ether was no different from mere babbling.[15] (Frege would have said that they lapsed into fiction, which is quite different from lapsing into meaninglessness.) The absurdity of this line is further illustrated by the following consequence. On this view there would be no way for *us*, who (let us suppose) never believed in the being of ether, to report what would appear to be those physicists' belief. For our words to have reference their words would have to have sense, but since this is being denied, our words too have no reference, and since on this view lack of reference implies lack of sense, *our* attempt to report their beliefs ends up being an empty sound as well. On such a view we do not merely fail to *say* any-

---

15 Compare this with Frege's mature view regarding names which lack a *sense* (in the same way). In a letter to Peano he writes that while a speaker might be ignorant of the agreement of reference of two names he 'will have to connect a sense with the name unless he is babbling senselessly' (PMC: p. 127). This suggests that Frege's recognition of empty names is not so much the renunciation of a formerly held principle as it is shifting a certain role, namely that of the kind of extra-linguistic entity the association with which is necessary for an expression's intelligibility, from one kind of entity to another. This perspective will be further developed in section IV of the following chapter.

thing, we do not even *mean* anything.[16] I think Frege was being, at the very least, reasonable in avoiding such consequences, bearing in mind that *for him*, that would have been the only alternative.

VI The application of Russell's argument in 'On Denoting' to Frege's distinction

To conclude this chapter I wish to discuss an issue which harks back to the discussion of Chapter 2, but which, for obvious reasons, was better postponed until after Frege's distinction had been set out. Most discussions of Russell's obscure passage give a prominent place to the question of whether his argument is directed against Frege's distinction and, if so, whether it succeeds. Some writers, helped by Russell's unstable terminology when translating Frege's, have simply assumed from the outset that Frege must have been the target, and on the basis of this have gone on to emphasize the differences between Russell's position and Frege's, concluding that the attack is a failure because Russell got Frege completely wrong.[17]

The discussion in Chapter 2 made it plain, albeit implicitly, that it is hardly likely that Frege's view was the chief target of Russell's argument – that role belongs to Russell's own former theory. But was Frege a secondary target? Did Russell think his argument did in fact *apply* to Frege's distinction? The textual evidence on this question is inconclusive, and I am therefore unable to make any definite statement on Russell's intentions in this respect. However, neither Russell's intentions, nor the overall differences between his distinction and Frege's, seem to me the important questions. What is important, rather, is whether the argument *applies* to Frege's distinction; to decide this, all we need know is whether it shares those features with Russell's former theory which are crucial to Russell's argument. The argument is confined to complex proper names, and there can be little doubt that Frege recognized such names.

Russell's criticism depended on there being 'aboutness-shifters', which give rise to the question 'how are propositions *about* them possible?' In Frege's context the question becomes 'how are thoughts about senses possible?', and

16 The obstacle may seem to be circumvented (as I have just illustrated) by roundabout reports such as 'they believed in there being such a thing as . . .'. But in this way we are reporting what is only a related belief and not the one in question. However effective the means one may devise to convey doxastic states, there is no getting away from the fact that on Frege's view, strictly speaking there cannot be any literal report of the apparent belief. Since in the absence of a component sense there is no thought which might serve as the object of the subject's belief, there is simply no belief to report.

17 The most striking example in this regard is probably J. R. Searle, 'Russell's objections to Frege's theory of sense and reference', *Analysis* 18 (1958) pp. 137–43.

the importance of having an answer is here as crucial as it was for Russell, because Frege too subscribed to a non-correspondence conception of truth, and thus must allow for such thoughts if anything is to *be* true of senses. Of course, Frege's position differs from Russell's in taking *all* thought constituents to be aboutness-shifters; but it is hard to see how this difference might *ease* the pressure of this difficulty for him. To see how Frege is in precisely the same boat as Russell we need only consider his account of indirect speech. The words within the scope of 'S said that . . .' do not have their usual reference or sense; their references are rather the senses those same words have outside such contexts. This implies that our using the same words both in and out of such contexts is an ambiguity in natural language, which should be avoided in a logically correct language. In a letter to Russell, Frege observes this point and says that 'to avoid ambiguity, we ought really to have special signs in indirect speech, though their connection with the corresponding sign in direct speech should be easy to recognize' (PMC: p. 153). If we ask, '*what* special signs can we use so that their connection with the sign used in direct speech will be easy to recognize?', it becomes apparent that Frege has placed himself, unwittingly, at the threshold of the 'symbolic' round of Russell's argument in OD, and it goes without saying that he has no more of an answer to the difficulty than Russell did. In fact, his remark in SuB, that one can speak about a sense by using 'the sense of the expression "A" ', strongly suggests that he was completely unaware of the problem. If the inverted commas flanking the expression about whose sense we wish to speak are understood as mention quotes, that would make the relation 'merely linguistic through the phrase'; and if they are understood as some special kind of 'sense quotes' then we are back to Russell's intractable problem.

However, although Frege was unaware of the problem that Russell's argument brought out, there is reason to believe he would have acknowledged it as fatal had it been pointed out to him. This is suggested by two independent passages, which show the same line of reasoning that we found in the 'symbolic' round of Russell's argument. As interpreted in Chapter 2, this claim was that the symbol for the second-level complex ('<C>') ends up being logically unstructured or, as we put it, we might just as well have used 'D'. This result was deemed untenable, because the relation to the original phrase would then be lost.

In Gl. § 36 Frege considers a proposal made by Jevons. It starts from the idea that one can represent the number five as the conjunction of five units, thus: '1 + 1 + 1 + 1 + 1'; but then, to indicate the crucial fact that these are *distinct* units, is modified thus: '1' + 1'' + 1''' + 1'''' + 1'''''. Frege comments that if we adopt this plan,

> it is hard to see why we still retain in our symbols a common element; why not write, instead of

$$1' + 1'' + 1''' + 1'''' + 1''''',$$

simply

$$a + b + c + d + e?$$

Yet the case for identical units has already been finally abandoned as hopeless, and it helps not at all to point out that they are to some extent similar. So our one slips through our fingers; we are left with the objects in all their peculiarity. The symbols

$$1', 1'', 1'''$$

tell the tale of our embarrassment. We must have identity – hence the 1; but we must have difference – hence the strokes; only unfortunately, the latter undo the work of the former.

(Gl.: § 36)

The failure of this proposal is of essentially the same kind as that of the '<C>' symbolism discussed in the obscure passage in OD. The occurrence of 'C' was intended to reflect the relatedness, and that of '< >' the distinctness, of C2 and C1. But since the structure of '<C>' conflicts with its value not being (a value of) a function of C, the relatedness ends up 'slipping though our fingers' and we are really no better off than if we had used a simple symbol, which would reveal the opacity that the proposed notation conceals.

The other case occurs in Gg. Volume I § 11, where Frege explains the merits of the description operator by noting a danger (which his theory avoids), namely the danger of forming ambiguous or empty names by prefixing 'the' to a concept-word:

If there were no irrational numbers – as has indeed been maintained – then even the proper name 'the positive square root of 2' would be without a denotation, at least by the straightforward sense of the words, without special stipulation. And **if we were to give this proper name a denotation expressly, the object denoted would have no connection with the formation of the name**, and we would not be entitled to infer that it was a positive square root of 2, while yet we should be only too inclined to conclude just that.

(Furth: p. 50)

That the object denoted would have no connection with the formation of the name is precisely the problem we faced when '<C>' was reduced to the hypothetical 'D' in Chapter 2. These two examples suggest that Frege would have conceded the defect in his theory, had it been pointed out to him expressly. Having concluded that Russell's argument not only applies, but would probably have been conceded as decisive by Frege, I now move on to consider some attempts to save Frege's distinction from the force of Russell's argument.

Dummett does not provide a full exegesis of the obscure passage in OD, but he does recognize that Russell's case hinges on there being second-level senses, and this suffices for him to try and counter it, on Frege's behalf, so to speak – which he does in a number of places (FPL: pp. 267–8; and IFP: pp. 87–8). While conceding that Frege's position is untenable as it stands – though he seems to have noticed only what in Chapter 2 was regarded as the derivative epistemic mode of the difficulty – Dummett suggests 'a simple emendation which can be made to the doctrine, which, with only a small perturbation in the system, dispels the objection'. 'The whole difficulty arises', he rightly observes, 'from the principle that the reference of an expression must be determined from its sense alone'; hence the crux of the emendation: 'The sense of a word may thus be such as to determine it to stand for one thing in one kind of context, and for a different thing in some other kind of context.' We may therefore regard an expression occurring in an opaque context as having the same sense as in a transparent context, though a different reference. The idea is that only in conjunction with the context in which the word occurs does a word's sense determine the referent (FPL: pp. 267–8).

The first thing to note about this proposal is that 'determination', in the thesis that sense determines reference, has been made to depend on a linguistic context, and is therefore no longer construed as a logical relation. To say that a sense determines reference only given additional conditions is tantamount, as already noted, to saying that it does *not* determine the reference.[18]

Dummett's emendation can, however, be purged of its linguistic bearings by appealing, instead of to the linguistic context of the word, to the (non-linguistic) notion of the type of occurrence a constituent sense may have in a thought. A sense will be said to have a secondary occurrence when it occurs in a thought which is itself only part of another thought (otherwise the occurrence is primary.)[19] We might then say that in a secondary occurrence a sense

---

18 Some years later, in IFP, Dummett retracted the claim that this emendation is in harmony with all of Frege's other views. 'It is *not* consonant with his views that an expression with a constant sense should vary in reference according to context; as we have seen, this conflicts, not merely with the principle that sense determines reference, but with the conception of sense as the mode of presentation' (IFP: p. 101).

19 Cases where the complete thought is a truth function of its constituent thoughts will be set aside as a different kind of occurrence (see OF § 23(b) and (e) pp. 375–6). This mimics Russell's distinction between primary and secondary occurrences as originally conceived for denoting complexes. Paradoxically, these labels were carried over to the theory of descriptions, despite that theory's dispensing with the kind of entity among whose occurrences we are supposed to distinguish.

refers to itself.[20] But even when this correction is made, the problem remains that the proposal simply fails to engage with the problem Russell was concerned with. To see why, we must clearly distinguish the problem of thoughts about *complete* thoughts from the analogous problem concerning senses which can only be *parts* of complete thoughts.

On Frege's view, complete thoughts also have reference, and a special provision is therefore needed if in indirect speech we are to speak about the content of the specific (embedded) sentence rather than about its referent (i.e. its truth value). Dummett's emendation tries to face up to this specifically Fregean difficulty without postulating, as Frege did, senses of higher levels. (Russell, it is worth noting, has no analogous difficulty with propositions about propositions.) But even when *this* difficulty is overcome with the modified Dummettian proposal, the problem Russell was concerned with remains unanswered. Russell's problem was concerned with senses which are only *parts* of complete thoughts, while in indirect speech 'S said that . . .' needs to be complemented with a *complete* sentence for the result to express a complete thought. Dummett's device thus fails to offer any help in handling senses of denoting phrases, even if it does for senses of complete sentences.

20 Strictly speaking this is incoherent, because a sense's referent (if the relation is to remain many–one) cannot vary any more than can the truth of a thought (besides infringing the principle that diversity of referents implies diversity of senses). What is meant, rather, is that in a secondary occurrence it is not the referent that is relevant to determining the truth value of the whole thought, but rather the sense.

Part III

Russell and Frege

Chapter 6

Russell and Frege compared

I Introduction: the strategy

The comparison between Russell's and Frege's views on singular reference has become inseparable from the exposition of those views themselves. A century after they were first set forth, the theory of descriptions and the sense/reference distinction remain such towering paradigms in philosophical logic and the philosophy of language that much of the subsequent discussions of these subjects may well be characterized (in the fashion of Whitehead's dictum concerning Plato's place in Western philosophy) as a series of footnotes to Frege's and Russell's seminal work. Most comparative discussions address themselves squarely to Russell's theory of descriptions and Frege's sense/reference distinction, and this is understandable in view of these being their most mature and final positions; but one more theory of Russell's, the PoM theory, and at least one more of Frege's, the Bs. view, ought to be involved in this comparison (I say 'at least' because one might also count the description operator in Gg.). Though not all pairs consisting of one Russellian and one Fregean theory make for an equally instructive comparison, our choice of which theories to compare calls for some justification, and focusing exclusively on the theory of descriptions and sense/reference distinction pair should not, without further ado, be regarded as the only way to proceed.

Another problem confronting us at the outset has to do with the absence of a neutral conceptual framework within which to conduct the comparison. To mention only two examples, Russell and Frege clearly differ in what they regard as a proper name, but is it a deep theoretical disagreement or can it be set aside as merely verbal? Without a notion which is neutral between the two positions, we can hardly phrase the question, let alone obtain a clear answer. Similarly, it is often assumed that Russellian propositions correspond to Fregean thoughts. Without wishing to challenge its correctness, such a view, I think, ought not to be left as a matter of mere intuitive recognition. Surely, to regard the two as essentially the same is to judge some features of each as more fundamental than others; and the grounds for this prioritizing ought to be made explicit. Problems such as these urge us to seek some theoretical apparatus exempt from an inherent bias towards either position.

Our discussion in the previous chapters revealed the following pattern: both Russell and Frege start with a first theory; some years later each discovers a specific, but fundamental, defect in it which leads to that theory's collapse. This leads, in turn, to forming a new theory, which supersedes the first. The defect in each case, it is important to note, was due to an oversight: they were both local defects the discoveries of which were *not* the results of any change of broader perspective. Given their respective views prior to these discoveries, these defects could and should have been detected beforehand. Curiously, there is also a striking similarity regarding the reception of these changes: the nature of these changes was not properly appreciated in subsequent philosophical tradition. Because in both cases the precise nature of the decisive defect was almost completely overlooked – though probably for quite different reasons in each case – they played practically no role in shaping the received understanding either of what provoked Russell and Frege to devise their respective new theories or of the very nature of these theories themselves. A principal thesis of the present work is that no understanding of the finished theories is complete without a full appreciation of the philosophical pressures to which they came as a response.

Thus far I have spoken of the parallel courses of events. When we turn to the contents of the theories involved, however, quite a different parallel suggests itself. There appears to be no Russellian counterpart to Frege's first theory (nor any Fregean theory whose content approximates to Russell's theory of descriptions); and the natural match seems to be between Russell's first theory and Frege's second. I am not saying that they are exactly the same, only that they are, at least prima facie, closer than any other pair one member of which is a Russellian and the other a Fregean theory; and this, in turn, suggests a certain course in addressing the two issues mentioned above.

Rather than start by comparing the theory of descriptions and the sense/reference distinction, we might do better to begin with PoM and sense/reference. This latter pair is more likely to enable us to extract useful generalizations which might reveal the common ground; and this should enable us, in turn, to delineate the remaining differences between them with greater precision. Since Russell's move from the PoM view to the theory of descriptions was revealed as a more local affair than it appears at first, such a course should facilitate a view of the differences between it and the sense/reference distinction as the compound outcome of the differences between the first pair and the change from PoM to the theory of descriptions discussed in Part I above.

Taking the pairing of the sense/reference distinction and PoM as our starting point has the additional advantage that, unlike any other pair, we have a substantial body of *primary* material relating to it. Both Russell's Appendix A in PoM devoted to Frege's views, and the remaining correspondence between the two philosophers, belong to a time when they subscribed to these theories. These sources may not be as instructive as one might have hoped –

among other things because our subject is not at the centre of attention – but they can still serve to check whether our discussion is broadly on the right track.

The comparison of the PoM and SuB positions, which therefore comes first, will occupy us for the greater part of the present chapter. After setting aside some widely held misconceptions regarding the two theories' commensurability, I will turn to delineating the common ground – an exercise designed to yield some of the necessary concepts – and then to the remaining differences. This will be followed by a critical discussion of some chief points of difference and some preliminary discussion of the pros and cons of each side. I will conclude with some remarks on the comparisons of sense and reference and the theory of descriptions, and the theory of descriptions and the '\' theory. Let us begin then with PoM and sense and reference.

II The PoM theory of denoting and the theory of sense and reference: some preliminaries

The main thrust of the present discussion can be usefully characterized by contrasting it with a remark made by Richard Cartwright in response to Russell's statement (in Appendix A of PoM), that Frege's distinction between *Sinn* and *Bedeutung* 'is roughly, though not exactly, equivalent to my distinction between a concept as such and what a concept denotes'. But, Cartwright protests,

> in fact the two distinctions are not even in the same ballpark. Russell's is a distinction between a denoting concept and what (if anything) the concept denotes. But Frege's is not a distinction between *Sinne* as such and their *Bedeutungen,* for the simple reason that it is not *Sinne* but linguistic expressions that have *Bedeutungen.* Of course, there is for Frege the relation of *Sinn* to *Bedeutung*, and it need not be considered merely derivative from the relation that a *Sinn* bears to the expression that has that *Sinn* and the relation that an expression bears to its *Bedeutung.* Nevertheless, in Frege's hands properties of that relation are used to elucidate a distinction within the general notion of the meaning of an expression – a use to which, in the text of *The Principles*, Russell never puts his distinction. There, as I have already noted, words have meaning in 'the simple sense' that they stand for entities other than themselves; no differentiations within this sense are contemplated.
>
> (Cartwright, 'On the origins', pp. 105–6)

This passage packs in it a great many of the characteristic misconceptions concerning the relation between Russell's and Frege's theories, which provides us with a useful opportunity to dispel them. The view I wish to advocate is that though Russell's and Frege's respective distinctions are not exactly the same, they are in *precisely* the same ballpark. What, then, are Cartwright's grounds for thinking otherwise?

He says that the Russellian and Fregean notions differ because, unlike a denoting concept, it is *not the sense that has the referent, but rather the linguistic expression.* But in the next sentence, noticing that this would render the relation of sense and reference 'merely linguistic', Cartwright backtracks by saying that this relation 'need not be considered merely derivative' from the relation each has to the expression. What he seems not to have noticed is that this admission, when thought through, completely undermines the thesis it was intended merely to qualify.

Using 'A' to indicate the expression's relation to its sense, 'B' for its relation to the referent and 'C' for the sense's relation to the referent, it ought to be plain, in view of our discussion in the last chapter, that regarding A and B as independent of each other would undermine the whole point of drawing the distinction. To say, as Cartwright does, that C is *not* merely derivative from A and B, is to concede that at least an element of C is independent of either of them and hence of the expression itself. Identifying C with this element, we see that admitting that the sense is even *relevant* to the expression's having the particular referent it has (i.e. admitting that B is not independent of the sense) amounts to making B redundant. Since the sense determines the referent, A + C will suffice to determine the referent, and B simply reduces to A + C. So although we can still speak of the referent as being 'of' an expression (provided we do not mistake this manner of speaking for the ultimate and precise account of the matter), it is *of* the sense in a far more fundamental manner: to be the referent *of* an expression just is to be the referent of that expression's sense. When this is acknowledged, the tables are turned on Cartwright's alleged contrast between senses and denoting concepts: it *is* the sense, and not the expression, that can properly be said to *have* reference.

A glimpse of what may have led Cartwright to overestimate this manner of speech is provided in the next sentence, where he says that the properties of C are used 'in Frege's hands . . . to elucidate a distinction within the general notion of the meaning of an expression – a use to which, in the text of *The Principles*, Russell never puts his distinction'. It is true, indeed, that Frege applied the distinction to *all* kinds of expressions, while Russell restricted it to denoting phrases, but how does this place them in different *ballparks*? Is Russell's distinction not a 'differentiation within the notion of meaning' of denoting phrases? The very notion of a 'general notion of meaning', so instrumental in expressing Cartwright's point, is quite un-Fregean, and is suspect from the outset. With both *Bedeutung* and *Sinn* serving specific technical functions, the appeal in Cartwright's remark to 'meaning' would seem untranslatable into German. What Frege does say, however, is that the distinction is a differentiation within the general notion of *conceptual content*; but this way of putting things leaves out the linguistic bearings on which Cartwright's contrast depends. Ultimately, the apparent plausibility of Cartwright's point turns upon a merely verbal accident: Russell's comment about having meaning in a simple sense employs the same word ('meaning') which Cartwright, not Frege, employs for indicating the notion within which Frege's distinction applies. What has been put forth as 'the simple reason' why the distinctions are so different thus crumbles under scrutiny.

Cartwright's citing of Russell saying that words have meaning 'in the simple sense' that they stand for entities other than themselves also fails, upon reflection, to establish the kind of striking difference Cartwright claims it does. If understood as covering denoting phrases as well, the matter is, presumably, not so simple, since Russell's denoting concepts give rise to just the same kind of distinction as Frege makes between a word's 'standing for' something qua object of cognition and what is thought or spoken *about* by its use. If, on the other hand, we confine our attention to *simple* proper names, then Frege too requires a simple, irreducible, relation between some words and some extra-linguistic entities (this matter will be explained in greater detail in section IV below). Russell and Frege differ, then, not on whether there is a need for such a simple relation, but rather on the kind of entities which are its relata. Russell does indeed stress the categorical difference between the two relations (i.e. A and C) more persistently than Frege does, but there is no reason to suppose any substantial difference between them on this point.

The precise extent to which Russell or Frege might be said to have been concerned with the meanings of expressions (in any substantial sense) is a matter I leave for Chapter 7; for the present I am content to rebut any suggestion of there being any substantial *difference* between them in this respect.

III The common ground: propositionalism, sensism and the implied metaphysical model

Having dismissed the view that the PoM and SuB positions are totally different, I turn next to elicit those features which the two theories share. They divide naturally into two clusters. The one is deeper and more stable – it goes beyond the two theories under consideration; the other is more specific and changeable. What follows does not purport to introduce anything new, but rather to generalize what has already been discussed, and rearrange it for the purpose of a comparative discussion.

Frege's and Russell's principal concern, as we saw, was not with anything linguistic, but rather with immutable, timeless, mind- and language-independent entities which language may *reflect* or express. Starting with the entities which correspond to complete indicative sentences – for which I will be using the term 'generic propositions' – they are the primary bearers of truth, and accordingly the relata of logical relations such as implication, i.e. the entities we are concerned with in proof and inference.[1] On this view it is plainly non-sensical to think of a generic proposition as being ambiguous, or vague, or true at some time (or in some circumstances) but not others. Truth itself is regarded as an unanalysable feature which generic propositions either have or fail to have, independently of anything else being the case. A curious consequence of this common repudiation of any correspondence conception of truth (which may well be regarded as a defect) is that the parity between true and false generic propositions becomes such that our apparent preference for truth over falsity, which otherwise might seem too obvious to need pointing out, is provided with no foundation. It appears to be completely arbitrary.[2]

Conspicuous by its absence is a distinct realm of *facts* which generic propositions might be compared to. (As mentioned earlier in relation to Frege, true generic propositions are the closest one comes to facts on this view.) The point is crucial because so long as a generic proposition's truth might be a matter of correspondence, insisting upon its non-linguistic character may be regarded as being of only limited importance; but in the absence of something it might correspond to, we are forced to leave behind the idea of its being a *representation* of any kind and, more generally, the idea of our discussion's being concerned with language, however abstractly considered. Generic propositions are immutable entities and this implies, in turn, the immutability of their constituent parts (if any).[3] False generic propositions are just as objective or 'real' as true ones.

Belief, knowledge (and what are known as 'propositional attitudes' generally) are, on this view, relations between a subject and a generic proposition. The generic proposition is the content, what is believed or known, and, except in special cases, it is independent of the act of cognition of which it is the object. So long as we are using 'meaning' in a loose, non-technical sense, we can say that generic propositions are the meanings of sentences, and their constituents (if any) the meanings of sub-sentential expressions.

1 Thus Frege writes, 'The sentence is of value to us because of the sense we grasp in it . . . I call this sense a thought. What we prove is not a sentence but a thought.' (PW: p. 206); and Russell, 'it is plain that when we validly infer one proposition from another, we do so in virtue of a relation which holds between the two propositions whether we perceive it or not' (PoM: § 37).

2 In contrast with other conceptions where truth is correspondence to fact. This feature is something Russell, at any rate, was acutely aware of. In 1904, in 'Meinong's Theory of Complexes and Assumptions', he gave it the following remarkably poignant expression: 'some propositions are true, and some false, just as some roses are red and some white' (Lackey: p. 75). This is all the more striking because at that time he felt compelled to endorse this view. Russell extricated himself from this embarrassment only in the MRTJ, but Frege never did: true and false thoughts, just like the objects named by 'the true' and 'the false', are so completely on a par that there is nothing to set them apart beyond the bare difference.

3 This feature is more familiar in relation to Frege's thoughts than to Russell's propositions but, as will become clear in the next chapter, this is a mere difference of emphasis.

While cognition and language are thus intrinsically dependent upon generic propositions (it is constitutive of saying, believing and knowing that something, i.e. a generic proposition, is said, believed and so on) this dependence is by no means reciprocal. There is no theoretical difficulty in supposing there are generic propositions which are never comprehended, and not only because they *happen* not to be comprehended, but also because they could *in principle* be outside the reach of human intelligence (and, correspondingly, human language). This possibility, though only rarely relevant to the generic propositions we are concerned with (as, in Russell's case, those about infinite totalities), is nonetheless significant for understanding the nature of generic propositions in general.

I call the cluster of tenets articulated above 'propositionalism'. It was subscribed to by both Frege (both with the earlier judgeable contents and with the later thoughts) and Russell (both before and after the theory of descriptions), and the two philosophers seem to have arrived at it independently of each other. My concern here is not to justify these tenets, but only to establish that they were indeed endorsed by both Russell and Frege. However, a certain seriousness towards propositionalism does seem to me required in the present inquiry, not out of reverence to either Russell or Frege, but rather because if we dismiss it as a mere myth we are far less likely to understand considerations which take this framework for granted.

At the risk of stating the obvious, this may be the place for a brief digression saying something about where this notion of a proposition comes from. I think the short answer must be that, at least by and large, it comes from mathematics. On a fairly natural view – at least far more natural in relation to mathematics than to any other kind of discourse – the contents of mathematical statements are embodied in timeless entities which are both the primary truth-bearers, and the epistemic objects. This much I think was so obvious to both Russell and Frege that they never bothered to argue for it in any detail (save implicitly, in criticizing alternative views, particularly in Frege's case). Despite their appealing to examples from natural language when discussing denoting in SuB and in PoM, it is worth remembering that both the problem of identity-statements in Frege, and that of statements about infinite totalities in Russell, appeared on their respective agendas first and foremost because of their respective roles *in mathematics*. This may not be clear from those discussions themselves, but becomes crystal clear when the broader contexts of the projects they were conceived in is brought into the picture.

The most common statements in ordinary arithmetic are equations, and these were considered by Frege to be identity-statements. This is why hardly anything could be considered properly worked out until this kind of statement in particular was worked out. That the discussion of infinite totalities is a characteristically mathematical issue hardly needs arguing for. I think Russell's and Frege's interest in the issues we are concerned with was to provide an account which would at the very least be workable and plausible as an account for mathematical statements, though, because of their view of the nature of mathematics itself, they must have also believed that whatever was right for mathematics would at least be the key to, or supply the general form of, what would be right for statements expressive of scientific, i.e. proper, knowledge generally.

Returning now to our main course of delineating the common ground, once the notion of a generic proposition, as characterized above, is taken on board, there are different ways in which it might be further specified. Here too we find a significant common ground between Russell and Frege which, however, is more narrow, and is confined to the pairing of the PoM and SuB positions. The principal reason for maintaining a distinction between this cluster of shared tenets ('propositionalism') and the other, which I will call 'sensism', is simply that Frege moved into, and Russell out of, sensism, while their commitment to propositionalism remained constant. Sensism is a variety of propositionalism – it is a particular view about how generic propositions are to be specified beyond the broad programmatic specification given above. The two most pressing questions left open by the more general account of propositions are these: Do generic propositions have constituent parts and, if so, what are they?

The similarity between Frege's notion of a name's sense and Russell's denoting concepts (of 'the'-phrases) seems so obvious that I feel free to waive the need for a distinct notion of *generic* sense, and simply use 'sense' to cover both the Fregean and the Russellian notions – though not Fregean thoughts. Confining ourselves to senses of proper names (i.e. names of objects other than value ranges and truth values) makes good sense not only because it happens to be the area where agreement lies, but also because it was considerations relating to names that led Frege, as argued in the previous chapter, to introduce the notion in the first place.

Both the Russellian and the Fregean notions are of abstract entities which are essentially constituents of generic propositions, they have no other theoretical function, which, though distinct from the corresponding entity which the generic proposition is conceived of as being *about*, secure by their very nature (so to speak) that the generic proposition in which they occur will be *about* an entity other than themselves (if about anything). The sense of a proper name is, in short, an aboutness-shifter.

The characterization of Fregean sense as 'a way in which the referent is given' is no obstacle to this assimilation with Russell's denoting concepts so long as we do not regard it as providing a definition or necessary feature of sense. As noted in Chapter 1, Russell employed denoting concepts to account for the very same puzzling phenomena (i.e. informative identity-statements) which prompted Frege to draw his distinction, and in essentially the same manner. The differences between them are more matters of emphasis than of principle.

Far more important than these differences, it seems to me, is the meta-physical structure which is implied by the positing of senses for proper names. At the ground level of this structure, which I will be referring to as 'level 0', we find entities which do *not* possess the property of inherent 'pointing' to another entity (i.e. aboutness-shifting). For each entity of level 0 there is a (potentially infinite) set of entities which 'point to', or 'determine', it; each of these could have, in turn, a potentially infinite set of entities determining *it* (these are what we earlier called second-level meanings, now 'senses'), and so on without limit. This metaphysical structure is implied by both Russell's and Frege's theories, though only a fraction of it seems directly relevant to the account of language and cognition.

When the entities of this structure are regarded solely in their role in rela-tion to linguistic expression, we notice that the status of an entity as a sense or as a referent becomes *relative*: the sense of one expression can be the ref-erent of another. The first advantage of having this model is that the dis-tinction between sense and reference can now be expressed independently of cognition and language, i.e. purely in terms of an entity's place in a meta-physical hierarchy, which makes the distinction an absolute rather than a rel-ative one. This is indeed far more fitting given that the distinction is first and foremost a metaphysical one, and that its role in the accounts of language and cognition must flow, given Frege's basic outlook, from this rather than the other way around. As soon as it is recognized that senses determining their referents is a brute metaphysical fact – regardless of either language or cognition – it becomes apparent that, except for level 0, the distinction is actually relative. Any sense will also be the referent of any member of the class of senses 'above' it; we have 'pure' or 'absolute' referents only at level 0 (which is what 'referent' *simpliciter* will mean henceforth, unless stated otherwise).

Although the implication of such a metaphysical structure is not the first thing to strike one when being introduced to these two views of denoting, it nonetheless follows when the matter is thought through. Moreover, both Russell, as evidenced by the obscure passage discussed in Chapter 2, and Frege, as evidenced by his appeal to second-level senses in his account of indirect speech, seem to have been aware of its being implied.

Ultimately, it should come as no surprise that both philosophers ended up with such a structure, because their motivations were very similar, and senses were called for to fulfil very similar roles in both cases. Assuming that the problem of informative identities was the 'primary case' leading Frege to the distinction, and that the problem of infinite totalities played a similar role for Russell, then we might generalize the line of reasoning leading to the posit-ing of senses in each case as follows. Starting from the assumption that we can and do reason and speak about some range of entities, the assumption that in so doing we establish a direct cognitive relation with those entities themselves has untenable epistemic consequences (namely that true identities are always tautologous in Frege's case, and that we apprehend infinitely complex propositions in Russell's case). To avoid this, an intermediate entity – an epistemic buffer, so to speak – is posited. This intermediate entity takes on, in place of the original entity, the role of being what we, or our words, directly relate to; at the same time, however, it enables us to preserve, in virtue of its 'aboutness-shifting', the initial assumption regarding what we think and reason *about*. Once such buffers are taken on board, it would be arbitrary, given that they are as objective and mind-independent as the referent, to rule against further buffers in some cases coming between us and the first buffers, and so on – hence the hierarchy. There is one more, by no means unimportant, topic which properly belongs to the common ground, namely the nature of the epistemic relation itself. But for reasons that will soon become clear, its discussion is best postponed until after some of the differences between Russell and Frege, to which we turn next, have been set forth.

IV The differences, and further similarities, in relation to the metaphysical model

When examined from the perspective of this common metaphysical structure, the disagreement between Russell and Frege can be put in terms of contrasting answers to the following question: what possibilities are there, as far as the considerations relating to proper names are concerned, for epistemically latching onto this structure? Frege, unlike Russell, prohibits any direct relation to entities of level 0, and hence the closest possible relation to a level 0 entity, for him, will *always* be via a level 1 entity. Russell, though he allows for such a route as well, recognizes the possibility of a *direct* relation to entities of level 0. There is nothing in this respect which Russell prohibits and Frege allows. This may not exhaust the differences, but it surely is a significant difference between them.

Given the epistemic role of the notion of a generic proposition, it is easy to see how this difference with respect to direct epistemic access leads to different views about what the constituents of a generic proposition might be. On the Fregean view there could hardly be any point in allowing generic propositions to have referents as constituents, since such generic propositions, had there been any, could never be grasped.[4] For Russell, on the other hand, since referents are epistemically accessible, it makes sense to allow generic propositions to contain either them, *or* the senses determining them, or both,

---

4 This is, of course, no argument against the *being* of such entities, but it does reveal why supposing that there are gets one no further. Similarly, Russell never argues against there *being* propositions containing infinite totalities; he only maintains that if there are, they are incomprehensible to us.

as the case may be. It was suggested in the last chapter that concept-word senses be identified for all intents and purposes with concepts *simpliciter*. In the light of this identification, the disagreement over the possibility of *objects* being generic proposition constituents turns out to be the *only* truly substantial difference between Russell and Frege regarding generic propositions in general. There is no other kind of entity about whose being a generic proposition constituent they disagree. Frege's taking a truth value to be the generic proposition's referent might seem like a major difference, but it strikes me as adding nothing substantial to the familiar conception of generic propositions as being either true or false. The route which starts from the notion of a generic proposition, and proceeds to characterize its constituents in the light of accessibility considerations, meshes well with what we know about the way Russell's and Frege's views developed, as well as with the (not unrelated) fact that their commitment to propositionalism was deeper and more stable than was their commitment to sensism or, for that matter, to any view that either of them held on what the constituents of generic propositions might be.

Returning now to the difference explained in the last paragraph but one, we ought to guard against a temptation to exaggerate it, and this in two ways. First, it would be incorrect to describe Russell's position as implying that *every* referent is epistemically accessible (even in principle) in the manner prohibited by Frege. He merely refrains from a sweeping exclusion of referents from becoming the objects of a direct epistemic relation *qua members of a level in the hierarchy* – as opposed to an exclusion on other, more specific, grounds (such as those regarding infinite classes). Second, by confining attention to the first two levels of the hierarchy one might form the false impression that on Frege's view grasping (the epistemic relation borne to senses) and thinking about (which is the relation borne to referents) are two relations whose very natures require different kinds of entities as relata, and thus that in entertaining the possibility of the one relation's obtaining to the other kind of entity one is not merely disagreeing with Frege, but committing some kind of category mistake. However, when it is remembered that one's epistemic relation to a sense can also go via a sense of a higher level, and that it is *precisely the same relation* which obtains between the two senses (when a second-level sense determines a first-level one) as between a sense (of level 1) and *its* referent, it transpires that a subject who apprehends a sense of level 2 bears precisely the same relation to its referent as he does, in apprehending a sense of level 1, to the entity of level 0, namely that of 'thinking about'. So although there is a relation which, on Frege's view, can be borne to senses but not to referents, there is also a relation which he admits may be borne to either senses or referents.

The epistemic difference just described is mirrored in Russell's and Frege's respective views regarding proper names. The expressions which are of the lowest possible level, i.e. names of objects, will, on Frege's view, *always* involve entities of level 1 (and thus relate only indirectly to an entity of level

0), while Russell recognizes a more directly related kind of name which does not involve level 1 at all, and whose employment corresponds to the epistemic relation Frege prohibits (the PoM term for this relation is 'indicate'). In discussing the differences between Russell and Frege there is a clear parallel between their contrasting views about which epistemic relations are possible, and which semantic relations, i.e. those between linguistic expressions and their extra-linguistic relata, are possible. (I reserve the discussion of the precise nature of this parallel for the next chapter.) Despite our immediate subject being the differences between them, the observation that it primarily concerns the epistemic access to one level of a shared metaphysical structure suggests yet another important common feature to which I turn next.

So far I have spoken of a 'direct' epistemic relation, by which I mean a relation the obtaining of which does *not* depend upon any *other* relation obtaining, in a manner general enough to justify its application to both Russell's and Frege's views. But now I wish to go further and argue that the direct relation which, on Frege's view, a subject bears to a sense he grasps, and that which, on Russell's view, a subject bears to an object he is acquainted with, is to all intents and purposes *the very same relation*. This might seem wrongheaded at first but, as I will try to show, when we adopt a broader and more abstract point of view, one which focuses on the role and nature of *the relation itself* rather than on the terms related, a different picture emerges.

Any view which allows the mind to engage with the world outside it, and to have knowledge concerning that world in particular, requires, at *some* point, a *direct* relation between the mind and some element of extra-mental reality. There may be need for an extended chain between the mind and the object this knowledge concerns, in which case the object known will be only indirectly related to the knowing mind, otherwise this relation can consist of a single link. In either case the fact remains that unless there *is* a direct relation at some point, there will be no relation between the mind and extramental reality at all. Since it is *epistemic* relations we are concerned with, a mind will invariably be one of the terms of this relation. What remains open, then, is only *which* kind (or kinds) of extra-mental item can take the role of the other term of this relation. Note that the considerations necessitating this direct relation are very general, and we have appealed to nothing which is specifically Russellian or Fregean.

This highly programmatic notion of a direct relation, the residue of the above transcendental line of reasoning, seems to me not only broad enough to capture the relation which obtains, both on Frege's view between the mind and a sense, and on Russell's view to either a sense or a referent, it may also be seen as providing the very essence of these relations. This is because there is hardly anything more to them than this 'thin' programmatic characterization. Both relations are irreducible and logically simple. They either obtain or fail to obtain completely, leaving no room whatsoever for gradation or vagueness (which is quite contrary to any intuitive or common-sense conception of epistemic relations). But it is precisely this thinness that seems to me to lend credence to the claim that Russell's 'acquaintance' (or in PoM 'perception') and Frege's 'grasping' are labels for what is at bottom *the very same relation*.[5] One is tempted to say that these terms have distinct senses, but the same reference.

It is a mistake to pass judgement on how similar these relations are solely on the grounds of the different kinds of entities they are a relation to – which, by the way, tends to overlook the fact that on Russell's view we have acquaintance with concepts, as well as with (at least simple) denoting concepts. From the perspective which looks first at the role of these relations in the broader scheme, the decision as to what this relation is borne to may be seen as advancing a particular claim about a relation whose fundamental identity has already been fixed.

A similar case can be made for linguistic expressions. Confining ourselves to logically simple expressions, a name's relation to its *sense*, on Frege's view, is essentially the same as its relation to its *referent*, on Russell's view. This may seem even more wrong-headed than the former epistemic equation, not only because for Frege a name is not the name *of* its sense, but also because Frege's view seems to stem from a denial that the name–bearer relation can be as Russell (or his own former self, in Bs.) conceived it to be. However, from a broader, more abstract, perspective, the matter looks otherwise.

Using 'significance' to label the property in virtue of which a (simple or complex) symbol can serve as an element of a language which might be used to speak about bits of extra-linguistic reality, it is a distinctive feature of both Russell's and Frege's views that a symbol's significance consists in its relation to some extra-linguistic entity.[6] In the case of a complex symbol (such as a complete sentence) this relation depends, clearly, on the significance of its constituent parts, and defined symbols may be considered as acquiring their significance via that of the symbols used in their definitions. But to suppose that such a dependence might apply to *all* symbols is plainly incoherent: at *some* point there must be simple, indefinable, symbols whose relation to extra-linguistic reality is *not* dependent upon any other symbol being so

---

5 When these observations are combined with the view, proposed in the previous chapter, that senses of concept-words can be identified with concepts *simpliciter*, we get the following result. Frege's conception of grasping such senses involves not only the same *relation* as on Russell's view, and not only a mind (or a subject) as one of its terms, but also the same kind of entity as the other term of this relation. The similarity in relation to concepts is thus so complete that it reinforces the view, advanced in the previous chapter, that it is in relation to the case of objects and proper names that the root of the disagreement with Russell lies, and that regarding other kinds of expressions the disagreement is, by comparison, derivative and less substantial.

6 Here we must remember to exclude incomplete symbols, which are ultimately eliminated by definitions.

related. Note that this reasoning, like its epistemological counterpart, is completely general, and is not dependent on any particular feature of either Russell's or Frege's view. This relation is embodied, on Russell's view, in the (simple) name–bearer relation, and on Frege's view, in any simple expression's relation to its sense. Both relations, like their epistemic counterparts, are left at a programmatic level.[7] Although I cannot think of a Fregean word for this relation after SuB (in Bs. it was, as we saw in Chapter 4, 'designation'), there can hardly be any doubt that such a relation is implied on his view as well.

Our course has been to start from an abstract characterization of a relation which, on highly general grounds, must occur *somewhere*, and then ask, what non-linguistic (or extra-mental) item does each of them place on the other side of this relation? The perspective thus obtained reveals the strata of shared views as being even more substantial, and this enables us, in turn, to locate the points of disagreement in relation to specific, relatively clear questions. This contrasts with the more common approach which, starting from names and their bearers, proceeds to note Russell's and Frege's differing conceptions of this relation, which can lead to their views appearing as two irreconcilable alternatives which may as well have stemmed from quite different fundamental assumptions.

These remarks conclude the comparative discussion which took the shared metaphysical structure as the frame of reference for delineating the remaining differences. But helpful as this framework is, I would hope, as a means for *characterizing* the differences between Russell's and Frege's finished positions at this stage, these generic notions are not the ones that will help us understand *why* they differed in the manner so characterized, or how this difference came about. For that purpose, we must return to those problems that they were consciously grappling with, put in terms that they themselves would have used.

V An apparent gap in Frege's argument

To begin with, we may recap the situation as follows: Russell and Frege employ what is essentially the same kind of theoretical device, namely a sense of a proper name; but except for 'the'-phrases in the singular (a special case of denoting phrases for Russell, and of proper names for Frege), about which they agree, they disagree about the range of linguistic expressions for which

---

7 A moment's reflection will suffice to recognize that the simple symbol's relation to the (possibly simple) extra-linguistic item must, in one sense, be exceedingly complex – its very conventionality, which implies a whole social machinery, tells against it being simple. But this complexity is not a *logical* complexity, and Russell and Frege are therefore justified in regarding it, for their purposes, as if it were simple. Similar remarks apply to the notion of a mind or a subject as one of the terms of epistemic relations.

this device is required. While Frege applies this treatment to expressions of *all* kinds, Russell thinks it is required only for a special subclass. This, in turn, brings with it a divergence over the kinds of entities which may constitute their respective notions of proposition (what was referred to as a generic proposition). While Frege's answer is 'only senses', Russell's is 'in some cases partly senses; in others, no senses at all'.

This relatively modest view of the differences is indeed how matters appeared to Russell in Appendix A of PoM (§ 476), when commenting that Frege's theory is 'roughly, though not exactly, equivalent to my distinction between a concept as such and what a concept denotes'. In the following paragraph Russell goes on to speak of Frege's theory as 'more sweeping and general than mine, as appears from the fact that *every* proper name is supposed to have the two sides [of meaning and indication]. It seems to me that only such proper names as are derived from concepts by means of *the* can be said to have meaning, and that such words as *John*, merely indicate without meaning'. The same view is also expressed in the last of Russell's letters to Frege, which I shall come to in section VI.

What, then, are the pros and cons of applying the distinction in Frege's sweeping manner as against Russell's restricted one? Since, fortunately, we have some area of agreement to start from, one might be inclined to enquire what case there is for extending the use of senses to account for expressions beyond the agreed class (i.e. 'the'-phrases in the singular)? No direct argument can be found in Frege for this, probably because he would never have regarded himself as *extending* the distinction to those cases where, in Russell's view, it would require further justification.[8] But we may examine Frege's argument for the distinction to see whether we might elicit from it any grounds favouring his position over Russell's. My aim here is not so much to adjudicate between Russell and Frege – though what follows has some bearing on this question too – as to discover the root of their differences. Granted that the distinction is needed for complex proper names (or 'the'-denoting phrases in the singular), what grounds are there for applying it to proper names generally (in Frege's terminology)?

The standard argument, as conveyed in Chapter 4, can be briefly recapitulated as follows: since substituting two co-referential[9] names in an identity-statement alters the generic proposition expressed, *something other than the name's referent* must determine the generic proposition's identity. This 'other thing', corresponding to various ways in which the referent is determined, is

---

8 My attention here is confined to proper names, because from Frege's course in SuB it appears that applying the distinction to complete sentences *is* regarded as an extension on his view as well.

9 Strictly speaking, we cannot help ourselves at this stage to the post-SuB notion of a referent, and must appeal, instead, to the pre-systematic notion of a name's bearer: what is spoken about by its use.

the name's sense. A similar argument, *mutatis mutandis*, was applied to class expressions as well.[10]

We do not falsify Frege's position by starting from proper names – since this is the course he himself takes. Accordingly, in the articulation of his case as canvassed in the last paragraph, we must take his use of *Gedanke* as indicating (in this context) a generic proposition rather than a thought (though it ultimately could be identified with a thought) because he could hardly be taken to be *arguing* for the distinction if he were appealing to a notion which presupposes it. So it is to a generic proposition, rather than to a thought, that the argument applies. Starting from an only partly determined generic proposition, he argues that it must be further determined in some ways rather than others.[11]

As noted already, the problem arises only with informative identities – not any true identity will do. Although admitting such identities does indeed exclude the possibility of *both* the names' contributions to the generic proposition being identified with their referents, Frege derives the stronger conclusion that *neither's* contribution can be so identified. This is clearly more than follows strictly from the premises, since it is enough that *either* 'a' *or* 'b' contribute something other than the referent to account for the fact that 'a = b' has a distinct cognitive value from 'a = a'. (If we abbreviate 'a name's referent exhausts its contribution to the generic proposition in whose expression it occurs' as 'S', Frege moves from 'it is *not always* the case that S' to 'it is *never* the case that S'; but 'it is *sometimes not* the case that S' is all he is strictly entitled to.)

The gap in Frege's argument becomes apparent when one follows it with Russell's alternative view in mind. Russell, translated into Fregean terminology, holds that some but not all names have senses, but this did not stand in the way of his using senses to account for the very same phenomenon to which Frege's argument for the distinction appealed. In his discussion in PoM, mentioned earlier, he accounted for the informativeness of an identity-statement by assuming that only *one* of the sides stood for a denoting concept. I am not suggesting that this gap refutes Frege's view (as against Russell's), because there may well be other arguments to the same effect, and the conclusion might follow given some additional, possibly unobjectionable, premise. The observation may amount to no more than a prompt, urging us to expose a suppressed premise but it is nevertheless noteworthy that an argu-

10 See letter to Russell (PMC: p. 157).
11 This perspective on the argument for the sense/reference distinction occurs in Frege's letters to Russell (e.g. that of 21 May 1903, in PMC pp. 156–8). I chose not to use that passage, however, because Frege's argument there, though parallel to the one below, is made for *classes* and their senses. This is because that discussion was prompted by a particular form of the contradiction regarding classes (cf. Frege to Russell 20 October 1902, in PMC pp. 149–50).

ment which Frege does in fact employ, and which might otherwise be thought conclusive, is inconclusive as it stands.

VI Can all expressions have sense?

It might be the case that even if there is a gap in Frege's argument to establish that the sense/reference distinction applied to *all* proper names, there is still no conclusive argument to decide between so applying it and restricting it, as Russell did, only to a special subset. Both positions may well be coherent, and in that case one's choice between them will have to rest on less than compelling grounds. But Frege goes further than extending the distinction to all names. He extends it to *all expressions whatsoever.*[12] Against this there might be some stronger, perhaps even compelling, argument.

If we purge the question at stake from its linguistic trappings, it boils down to the following: can it *sometimes* be the case that the (complex) epistemic object will *contain* an object of level 0, or should this possibility be completely ruled out? On this matter I am unable to recommend any watertight and conclusive argument, pro or con. Instead, I will first dispose of an argument that might appear to be such, but which I believe is fallacious, and then introduce a consideration inspired by a remark of Russell's, which though perhaps not compelling as it stands, may point the way to one that is, and which is clearly worth considering.

One line of reasoning which might be, and, I suspect, has been, thought to tell against Russell's position in response to the question just posed needs to be dismissed from the start. Some of Frege's statements could be read as suggesting that a *concrete* object cannot be the constituent of a generic proposition; and indeed there are solid grounds for believing that Frege thought mountains and persons are just not the kinds of things that can be parts of a thought – he says so explicitly on many occasions and in a letter to Russell in particular (PMC: p. 163). But what I wish to dismiss is a particular ground for holding this view, to wit, that since thoughts are the meanings of sentences, and meanings are abstract, to allow concrete objects such as mountains or persons to be their parts is to commit some kind of 'category mistake'. This point seems intimated (though not explicitly asserted) in the following passage by David Bell:

> Russell notwithstanding, the person Julius Caesar is no part of the meaning of the expression 'Julius Caesar', nor of any expression in which this

---

12 To this there is an exception in Frege's Roman letters, or free variables (Gg.: Volume I, § 17) which are said not to denote as other symbols of the concept-script do, but rather to 'indicate' (*andeuten*) (§ 17, see also Furth's comments on p. xxxvi of the same volume). Though this exception seems to me important, I will not pursue the matter here.

occurs. For as Wittgenstein has shown, if he were then it would be the case that part of the meaning of the sentence 'Julius Caesar is dead' used to be bald, crossed the Rubicon, and is buried in Rome. But *meanings* do not cross rivers or lose their hair.[13]

But there is just no reason why an abstract entity (such as a class) cannot have concrete parts. Whatever reason there might be against allowing generic propositions to have entities of level 0 as constituents, their abstractness is surely not even a plausible candidate for being a valid one. However strange it may seem to say that the meaning of a name crosses a river, this strangeness is only a superficial effect, and if one chooses, as Russell did, to call a name's bearer its meaning, this strange statement is perfectly in order. Besides, even if some argument along those lines were successful, it would only tell against the occurrence of concrete referents in thoughts, but since not all referents are concrete, this would be no argument against including abstract referents in thoughts.

I turn now to the case which might be made in favour of Russell's view. Its source occurs in the last of Russell's surviving letters to Frege (12 December 1904). Russell writes (I leave some terms of art untranslated),

> Concerning Sinn and Bedeutung, I see nothing but difficulties which I cannot overcome. I explained the reasons why I cannot accept your view **as a whole** in the appendix to my book, and I still agree with what I there wrote. I believe that in spite of all its snowfields Mont Blanc itself is a component part of what is actually asserted in the Satz: 'Mont Blanc is more than 4000 metres high'. We do not assert the Gedanke, for this is a private psychological matter:[14] we assert the object of the Gedanke, and this is, to my mind, a certain complex (an objective Satz, one might say) in which Mont Blanc itself is a component part.
>
> (PMC: p. 169)

So far we have no more than the usual statement of Russell's side of the debate. He then continues,

---

13   D. Bell, *Frege's Theory of Judgement* (Oxford: Clarendon Press, 1979) p. 60.

14   This retracts an implicit understanding, which Russell observed in the correspondence until then, that *Gedanke* does not indicate a psychological entity, but rather a generic proposition (see e.g. Russell to Frege, 20 February 1903, in PMC pp. 154–6). This, however, does not affect Russell's point that he finds no reason to recognize an intermediate entity between the psychological entity (as with the corresponding linguistic entity) and the proposition (or '*ein objektiver Satz*', as he calls it here).

If we do not admit this, then we get the conclusion that **we know nothing at all about Mont Blanc** [itself[15]]. This is why for me the *Bedeutung* of a Satz is not the true, but a certain complex which (in the given case) is true.

(PMC: p. 169)

The last but one sentence points to what seems a major consideration. Since Mont Blanc is here only a place-holder for an arbitrary referent, Russell's statement implies that if *all* expressions have senses then (in a privileged sense of 'know about' which requires a *direct* cognitive relation to the object) we know nothing about *anything* in the realm of reference. It might be suspected that this strong sense of 'know about' is introduced only to counter Frege's view, but in OF Russell had taken the same line regarding propositions containing denoting complexes.[16] It is natural to suppose that when one knows a proposition which, according to the theory of denoting, is *about* x, one *ipso facto* knows something about x; but Russell seems to reject this implication, and he reserves this way of speaking for the case where the object is actually a constituent of the proposition known. The difficulty is that though Russell may be entitled to prefer what may be labelled 'primary aboutness' as a more secure and direct kind of epistemic relation to 'secondary aboutness', for Frege, who recognizes only one kind of aboutness, this would carry no weight against his view. He would simply maintain that this is what aboutness is.

What our considerations so far have not addressed is that at least part of the significance of designating some kind of entity as a possible constituent of the direct epistemic object is that it *guarantees* the being of such an entity when the epistemic event occurs. Both Russell and Frege felt bound to supply belief with the same kind of epistemic object whether or not it is true. But in Frege's case this guarantees only the presence of a sense, which opens his position to the following threat, aptly articulated by Dummett (who, since he does not quite regard senses as entities, is not expressing his own view) as follows:

> if it is only by the medium of senses, as thought-components, that we
> can apprehend objects, we appear to be threatened by the same danger

---

15 This word was omitted in the published English translation of the correspondence. The original reads '*wir über den Mont Blanc selbst überhaupt nichts wissen*'. The difference is perhaps only rhetorical, but it pertains to the very point I wish to bring out.

16 'Whenever a denoting concept occurs in a proposition, it is the meaning, not the denotation, that occurs. It follows that, unless we happen to be acquainted with the denotation, and know that it is the denotation, we can know no proposition about it, although we may know numbers of propositional functions which it fulfils, and know it fulfils them' (OF: p. 368). This passage occurs just a few pages before the discovery of the theory of descriptions.

as threatened the empiricists who saw us as enclosed in a world of mental images and sense-impressions . . . How can we know that we ever do reach the object, or that there really is any object, if a sense always interposes between us and it, a sense that carries no guarantee of any corresponding referent?

(IFP: p. 133)

Despite Frege's acute awareness of the dangers of the epistemic object's being *subjective,* he seems hardly to have been aware of the danger of a global reference failure of the kind indicated in Dummett's words. By recognizing senses as objective and mind-independent entities, Frege does indeed avoid the most fatal threat faced by the empiricist position, because in grasping senses we already relate to something which is objective and shareable – part of the furniture of *the* world, rather than of each of our own 'private worlds'. Grasping senses is unlike having ideas. But making senses the *only* kind of directly accessible epistemic objects there are yields, together with the principled possibility of empty senses, the theoretical possibility that *none* of the senses we actually grasp has a referent. In that case our whole discourse, including what we assume to be scientific, could end up, unbeknownst to us, being fictional. Russell's acquaintance, by contrast, *guarantees* that, at least in those cases where we have 'primary aboutness', there will always be a referent.

Frege's discussion of identity-statements assumes from the outset that we are capable of knowing that two names have the same referent, but how could we ever be in a position to judge that, unless we had, at least in some cases, independent access to a referent? Where would the idea that there are referents behind the senses have come from? If senses without referents are possible, then there is indeed a threat, not so much that none of them has a referent at all, but rather that those senses we actually grasp have none. If our minds were so designed that they could relate only to entities in the realm of sense, it would seem that we would have no means of telling whether this was the case.

Adopting the conceptual view of name-senses proposed in the last chapter, we can describe Frege's view as confining *all* our knowledge of referents to what Russell was later to call 'knowledge by description',[17] and our very conception of any referent thus reduces to that of *whatever* answers to, or is determined by, the sense grasped. Such a view is not incoherent, but it is bound to repel someone like Russell who not long beforehand had emanci-

17 An expression which is only apparently anachronistic. The contrast between a direct cognitive relation (for which in PoM the word is 'perception' – even when abstract entities are at stake) and a more remote, indirect, one, is evident in Russell long before the theory of descriptions. 'Knowledge by description' was merely a new label for the cognitive relation to an object which in the former theory was mediated by a denoting concept.

pated himself from the idealism in which he was schooled. It is doubtful whether Frege was aware of his position having these consequences, and it is very unlikely that he would have consciously welcomed them.

In relation, then, to the question of whether direct epistemic access to referents – albeit in the context of a generic proposition in which they occur – should be recognized as possible, we have not succeeded in gleaning any conclusive argument pro or con, but we have discerned what I think is a strong case against an apparent consequence of Frege's position. This draws us to another, prior, question: where does the burden of proof lie? Are we entitled to assume that such access is possible unless proven otherwise, or is the Russellian position in need of proof? Fortunately, the *being* of entities of the kind to which such access is in question is not disputed, and our question is an instance of a more general one: given a kind of entity, is there a presumption in favour of, or against, its being accessible to a direct epistemic relation? For my part, I think that a presumption pro is much more plausible than either the contrary presumption, or the absence of any presumption. My point here is not to argue for this, but merely to indicate that this is what settling the differences between Russell and Frege might depend upon.

VII The taxonomic difference: a diagnosis of Frege's position

We noted earlier that no conclusive argument could be elicited from Frege's case for the sense/reference distinction for proper names which would decide between his view and Russell's, as to whether all, or only some, names had senses, and that Russell's view is coherent. But the very fact that Frege did not feel the need to argue for the application of the distinction to all names may well be the key to the most important and consequential difference of all. When Frege found the need to recognize some names as having senses, he was led to apply the moral to all names simply because on his conception of a proper name there was no boundary at which to stop and ask, 'does it apply to this case as well?' (as he did explicitly when turning to sentences). If some names require senses then, by parity of form (as Russell would have put it), so must all. This is, clearly, the suppressed premise of Frege's argument criticized earlier – one which, crucially, was not shared by Russell. I call this point of difference between Russell's and Frege's views 'taxonomic' because it concerns the manner in which expressions are classified. Frege conceived of proper names as a unitary class for the purposes of logic: if an expression stands for (in the sense of 'serving to speak about') an object, it is a proper name (Gl.: § 51, SuB: p. 57, PW: p. 178). Russell, on the other hand, observed a divide between simple and complex proper names (or 'the'-phrases in the singular). This view was quite independent of the theory of descriptions, but without it the theory of descriptions would have never been discovered.

This taxonomic difference is, in my opinion, the most consequential difference between Russell and Frege (in this field of inquiry), and it explains more than anything else why Russell did, and Frege did not, arrive eventually at the theory of descriptions. But it is not discussed in the correspondence between them, and neither party defends his side of it elsewhere: it is simply laid down without argument by Russell, and introduced as if it were an innocent verbal convention by Frege. Its significance seems to have completely escaped them in their correspondence. This is explained, at least in part, by Russell's adopting Frege's terminology rather than his own when discussing Frege's position (both in PoM Appendix A, and in the correspondence). It is difficult to trace this difference to some more fundamental grounds, but some explanation of Frege's tendency to assimilate simple and complex names when drawing the sense/reference distinction can nonetheless be offered.

Before SuB, Frege's view was that the content of a name (any name) is its bearer (strictly speaking, even identity-statements are no exception, because there the name coincides with the bearer). Since complex and simple names could stand for the same object, it followed that they had the same content and that the distinction between simple and complex names could be relegated, together with many others, to the waste bin of logic.[18] This was in perfect accord with the ambition that a conceptual notation should ignore all distinctions which do not affect content. (Note that, since the object could be simple, what this kind of assimilation ignores is the complexity of complex names.) When, more than a decade later, he came to argue for the need for a notion of sense, he may well have been uncritically taking over this assimilationist view. I will come to the question of whether he was right to do so in a moment.

While this might explain, to some extent, Frege's indiscriminate attitude when drawing the sense/reference distinction, it cannot explain why, unlike Russell, he did not distinguish between complex and simple names at the outset, i.e. in Bs. The answer to this, I suggest, lies in Frege's general tendency in Bs. to dismiss grammatical distinctions without much ado. Russell, by contrast (though surely aware that a complex and a simple name could have the same bearer), was more cautious, and regarded grammatical distinctions as prima facie evidence of logical distinctions (as noted in Chapter 3 above).[19] Grammar distinguishes 'the'-phrases from simple proper names and suggests

18   As Russell had shown in PM, the assimilation will not lead us into falsehoods, so long as the name has a referent. And as for those names that do not, the pre-SuB Frege would not count them as names at all (see 'Dialogue with Pünjer on Existence', PW: p. 60).

19   This difference shows in many places. Unlike Frege's judgeable contents in Bs., Russell could recognize propositions as distinct even when they were logically equivalent; he recognized the subject/predicate distinction (though not its exclusivity), and resisted the temptation to assimilate complete indicative sentences to proper names (which is implicit in Frege from as early as Bs. § 3).

rather obvious similarities with other denoting phrases, but Frege's single-minded content-directedness led him to regard only the fact that both kinds of names serve to speak about objects, and to dismiss the grammatical evidence which suggests a difference. I turn now to the question of whether this assimilation is justified.

VIII Frege's suppressed premise: are all names on a par?

What arguably constitutes the most striking vindication of Russell's position – its role in pointing him to the theory of descriptions – belongs to a later stage of our discussion. But, confining ourselves to the stage when Russell and Frege held the PoM and sense/reference positions respectively, what are the pros and cons of each of these taxonomic views? The attempt to make the situation clear in relation to Frege raises fundamental issues regarding the nature of the sense/reference distinction. On Russell's side, whatever needs to be said for or against his notion of a logically proper name need not wait until we come to the theory of descriptions, because the fundamental logico-semantic notion (stripped of the empiricist trappings it was later to acquire) is already in place in PoM.

The choice between the two taxonomies has been linked, in our discussion, to Frege's assumption that what holds of the names which gave rise to the puzzle about identity holds of names generally. This assumption, which was found to be crucial to his position, would have been disputed by Russell. Since Russell would agree that the puzzle arises (and hence that a notion of sense is called for) when at least one of the names used is complex, the question confronting us is whether the puzzle would arise just the same when *both* names are simple. If it does, then Frege would be justified in thinking that the moral he drew from the puzzle should be applied to *all* names. If not, then (as far as the considerations relating to the puzzle are concerned) Russell would seem to be justified in thinking that there is no need for the distinction for simple proper names. Having taken on board the need for a notion of sense for *complex* proper names, can a similar case be made for simple proper names? Are both kinds of names on a par? Before we can address this question directly we need to be more precise about what is to count as a simple proper name in the present context. The following example from Frege makes it plain why we cannot take lexical simplicity in natural language at face value.

In a footnote in SuB Frege considers the name 'Aristotle' and says that different speakers may attach different senses to it, illustrating this with 'the pupil of Plato and teacher of Alexander the Great' and 'the teacher of Alexander the Great who was born in Stagira' (G&B: p. 58).[20] My concern

---

20 'Thoughts' (CPF: pp. 358–9) contains similar remarks regarding the name 'Dr. Gustav Lauben'.

here is not with the variation between different speakers, but rather with another crucial matter which Frege does not make as clear as he might have. Does he mean to imply that the sense of 'Aristotle' *contains* the senses of words like 'Alexander' occurring in the paraphrase, and that the true logical form of the name (when those senses are attached) is therefore complex? On that view, replacing 'Aristotle' with 'the pupil of Plato and teacher of Alexander' would leave the thought expressed unchanged.

I think this is indeed the only viable interpretation, because unless the occurrence of, for example, 'Alexander' (in Frege's remark) is assumed to have the same sense that it has (at least for that speaker) in other occurrences, and thus to form *part* of the sense of 'Aristotle' (in that idiolect), then it is hard to see why supplying the paraphrase should be regarded as illuminating the sense of 'Aristotle' at all. Grammatical simplicity *may*, on Frege's view, disguise a logical complexity which can be made explicit by paraphrasing the simple name into a 'the'-phrase. Frege's move here is essentially the same as Russell's rendition of fictional names as disguised descriptions in EIP. Whether the 'Alexander' occurring in the sense-giving phrase will then be subject to similar treatment is irrelevant, so long as the process can be assumed ultimately to terminate. Nor does it matter whether these particular phrases are correct or complete accounts of the sense in question, provided they illustrate the form such an account takes.

Before we can grant Frege the crucial assumption of the parity of all names in relation to the puzzle, we must make sure that this kind of move will *not* apply to either of the two apparently simple names – if such a pair can indeed be found – said to give rise to the puzzle about identity. Almost all of Frege's examples employ pairs of complex names (or, counting the geometrical example from Bs. § 8, at least one complex name). The single exception occurs in a letter to Jourdain (more accurately, a draft, since this part was omitted from the final version). This example has been cited in support of the contention that the puzzle of identity does not depend upon the names in it being complex:[21]

> Let us suppose that an explorer travelling in an unexplored country sees a high snow-capped mountain on the northern horizon. By making inquiries among the natives he learns that its name is 'Aphla'. By sighting it from different points he determines its position as exactly as possible, enters it in a map, and writes in his diary: 'Aphla is at least 5000 meters high'. Another explorer sees a snow-capped mountain on the southern horizon and learns that it is called Ateb. He enters it in his map under this name. Later comparison shows that both explorers saw the same mountain. Now the content of the proposition 'Ateb is Aphla' is far from

21 See FPL: pp. 96–8.

being a mere consequence of the principle of identity, but contains a valuable piece of geographical knowledge.

(PMC: p. 80)

At this point Frege proceeds with the familiar claim that the mountain itself cannot be part of the thought, and hence that there is need to recognize a sense which can. But the question that concerns us at present is: what precisely is the role of the background story? The answer should apply, more generally, to similar stories in other examples as well. Clearly, it is only by means of the story that we are persuaded that the difference between the two names marks a *cognitive* difference, and if it is omitted the assertion that Ateb is identical with Aphla could mean no more than that one and the same mountain has these two names. In that case the assertion that Ateb is Aphla would not give rise to the puzzle. But granted that, what needs to be decided is whether or not the story is, in effect, a means for *providing the senses* which these names have in this context – just as Frege, presumably, had done more explicitly in relation to 'Aristotle'. We can obtain a clearer view of the matter by comparing this case first, with what Frege says about 'Aristotle' and second, with the more familiar geometrical examples Frege devised to illustrate the puzzle in Bs. and in SuB.

The 'Aristotle' example serves to show that a single, apparently simple, name can conceal quite different epistemic objects, despite the bearer being the same. To generate the puzzle from this case all we need do is suppose that each of the two speakers (one of which attaches the sense 'the pupil of Plato and teacher of Alexander the Great' and the other the sense 'the teacher of Alexander the Great who was born in Stagira') uses a slightly different name. We then get an informative identity of the form 'a = b'. To this we may add, just to make the case psychologically more plausible, some story explaining how each speaker has come to attach the particular sense he does to 'his' name.

Alternatively, we could modify the Aphla/Ateb story by stripping the narrative down to its bare essentials, and encapsulate it in the comparison of two descriptive phrases such as 'the most salient mountain on the southern horizon from point a', and 'the most salient mountain on the northern horizon from point b'. Moreover, this exercise reveals, upon reflection, that the Ateb/Aphla case is at bottom yet another geometrical example of the kind Frege used in SuB and in Bs., where a single point is defined first in relation to one set of points, then in relation to another.[22] It may be worth noting that it is not the epistemic state of either of the explorers which gives rise to

---

22 The description 'on the northern (or southern) horizon' locates an object on the line from the observer to the relevant pole of the Earth, the distance (from the observer) being determined by the Earth's curvature and the topography along that line.

the puzzle, but rather that of the subject who compares their reports; to him, who never encountered the mountain, 'Ateb' and 'Aphla' would seem to be nothing other than labels of epistemic objects characterizeable by descriptive phrases such as those given above. The move from spatial relations (as in the geometrical examples) to relations like 'teacher of' or 'born at' (as in the 'Aristotle' case) is logically insignificant; nor does it matter whether one or two names, or one or two subjects, are involved. What is essential to all these cases is that names which have the same bearer are associated with different epistemic objects.

In any example I know of, including all of Frege's, at least one of these epistemic objects is complex, and the complexity is instrumental in establishing their diversity, because this diversity follows from the fact that the two senses are composed of distinct sets of constituents – which, though not strictly necessary, is *sufficient* to establish that they are indeed distinct. The background stories in the Ateb/Aphla and similar cases are a means of characterizing this epistemic object: they tell us not only *how* a subject acquired a belief (such as 'Ateb is 5000 meters high') but determine the very *content* of his belief – telling us what *his* use of the name would express. This is required because characterizing the belief in terms of simple names alone was found to obscure vital distinctions.

There is another, more general, consideration which steers us towards reading the Ateb/Aphla example in this way, and which appeals to Frege's own principles. With the same harshness with which Frege banished formerly respected logical distinctions from conceptual content in Bs. we can ask, regarding these background stories, 'do they pertain to the *content* (such as of the explorers' assertions), or are they mere psychological paraphernalia?' Before deciding which of the two they are, it is crucial to observe that they must be either one or the other, and that there is no halfway house. They cannot be kept on the sideline – as something which 'goes along' with the different names but has no part in their contents (that being how Frege dealt with BW in Bs.). That one cannot prevaricate on this question must be regarded as one of the morals Frege drew from the failure of the Bs. account in SuB. One cannot both forbid something from affecting the content's identity *and* use it to account for a *cognitive* difference. I conclude, then, that the Ateb/Aphla example does *not* establish, as one might think, that the puzzle would arise with two simple names. Can we infer this as a general result? Going beyond any of the examples Frege might have considered, can we find any pair of proper names which will give rise to the puzzle and which cannot be analysed as complex?

It might be argued that all apparent simple proper names are ultimately complex, and had this been Frege's view then the principal disagreement with Russell would reside not in whether simple and complex names are on a par with respect to the puzzle, but rather in the more fundamental question of whether, ultimately, there are simple names at all. Although Frege's concept-script in Gg. contains no simple names of objects, there are no real grounds to suppose that he would have excluded them in principle. Their absence in Gg. can be explained by the purely conceptual nature of arithmetic, and Frege gives no reason to suppose that the concept-script of some empirical science might not employ simple proper names (indeed, it is hard to imagine how this could fail to be the case). I therefore proceed, in what follows, on the assumption that Frege did *not* maintain that all proper names were ultimately complex, despite his having made no explicit statement on this matter.[23]

Bearing in mind that the question of parity is being pursued in the interest of a comparison with Russell, we must take special care not to employ 'simple proper name' in a way that will prejudge the matter in favour of either party. Since a 'simple proper name' cannot just mean a name whose bearer is a simple object (both Russell and Frege recognize the possibility of such an object's having a complex name), nor, as we have already seen, can it be a matter of lexical simplicity in natural language, the notion we are concerned with seems to come down to the simplicity of the *epistemic object* associated with the name. On the presumption that logical and epistemic simplicity coincide, we can identify this notion with that of a simple name *in the concept-script*. Adopting this characterization, however, confronts us with a dilemma which seems at first insoluble.

If we take Russell's line and identify the epistemic object with the name's bearer, then we clearly block any possibility of the puzzle arising with two such names. This was, in fact, one of the horns of the original dilemma confronting Frege. But if, in line with Frege's view, we allow the epistemic object to come apart from the bearer, then we seem to have conceded that simple names, too, have senses – which is the very question which this whole exercise was designed to settle. Fortunately for the purposes of this comparison, the matter is not so simple, because even if we take a simple name to be one whose *sense* is simple, this still does not quite settle the matter.

This is because it might still transpire, for instance, that although there are simple name senses, they could not give rise to the puzzle. To generate the puzzle, more is needed than the mere being of such names. If, for example, it transpired that there could be *no more than one* simple sense for each

23 Although it is open to Frege to deny the existence of simple proper-name senses, he could *not* consistently deny simple senses altogether. Because parts of senses are supposed to be themselves senses, unless there are simple senses, the analysis of a thought into its constituents would *always* be an infinite process – thus making all thoughts of a kind Russell supposed we could never grasp, i.e. infinitely complex. Such an outcome, besides being epistemically absurd, would defeat the whole point of analysis: there would be nothing towards which we would be progressing. Frege says explicitly that what is indefinable is logically simple, so we have every reason to suppose that the senses of the primitive signs of the concept-script in Gg. are simple. There must, then, be simple senses even if none of them are of the kind which have *objects* as referents.

simple object, then the puzzle, which depends upon there being *two* such names with the same bearer, could never arise. (In that case we might still have two names in the lexical sense, but they would not count as distinct names in the epistemic sense required.) My present point is not to establish that this is indeed the case – though I think something along these lines is – but only to illustrate that even if we admit simple name senses, this does not necessarily settle the question of whether all names are on a par with respect to the puzzle in Frege's favour.

Despite the fact that there is nothing in Frege's writings on the basis of which we can *preclude* the possibility of an informative identity involving two simple names, this possibility seems very unlikely and it is worth bearing in mind that we cannot make do with the mere possibility. To uphold Frege's suppressed premise what is called for is an informative identity involving two simple names which is roughly *as persuasive as the familiar examples* (where at least one of the names, and usually both, are complex). For my part, I know of no such example, and there are some indications (though not a conclusive argument) suggesting that there might be none to be found. The difficulty I have in mind concerns the very intelligibility of there being *two* such name senses determining the same object, both of which are accessible to the same subject. We can *say* that the names' senses are distinct, but any attempt to get a grip on what this distinctness amounts to seems to slip through our fingers.

Since there seems to be no clear intuitive content to the idea of a simple name sense – let alone two co-referential ones – we might take the primitive functors of the concept-script in Gg. to have simple senses (which, though not explicitly stated, seems to follow on Frege's principles) and ask, regarding, for example, negation, do we know what it would be to conceive of it as the referent of a sense which is both simple (and thus does not correspond to any of the possible definitions appealing to other logical constants) *and* distinct from the sense of negation we had grasped at first? And do we have a sufficiently firm grip on this difference for it to serve as compelling evidence that two thoughts, differing only in their respective simple senses of negation, cannot be identical? This seems hardly credible, and yet something like it would be required to establish the parity of simple and complex names with regard to the puzzle. The problem is not confined to logical notions, and can be appreciated in relation to any concept. It seems to be essentially the same as this: can two *simple* (i.e. indefinable) concepts have the same extension? Some principled reason seems to tell against this possibility. We clearly cannot *need* both, and we cannot explain what the difference between them amounts to. This contrasts markedly with cases where at least one of the pair is complex.

Turning now to proper names, I can think of only three cases in Frege's writings which *might* be counted as simple names in the required sense: the

'I' of soliloquy, 'the true', and (a particular case of) a name of a point in a geometrical construction, but in each of these cases one finds it difficult to conceive of there being *two* such names. The first case occurs in the late (1918) paper 'Thoughts', where, in discussing the word 'I', Frege says that there is some peculiar way each person is given to himself, and to himself only, which he identifies with the sense each of us attaches to his use of 'I' (known as the 'I' of soliloquy). Since I cannot imagine (say, in my case) what the complexity of this sense might be, it seems just possible that it might be simple. Alas, to give rise to the puzzle we need *two* such senses with the same referent, and Frege rules against two such senses being accessible to the same mind even if they have *distinct* referents.

The second case of what might be a proper name with a simple sense is the pair 'the true' and 'the false'. Despite the fact that these are 'the'-phrases, it is hard to imagine what complexity their senses might express. But again, can we think of *another* name of the same object, which has a sense which is both *simple* and *distinct* from that of the first?

The third case occurs in Bs., where Frege tries to demonstrate the same cognitive difference which he was later to codify as a difference of sense. He draws the following contrast:

The same point is determined in a double way:

(1) It is given directly in experience;
(2) It is given as the point B corresponding to the straight line perpendicular to the diameter.

To each of these two ways of determining [*Bestimmungsweisen*] it there answers a separate name.

(Bs.: § 8)

The BW under (1) above would seem to be exemplifying a *simple* BW if anything in Frege's writings is, and thus might be considered as a simple sense once that notion is introduced. But while it is easy to multiply BWs of the kind (2) belongs to, I fail to see how another *simple* sense, of the kind exemplified by (1), and having *the same referent* might also be available to *the same subject*.[24]

---

24 The difficulty at this point can be complicated and obscured – though not, I think, circumvented – by introducing relativization to time. Following Frege's example, I think that we obtain a clearer view of such issues if we lay time aside and regard all the elements involved as being timeless or, what in this context amounts to the same, relative to the same instant of time.

To sum up, when we consider those cases where a Fregean sense might be simple (whether or not its referent is an object), we encounter what seem to be principled obstacles to a *pair* of such senses serving as (parts of) the epistemic object in an informative identity. It is thus far from clear that such a pair could give rise to the kind of situation described in Frege's puzzle.

In any case, the burden of proof seems to me to rest squarely with those who maintain that a pair of genuinely simple proper names *can* give rise to the puzzle – and there is no obligation for the Russellian side to prove it impossible. The situation here parallels the one regarding Russell's argument which we encountered earlier in Chapter 2: one cannot expect an impossibility proof; the onus is on the other side to supply a feasible example showing that it *is* possible.

As for the comparison of PoM and the sense/reference distinction as a whole, nothing we have found amounts to a decisive refutation of Frege's view on the points of difference; we have merely noted, on a number of issues, the *absence* of compelling grounds in his favour, where some – perhaps even Frege himself – might have supposed that there were such. But although Frege's view must be assumed consistent unless proven otherwise, Russell's more discriminatory position seems to have been guided by a more acute, even if unarticulated, vision of difficulties of which Frege seems to have been quite unaware.

IX The theory of descriptions versus sense and reference: an adjustment on the Russellian side

I turn next to the comparison of the sense/reference distinction and the theory of descriptions. In accordance with the strategy explained at the beginning of this chapter, all we should need to do is adjust the comparison between PoM and the sense/reference distinction – which, as we found, boiled down to a difference over the accessibility of level 0 of the shared metaphysical model – to take account of the change from PoM to the theory of descriptions on the Russellian side. Here, in contrast with the discussion in Chapter 3, I will be examining the effect of this shift in Russell's view exclusively from the perspective of its relation to Frege's sense/reference distinction.

To effect this three-cornered comparison I will adopt a particular perspective which so far has been deliberately neglected. All the theories under discussion provide, *inter alia*, solutions to the problem of empty singular expressions (names or descriptions), the problem being how can sentences in which such expressions occur be meaningful (and sometimes even true)? The neglect has been deliberate, partly to counter a common misconception which allots this problem a far greater role than is borne out by the evidence. Although Russell and Frege certainly *employed* the theories we are considering to handle this problem, it was not a major concern of either, and there is no question of the theories having been devised for that purpose. Approaching the matter thus also brings out a few more points of similarity which are only obliquely related to our principal subject.

With respect to empty expressions, and with respect to true negative existentials, three kinds of devices may be discerned in the writings of Frege and Russell (the distinction between the first two has been already discussed in relation to Russell in Chapter 3):

(a) The distinction between existence and being in Russell, and Frege's corresponding contrast of what is *Wirklich* (commonly translated as either 'real' or 'actual') with what is *Unwirklich* (yet objective). The two distinctions correspond by and large to that between concrete and abstract entities, and serve to counter challenges to the objectivity of some purported entities such as numbers and senses.
(b) The notion of existence as applied to concepts or classes. Thus a concept is said to exist just in case at least one entity falls under it. In this sense existence is understood (explicitly by Frege in Gl. §§ 46 and 49) as a second-level concept – what is expressed in standard predicate logic by the 'existential quantifier'.
(c) The distinction between sense and reference (or meaning and denotation in Russell). The significance of some, apparently empty, expressions is accounted for by saying that though they have no referent, they nonetheless have a sense. Similarly, Russell acknowledged that some denoting concepts may fail to denote anything (PoM: § 73, see also EIP).

On Russell's view, but not on Frege's, there is an intrinsic tie between (b) and (c), because denoting concepts are derived from *concepts*. A denoting concept will have no denotation only when the concept from which it derives does not exist in sense (b). For Frege, (c) was the favoured device for dealing with fictional names, while Russell employed (c) to this end only for the brief interval between EIP and OD, as we saw in Chapter 3.

Two points concerning Russell's position before the theory of descriptions are important here. First, he was aware that most of the kinds of cases he employed device (c) for could also be accounted for by means allied to device (b); but he resisted reducing them to (b) because he thought (c) was more fundamental. (His response to the Fregean account of 'all' and 'some' would have been that it was true as far as it goes, but not the ultimate account.) Second, he found a method in which *some* cases, formerly handled by (a), were transformed into a form amenable to treatment by (c); i.e. by treating names as disguised denoting phrases.

Bearing this picture in mind, we see that the change brought about by adopting the theory of descriptions is that the single type of case for which Russell needed (c), and for which no corresponding account by means of (b) was available (i.e. 'the' denoting phrases), is reduced to a special case of (b). This removes, from Russell's point of view, the rationale for keeping (c) at all.[25] Since this is the *only* type of expression for which Russell's and Frege's views overlapped, Russell's withdrawing 'the' cases from (c), and hence abandoning (c) altogether, makes the resultant position appear more detached from Frege's than it really is. What drove Russell to make this change, it is important to bear in mind, was not anything which challenged the fundamental views he shared with Frege, but rather the discovery of a specific and relatively local fault concerning (c) which, as we saw in the previous chapter, we have no reason to suppose Frege was even aware of.

It can now be seen clearly how crucial to his later discovery of the theory of descriptions was Russell's separation of 'the'-phrases from proper names and his assimilation of them into denoting phrases. The theory of descriptions would never occur to one as an account for both simple and complex names, and if Russell had endorsed senses for all proper names, as Frege did, the discovery of the theory of descriptions would not have made senses redundant.

The picture of two positions which are in agreement concerning a limited domain, which is then withdrawn due to Russell's changing his mind in response to a specific problem, is not, however, the full picture of the effects of the theory of descriptions on the comparison. In another dimension, and on what may be seen as a much wider front, the change actually brings Russell's position *closer* to Frege's than before. I have in mind the change regarding denoting phrases other than 'the'-phrases in the singular. I will first explain how this change is tied in with the adoption of the theory of descriptions, and then point out a rather peculiar perspective, which it suggests, on the relation between the theory of descriptions and Frege's position.

Only with the discovery of the theory of descriptions did Russell drop his misgivings about the Fregean account[26] of denoting phrases *other than 'the'-phrases*; only then did he accept the (b) rather than the (c) account as fundamental. The reason why this change had to wait until the theory of descriptions seems to be that Russell regarded denoting phrases as a unitary phenomenon, and insisted upon 'the' belonging with 'all' and 'some' despite

---

25 This is not quite how Russell conceived the move at the time. He thought that the variable meant the same as 'any term' and thus that the theory of descriptions does not eliminate denoting concepts altogether but only effects, as noted at the end of Chapter 3 above, the reduction of all denoting concepts to a single case. See PoM: § 86, OF: pp. 387–8: as well as a passage from a letter to G. E. Moore cited in Hylton, *Russell*, p. 256.

26 I say 'Fregean account' though probably this is not how things appeared to Russell. Russell received the notion that he called 'formal implication' from Peano, not Frege. This is evidenced by his subsuming the generality expressed by bound ('apparent') variables under the notion of formal implication even when no implication is involved. However, I take this *not* to be a substantial difference between his and Frege's views of generality as far as this device is concerned. The difference is thrashed out in Frege's 1892 essay 'On Mr. Peano's Conceptual Notation and My Own' (PW: pp. 244–7), and the Peano–Russell stand is renounced in Russell's introduction to the second edition of PoM (p. vii).

its obvious peculiarity. Accordingly, so long as his account of 'the' could *not* be brought into line with those of 'all' and 'some', Russell regarded the other device, denoting concepts, as the more fundamental device common to all members of the group. When the possibility of treating 'the'-phrases by means of the variable/quantifier device was discovered, he shifted his account of denoting phrases *in toto* to one involving that device. The taxonomic view we noted earlier emerges from this as a guiding principle which he stuck to throughout. His insistence on a unitary treatment – whatever it may be – for all the various kinds of denoting phrases may therefore be regarded as one of the most crucial features of his position.

The observation that the theory of descriptions brings Russell's account of 'the'-phrases into line with Frege's account of the other kinds of denoting phrases, is one that sheds a rather surprising light on a deeply rooted partiality in their respective receptions. It has somehow become natural for anyone raised in the analytic tradition to regard the Fregean account of 'all'- and 'some'-phrases as an innocent fact of elementary logic, while Russell's account of 'the'-phrases is regarded as a highly controversial *theory*. Anyone familiar with predicate calculus knows that this is how 'all'-phrases are to be analysed, while the theory of descriptions, despite appealing to precisely the same devices,[27] is judged by different criteria. Upon reflection, however, such partiality has little foundation in the nature of the two positions themselves.

The sense in which each is an account of the respective kind of phrase is exactly the same (whatever that may be), and all the criticism relating to the adequacy of the theory of descriptions as an account of phrases in natural language should apply therefore, to precisely the same degree, to Frege's account of 'all'. If Frege's account is not meant to capture our actual use of those phrases in natural language, but is only a formal logical device (whatever that may mean), so is Russell's. If Russell's account is highly artificial, so is Frege's. If one's complaint against the theory of descriptions is that there is no generality to be observed in 'the'-phrases, then there is similarly no conditionality to be observed in 'all'-phrases. Regardless of *what* standard of adequacy is appropriate here – a matter I hope to throw some light on in the next chapter – I urge that it must be exactly the same for both. This is not to say that anyone who adopts Frege's account of 'all' must also adopt Russell's account of 'the'; but only that certain kinds of objections – those most commonly raised against the theory of descriptions – must be applied either to both or to neither.

Much of this discriminatory attitude, and the controversy surrounding the theory of descriptions, appears to hinge on the contextual definition and

---

27 This ignores the appeal of the theory of descriptions to the relation of identity, but this does not affect the present consideration.

the fact that Russell's position implies denying 'the'-phrases the status of genuine terms (in the linguistic sense of 'term'). But does that really distinguish the theory of descriptions? Does not Frege's account of 'all' render 'all'-phrases non-terms in just the same way as the theory of descriptions does for 'the'-phrases?[28] Russell's most definitive statement of the theory of descriptions, in PM, encapsulates the theory in a definition, while Frege gives the impression of having stumbled over his accounts of 'all' and 'some' in the course of illustrating how the symbols for expressing generality and conditionality can be combined in a single formula (Bs.: § 12, Gg.: Volume I § 13). But Frege could just as well, it seems to me, have introduced an 'all' operator with a contextual definition in Russell's fashion without altering anything substantial in his account. Similarly, Russell, instead of setting out to provide an account of denoting phrases, could have simply set forth the familiar analytic formula and then, avoiding the description operator altogether, timidly suggested that for logical purposes it captures all we need regarding the working of 'the'-phrases.[29] Such a course, it seems to me, would alter nothing of theoretical substance in either account. The difference seems to lie, rather, in (pardon the phrase) different modes of presentation. After all, the two accounts employ the very same, and not merely analogous, logical devices.[30] How, then, could there be any substantial difference of *kind* between them? Our pre-theoretic inclination to regard 'the'-phrases as terms is probably stronger than it is with 'all'- and 'some'-phrases – but these are mere mental habits which do not constitute a logical difference.

Looking back at Frege's handling of the epistemic problem of identities in Bs., it may be observed that at that time he already had at his disposal all the conceptual tools which would have enabled him to leap straight to the solution of that problem which is embodied in the theory of descriptions, and thus to circumvent senses altogether (with the notion of the generic proposition remaining unchanged). What seems to have led him to taking the other route was, first, his failure to distinguish between simple and complex names which, in turn, prevented him from seeing that unless at least one of the names is complex, it is at least doubtful whether any epistemic difference

28 Though Russell, as noted earlier, would probably not regard the now standard account of 'all Fs are Gs' as distinctly Fregean (see note 25 in this chapter), and Frege's notion of conditionality differs somewhat from the modern one. Such details, however, do not affect the point at stake. It may be remembered that 'all' is *not* regarded by Frege as primitive. The primitive notion is something more like 'everything'.

29 This is indeed in line with Russell's and (sometimes) Frege's view of definition as a mere notational abbreviation bearing no theoretical significance and thus being always dispensable. (For a clear Fregean statement to that effect see PW: p. 208.)

30 Again, this ignores some fine differences between Russell's and Frege's respective accounts of quantification, which do not affect the point at stake.

could arise; and, second, an insufficient separation of the issues of identity and of definition. Since Russell too, though for different reasons, took a substantially similar course, the role of the argument of the obscure passage emerges, in his case, as the crucial force which made him give up the deep pre-systematic bias in favour of regarding 'the'-phrases as terms.

The comparison of the theory of descriptions and the sense/reference distinction, when approached via the comparison with Russell's first theory, may be summed up as follows: Frege and Russell arrived at essentially the same theoretical device to resolve essentially the same kind of problem. The difference lay in their views as to the range of its application. Russell applied it only to a special subclass of the expressions to which Frege did, because he employed a different, more discerning, taxonomy. Then, driven by the discovery of a fundamental flaw in that device (of which Frege seems to have been unaware), Russell was led to an alternative account for this special subclass by a novel combination of means which were acceptable to both (though Frege formerly did, and Russell did not, regard them as fundamental). By withdrawing these expressions from the treatment of this mischievous device, Russell created a situation where, in view of his restricted employment of it beforehand, he no longer needed this device at all. Consequently both the special logical relation it required, and the elaborate metaphysical structure it gave rise to, could be abandoned. None of this affected the deeper strata of agreement delineated earlier as 'propositionalism'.

X Frege's description operator and the theory of descriptions

In Gg. (Volume I: § 11) Frege introduces a primitive first-level function, symbolized '/ξ', which, given a course of values containing a single object as argument, returns that object; and given any other argument, returns that argument. In that section Frege says,

> We have here a substitute for the definite article of ordinary language, which serves to form proper names out of concept-words. For example, we form from the words 'positive square root of 2', which denotes a concept, the proper name 'the positive square root of 2'.

Although this function, in conformity with general Fregean principles, is assigned a value for *any* argument, and hence the resultant expression might be one which will *not* be counted as a 'the'-phrase, the fact remains that it is solely for the sake of those cases where the argument *is* a singleton, and the resultant expression *can* serve as a substitute for a 'the'-phrase, that this operator is introduced – in all other cases it is simply 'idling'. In view of this, it seems reasonable to judge the view in Gg. § 11 on its merits as an account of

'the'-phrases and to compare it with other accounts we have been considering. Our doing so should *not* be understood as giving any special weight
to its relation to natural language, nor as telling against there being such a
relation. The primary question facing us is, what form should 'the'-phrases,
given their indispensability in mathematics, take *in the concept-script*? Thus
conceived, the description operator's relation to the sense/reference distinction in particular calls for special attention, because the very idea of regarding it as embodying a view of 'the'-phrases distinct from the sense/reference
distinction (which regards 'the'-phrases as proper names) might be thought
mistaken; and indeed it would be mistaken if this was understood as implying that it might be an *alternative* to the sense/reference distinction. Like
all symbols of the concept-script in Gg., – barring the exception of Roman
letters noted earlier – the description operator itself (as well as the symbols
it combines with to form the substitute for a 'the'-phrase) is assumed to have
both sense and reference. So we are dealing here with a view *contained* within the broader sense/reference view. However, there are a number of reasons
for regarding it as a distinct view.

In the first place, given that 'the'-phrases are for Frege proper names then,
since this view is clearly *not* intended to encompass simple names, the description operator implies a distinction, for logical purposes, between 'the'-phrases
and other names – a distinction to which the sense/reference view was oblivious. Second, it implies far more about the senses of 'the'-phrases than could
be gathered from the mere contention that they have senses. It tells us that
these senses contain, besides the sense of the particular concept involved, the
senses of the description operator, and of the abstraction operator. Third,
while Frege's admitting the possibility of names which have no reference leads
to supposing that a 'the'-phrase whose concept-word expresses an 'empty'
concept would be such a name, the description operator, by guaranteeing a
referent to all names formed by its means, implies that 'the'-phrases will *never*
lack reference. Finally, the discussion of the description operator does not
involve the sense/reference distinction in any essential way, and it is no more
linked by Frege to the sense/reference view than any other symbol of the concept-script – the two discussions seem to be quite independent of each other.
The description operator might have been introduced, for example in Bs.,
without any substantial change. In view of all this, it seems to me plausible
to regard the description operator as a distinct development in Frege's thinking about 'the'-phrases, albeit one made within the sense/reference framework, and I shall be so regarding it in the present discussion. The comparison
of the theory of descriptions and the Fregean description operator has a clear
advantage which none of the other pairs of views we have examined, one
Russellian the other Fregean, has enjoyed. For once, both parties respect the
same taxonomic boundaries – since both clearly set aside simple proper
names. This is conducive to the comparative enterprise. The description

operator characterizes 'the'-phrases both at the level of reference[31] and (implicitly) at the level of sense, while Russell's theory of descriptions may be regarded as confined to the level of reference. However, I do not think that this difference matters for our purposes.

The particular angle on the two theories which will guide us in the present discussion (and will be developed more fully in the following section) observes that in both the Russellian and the Fregean proposed analytic formulae (ignoring for the moment that the theory of descriptions analyses whole sentences, while Frege's operator deals with what can only be part of a sentence) we find both a 'regular' concept-sign (or signs) which will vary from one 'the'-phrase to another, and signs standing for logical constants which are the same in all the phrases of the kind in question. By regarding the conceptual component as simple, we can effectively set it aside as being the same in both analyses, and narrow the comparative question at issue to this: what precisely is the logical-constant component in the analysis? Should it be regarded as irreducible, or is it structured? And if structured, *how* structured? It is to these questions that the theory of descriptions and Frege's description operator provide alternative replies.

Confining attention to the 'the' case, once we have distinguished between a conceptual and a logical component, we can say precisely what the latter is needed for: it is needed to 'take us' from a concept which determines a singleton to its single member, and the only substantial question which remains is *how* it does it, the aim being to discover the minimal set of primitive notions which will produce this effect. From this perspective on the problem they both deal with, the fundamental comparability of the theory of descriptions and Frege's description operator becomes apparent.

One point which clearly distinguishes Frege's view from Russell's is that it preserves the intuitive recognition of 'the'-phrases as genuine terms (in the linguistic sense). This, I think, may well be considered an advantage but, at least in view of their programmatic aims, not a very substantial one. As noted earlier, Frege was content to 'sacrifice' surface structure in relation to 'all' and 'some' without much ado. This may be the only clear advantage the description operator has over the theory of descriptions.

Another difference – though its precise statement is complicated by the fact that talk of the phrase's referent in the theory of descriptions becomes very roundabout – consists in the fact that Frege's view guarantees a referent (or value for the function) even when the number of objects falling under

---

31 By which I do *not* mean the reference of the *phrase*, or (more accurately) its sense, but rather those elements (function and argument) in the realm of reference which *determine*, on this account, the phrase's referent (as value). This determination is clearly distinct from that effected by the phrase's sense, though it is the same object that is determined.

the concept involved is other than one. Russell, in OD, commented on this, saying that Frege

> provides by definition some purely conventional denotation for the cases in which otherwise there would be none. Thus the 'The King of France', is to denote the null class; 'the only son of Mr. So-and-so' (who has a fine family of ten), is to denote the class of all his sons; and so on. But this procedure, though it may not lead to actual logical error, is plainly artificial, and does not give an exact analysis of the matter.
>
> (Marsh: p. 47)

Although this feature of Frege's view is indeed a weakness, I do not think it should be regarded, at least in this comparative context, as carrying much weight: neither Russell (as exemplified by the theory of descriptions) nor Frege gave much weight to naturalness.[32] However, this difference implies, in turn, another difference which is more striking: the two views assign different truth values to the same sentences. Regarding sentences whose grammatical subjects are 'the'-phrases under whose associated concepts there falls no object, or more than one. On Frege's view some of these (like, 'The only son of Mr. So-and-so has ten members') will be true, while on Russell's view they are all false.

There is reason to believe that Frege's view, at any rate, has little to do with the merit of the case at hand. In Gl. (in a note to § 74) he lists the prerequisites for a meaningful use of a 'the'-phrase in the singular as follows: '1. that some object falls under the concept; 2. that only one object falls under it' (adding that if either fails, the expression has no content). These same conditions are required for truth by Russell's theory of descriptions, and this suggests that where the truth value prescribed by Frege's view differs from that prescribed by the theory of descriptions, Frege's position has less to do with a conviction that such sentences are true than with the desire to conform to general principles regarding functions (which Russell, by the way, would not dispute), namely that they shall have a value for *every* argument. But again, although the Fregean position on this point can hardly be regarded as an asset, none of this seems to me decisive. Like the charge of

---

32 Consider the following Fregean statements: 'To those who feel inclined to criticize my definitions as unnatural, I would suggest that the point here is not whether they are natural, but whether they go to the root of the matter and are logically beyond criticism' (Gl.: p. xi); 'If the logician tried to take account of objections on the score that what he said was unnatural, he would be in danger of involving himself in disputes over what is natural – disputes which logic is quite incapable of resolving on its own and which, therefore, do not belong to logic' (PW: p. 146); 'Languages are not made to match logic's ruler . . . The main task of the logician is to free himself from language and to simplify it. Logic should be the judge of languages' (letter to Husserl, PMC: p. 68).

'unnaturalness' raised by Russell in the passage just quoted, it carries little weight. Giving 'an exact analysis of the matter', on the other hand, is a far graver matter.

By far the most striking achievement of the theory of descriptions seems to me to be its providing an account of 'the'-phrases without introducing any new primitive notions. Not only does it require no more tools than are required in any case on Russell's view, but those same tools are also required on Frege's view too, and this before we ever turn to the problem of 'the'-phrases.[33] Frege's description operator, by contrast, is a new primitive notion (serving no other purpose); this requires, in turn, a special axiom to govern its use, to the effect that the result of applying the operator to the value range of the concept 'identical with a' is a. The reduction in the theory of descriptions of 'the'-phrases to notions which are indispensable regardless of the account of 'the', makes the relations between it and the other kinds of denoting phrases transparent, in a sense to be explained in the next section. Even if we suppose that the two theories are otherwise on a par, this achievement alone would suffice, in my view, to tilt the balance in favour of Russell's theory.

In view of our earlier discussion of Frege's unitary treatment of proper names and 'the'-phrases, and its role in leading him to a sweeping application of the sense/reference distinction, the description operator appears as his coming round at last to Russell's taxonomic view. Ironically, there is also a respect in which the theory of descriptions signifies Russell's coming round at long last to Frege's view. The whole discussion of denoting revolved, from Russell's point of view, around the notion of the variable. The variable was for him not a solution, but the heart of the problem. Frege, by contrast, was less troubled by our capacity to deal with infinite totalities, and was content to take the notion of the variable for granted. After all the twists and turns, Russell ends up taking the notion of the variable – as he explains in the first sentence of his statement of the theory in OD (p. 42) – for granted as well.

XI The progression towards transparency

To conclude this comparative chapter I wish to take further advantage of the distinction introduced in the previous section between the logical and conceptual components in the account of 'the'-phrases to present a particular angle on *all* the views so far considered of 'the'-phrases in the singular

33 This ignores some not unimportant differences between Russell's and Frege's understanding of universal quantification. For Frege this involves a second-level function, while for Russell (as indicated in the final section of Chapter 2 above) what we have is an assertion about a class of propositions, i.e. those defined by the associeted propositional function. However, these differences seem to me not to affect the comparative issue at stake.

(henceforth simply 'the'-phrases). This distinction is conducive to the comparative task not only in providing a more general and abstract perspective
on the different views at stake, but also in suggesting a particular manner of
arranging these views in relation to each other, an arrangement which forms
a progression with each view embodying a further step towards what may be
seen as a certain goal. By its very essence the distinction prescribes that the
progression will not emerge if we restrict our view to 'the'-phrases alone: their
relation to other kinds of phrases is essential to this structure. Before entering this exercise we need to extend and enrich the distinction between the
conceptual and logical-constant components so that it will encompass not
only 'the'-phrases but also denoting phrases generally, as well as views of
such phrases which do not take the form of analytic formulae as the theory
of descriptions and Frege's description operator do.

The distinction between a *conceptual component* and a *logical-constant component* (henceforth simply 'logical component')[34] is best explained with reference to the following comments by Russell in PoM § 72 (they were already
cited in Chapter 3, though with a different interest in mind):

> The word *all* has certainly some definite meaning, but it seems highly
> doubtful whether it means more than the indication of a relation. 'All
> men' and 'all numbers' have in common the fact that they both have a
> certain relation to a class-concept, namely to *man* and *number* respec-
> tively. But it is very difficult to isolate any further element of *all-ness*
> which both share, unless we take as this element the mere fact that both
> are concepts of classes. It would seem then, that 'all *u*'s' is not validly
> analyzable into *all* and *u*, and that language, in this case as in some oth-
> ers, is a misleading guide. The same remark will apply to *every, any, some,
> a,* and *the.*

This suggests the arrangement of denoting phrases in the following matrix:
the rows are the various class concepts (of which there may be infinitely many),
and each of the columns a particular *kind* of denoting concept. Each particular denoting phrase thus expresses a particular element of this matrix.
This arrangement may seem a very meagre achievement – after all, it is
suggested quite strongly by the linguistic evidence – and yet it codifies the
not insignificant fact that, e.g. '*the* author of *Waverley*' and '*all* authors of
Waverley' are intrinsically related. Each has a distinct but fixed relation to

---

34 This terminology is *not* meant to imply that the logical-constant component is not conceptual. Nonetheless, it is clearly distinct from the non-logical, or *merely* conceptual, component, in a manner that will become plain shortly. The conceptual component may, of course,
contain an object as a part (as, e.g. Alexander in the content of 'teacher of Alexander'), but
it cannot simply *be* an object.

the same concept, and this relation is exactly the same as that had by other 'the' and 'all' contents to their respective class concepts. I call the feature which the above pair have in common the 'conceptual component' of the phrase's content (on this Russellian view), and the distinct relation each of them has to that concept the 'logical component'.

My choice of 'component' is intended neither to imply nor to deny its being contained in the phrase's content as a part. In the passage just quoted Russell explicitly denies that the logical component forms a distinct part of a denoting concept. What 'component' is designed to indicate is the weaker relation where an entity makes a contribution to the content's identity – whether or not it forms a *part* of it. (What in Chapter 4 was characterized as a 'functional', as opposed to 'compositional', view of generic propositions, exemplifies this neutral sense of 'component'.) We can now turn to the progression suggested by this distinction.

The first step in this progression is the Bs. view, but the distinction in the light of which it *is* the first step is best explained with reference to the second, which is Russell's PoM view. This view, as we saw, suggests the arrangement of all denoting phrases in a matrix, where the rows are the various class concepts and each of the columns a particular *kind* of denoting concept. To see that this kind of systematization of the relations between denoting phrases is not as trivial as it may seem – the classification deals, it must be remembered, primarily with contents, and only derivatively with expressions – we only need to look back at Frege's position in Bs. For Frege 'the'-phrases were proper names, but because he identified a name's content with its bearer (which might be simple, even when the name is complex), for him there could be no scope for a name's complexity to reflect anything in its content, i.e. anything which might have a logical role.[35] This view, then, acknowledges no conceptual component in 'the'-phrases, nor any logical-constant component. The complexity of 'the'-phrases is, in other words, discarded: they might just as well have been simple. The complexity could perhaps be said to reflect the BW which 'goes along' with the name, but this, as we observed earlier, is no part of the content. The contrast with Frege's treatment, in the same work, of 'all'- and 'some'-phrases is striking, but before we consider that, let us first return to PoM.

We noted that Russell's PoM view makes the relation between 'the' on the one hand and 'all' and 'some' on the other *systematic* in a way which Frege's Bs. view does not, but the limitation of this systematization is evident when we ask *how* are (the contents of) a 'the'-phrase and the corresponding 'all'-phrase related? In reply Russell could only say that each bears a

---

35 Accordingly, though this only becomes clear in Gl. (which I regard as propounding the Bs. view), 'the'-phrases under whose associated concept no object, or more than one object, falls were deemed to have no content at all (Gl.: § 74n).

particular and distinct relation to the same class concept: but each of these relations is itself regarded as simple, so that any prospect of illuminating the relation between them is blocked.[36] This does not, however, block all prospects of exploring, as Russell did in PoM, logical relations between such phrases (and thus, derivatively, between whole propositions whose expression involves such phrases). But this exploration dealt only with the *denotations* of these phrases. What we are after, on the other hand, are the structural relations between the propositional constituents, or the phrases' contents, themselves.

If Russell's PoM position exemplifies a view which makes the logical component opaque, Frege's accounts of 'all' and 'some' (which remains essentially unchanged from Bs. to Gg.) vividly exemplify the contrasting transparency. Instead of being told that each of the phrases (assuming a constant conceptual component) has a distinct irreducible relation to that class concept, we are presented with a *structure* combining logical constants and conceptual components (i.e. $\forall x\ (Fx \rightarrow Gx)$ for 'all Fs are Gs', and $\sim\forall x\sim (Fx\ \&\ Gx)$ for the corresponding 'some' proposition). The progress is embodied in the fact that the logical component has now become composite, which makes it possible that at least some of its components might be already familiar – that is to say, logical constants which occur either in the account of logical relations not specifically concerned with denoting phrases, or (at least) such that occur in the account of other kinds of denoting phrases. (That these accounts do not assign 'all'- and 'some'-phrases distinct contents but provide, instead, analyses of complete propositions in whose expression they occur, is not relevant to our present concern.) This constitutes logical transparency of just the kind that Russell's PoM account lacked. So although PoM embodies some progress over the Bs. view with respect to 'the', i.e. by regarding it, too, as combining conceptual and (albeit unstructured) logical components, it may be regarded as a retrograde step in relation to 'all' and 'some'.[37]

Let us sum up the progression so far. Although Frege's position makes the relation between 'all' and 'some' transparent where Russell's view leaves

---

36 Russell does not actually *assert* that these relations are simple, but his failing to provide any further details regarding them produces, in effect, the same result (mark the analogy with the view taken of the structure of '<C>' in Chapter 2 above). But its being an omission rather than a denial does, however, leave the door open for a possibility that at some later stage an analysis will be given – a possibility which Russell ultimately made good.

37 This is not quite true of Russell's view in PoM, because he was clearly aware of the relatedness of 'all' and 'some' (which, in that form, he learned from Peano). However, since he did not regard the accounts from which this relatedness emerged as the fundamental ones, and thought that the account in terms of denoting was more fundamental, we might ignore this aspect of his position in the present discussion and regard the view articulated above (which Russell clearly did hold as well) as occupying a position in the progression.

matters opaque, Russell, by including 'the'-phrases in the same scheme, surpasses the Bs. view with respect to the relation of 'the' to 'all' and 'some'. He regards 'the' as determined by a conceptual component (from precisely the same stock as we find in 'all'- and 'some'-phrases) and a logical component (which is assumed to be distinct from either, but the same for all 'the'-phrases). What Russell gains in breadth he loses in transparency, while Frege's view achieves greater transparency over a narrower domain.[38]

I move on now to the next two Fregean views. The sense/reference distinction embodies an important advance over Bs. with respect to 'the'-phrases in that (at least when the sense of such phrases is complex) it contains a fairly clear acknowledgement of a conceptual component. This, at any rate, is what we had concluded earlier from his remark about 'Aristotle'. The case for admitting such a component was poignantly put by Russell when, explaining the difference between proper names (distinguished, on his view, by the *absence* of such a component) and 'the'-phrases, he wrote,

> A man's name is what he is called, but however much Scott had been called the author of *Waverley*, that would not have made him be the author; it was necessary for him actually to write *Waverley*, which was a fact having nothing to do with names.
>
> (KAKD: p. 226)

This fundamental point is implicitly acknowledged by Frege in SuB as it was not in Bs., but we still have nothing which could be regarded as even an implicit acknowledgement of a logical component – not even in the crude form it was given in PoM. Although the sense/reference distinction implies that 'the author of *Waverley*' has *something* to do with the concept 'author of *Waverley*', it does *not* imply, as both Frege's own view of 'all' and 'some', and Russell's PoM view do, that the same relation obtains between other 'the'-phrases and their respective concepts. The matter is left completely open.

It is precisely in this respect that the description operator in Gg. goes a step further. It provides not only a more precise and explicit commitment to a conceptual component in 'the'-phrases than could be extracted from SuB, but also a clear commitment to a logical component, which is said to be the same for all 'the'-phrases. This logical component is not quite simple – at any rate it has more structure than Russell's PoM analogue – and it thus offers

---

38 Here the effects of the diverse taxonomies become evident. Because Frege regards simple and complex names as a single category, he is unable to make the move Russell does: it would be totally unsuitable for simple names. Russell, on the other hand, though he has effectively the same position as Frege regarding *simple* names, is not restricted in a similar way, because he regards 'the'-phrases as a separate category from a logical point of view.

some degree of transparency. As noted earlier, one implication is that the sense of the abstraction operator forms part of the sense of the phrase, and this component cannot be suspected of being ad hoc precisely because it occurs in other contexts which have nothing to do with 'the' as well. The case is different, however, with the description operator itself, which is as opaque as its PoM counterpart: it plays no role in any other context and has no parts. So although *some* move towards transparency had been made and we find, for the first time on Frege's view, a clear distinction between a conceptual and a logical component in 'the'-phrases, nevertheless the transparency remains very limited. In particular, it sheds no light on the relation of 'the' to either 'all' or 'some'. So much for Frege's description operator.

By this point it should come as no surprise that I place Russell's theory of descriptions at the terminus of the progression: transparency of the kind formerly available only in relation to 'all' and 'some' is extended to 'the'. It is of the utmost importance to observe that, except for the notion of identity, which can hardly be suspected of being ad hoc, the theory of descriptions does *not* require any logical notions over and above those already occurring in the accounts of 'some' and 'all'. This, it seems to me, is where its chief merit lies, a merit that was already noted in the previous section.

If it is indeed in its transparency, rather than in anything else, that the chief merit of the theory of descriptions lies, then the following synoptic view of our course regarding this theory, from the very start of this work, emerges. Earlier (in Chapter 3) we dismissed the prevalent view which emphasizes the merit of avoiding the ontological commitment to, e.g. a non-existent present King of France, in favour of the view that Russell was seeking to avoid untenable results regarding denoting concepts (discussed in OD and in Chapter 2 above). In the present discussion we focused on another aspect of this theory which, at least on the face of things, has little to do with either of these difficulties. The greatest merit of the theory of descriptions may well lie in relation to problems quite unlike those Russell was consciously concerned with when devising it. Nonetheless, this merit may still have played a decisive role in persuading him to accept this analysis as definitive.

Chapter 7

The Russell–Frege enterprise and natural language

I Introduction

One of the chief themes in our discussion so far has been that Russell's and Frege's theories are not concerned in any fundamental sense with language; and our remarks about the relation to language were persistently negative. This gives rise to the following question: conceding that they indeed were not concerned primarily with language, is there not *some* sense in which they were concerned with it after all? In the present chapter I try to paint what seems to me the correct picture of the matter.

I begin from what seems to me a decisive case for *dis*sociating Russell's and Frege's theories from natural language. I then proceed, by a rather roundabout course, to describe how their appeal to linguistic notions (such as 'proper name') ought to be understood in the light of general features of the enterprise they were engaged in. The focus on proper names is convenient because the underlying assumption is that what holds for names will apply *mutatis mutandis* to other kinds of expressions as well, and will thus illuminate the place of language in the enterprise generally. In this discussion I treat Russell and Frege as representing a single standpoint, and I shall accordingly be speaking of the 'Russell–Frege enterprise', or a 'Russell–Frege view', and so on. This is not to suggest that the differences between them are insignificant; rather, I am addressing the substantial area of agreement between them on broader programmatic issues. Part of this common ground was already delineated in Chapter 6 above, and further reason for grouping Russell and Frege together will emerge in the course of the present chapter.

Except where what is said is applied explicitly only to Russell or only to Frege, I have tried to cite evidence from both to support grouping them together on particular issues as they arise. This has not always been easy. Often one finds, for example, Frege driving home a point of principle which is only casually made by Russell or vice versa. For the most part these are matters of emphasis rather than substance. In some cases I have presumed agreement even in the absence of direct evidence from one, but only when this appeared highly plausible in the light of, first, views on related matters, and second, the alternatives on the particular issue in question. For example, in Frege there is much more than in Russell about concepts having sharp boundaries and the dismissal of vague concepts. I have assumed this goes without saying for Russell too, because this is fundamental to his conception of logic. In section IX of the last chapter I insisted that the relation of Russell's and Frege's theories to natural language was essentially the same; I turn now to address the question of what that relation is.

II Ordinary names and logically proper names

I believe there to be a constraint, to be laid down at the outset, on what the relation of the Russell–Frege enterprise to natural language might possibly be. My point is simple: whatever else Russell and Frege might have been doing, it was clearly *not* their primary interest to offer accounts of the functioning of a natural language. So far this claim was implied by the emphasis on the non-linguistic nature of (generic) propositions – which *were* their principal concern. My aim here is to show, by focusing on their respective theoretical notions of a *proper name*, that tenets they were clearly committed to, or corollaries thereof, are so obviously inapplicable to names in natural language that the thought that such an application was intended becomes incredible.

It will be convenient in what follows to use 'logically proper name' (in a generic sense) as a label for their theoretical notion, a logically proper name being what one takes to be a proper name for the purposes of logic. Just to set this generic use in context (and perhaps undo some Fregean misgivings), we might add the corresponding pair of a 'logically proper concept-word', and 'logically proper concept' which, for reasons Frege insisted upon on many occasions, must be regarded as distinct from concepts of the kind we might plausibly assume ordinary language concept-words to express.[1] The discrepancy between logically proper and ordinary names is more straightforward in Russell's case, and I shall therefore begin there.

For Russell the notion of a proper name (confining ourselves to *simple* names, since complex names are regarded as belonging to a different category) is strictly correlative to that of an object.[2] Barring difficulties over combinations, Russell's broadest theoretical notion is that of a term, and the principal

---

1 'For a given concept', Frege writes, 'every object must either fall under it or not, *tertium non datur*' ('Introduction to Logic', in PW: p. 195). 'A sign for a concept that does not satisfy this requirement is to be regarded as meaningless from the logical point of view' (letter to Peano in PMC: p. 115). Frege is here speaking of the post-SuB notion of a concept, but the difference does not affect the demand for absolutely sharp boundaries.
2 I use 'object' for convenience despite Russell's term for this in PoM being 'thing', and despite 'object' having a different technical sense in PoM (see § 58n) encompassing both terms and 'combinations' (as discussed in Chapter 1 above). Doing so seems to me unlikely to lead to confusion, and enables us to avoid a persistent awkwardness when we turn to Frege.

division of terms is into objects and concepts. Any statement about terms in general can therefore be safely assumed to hold good of objects.

Early in PoM we come across the following unequivocal statement: 'every term is immutable and indestructible. What a term is, it is, and no change can be conceived in it which would not destroy its identity and make it another term' (PoM: § 47; see also § 443).

From which it follows – despite the innumerable examples apparently to the contrary – that, for example, Plato or Socrates cannot be objects in the relevant technical sense nor, more generally, can human beings and medium-sized tangibles of the kind common sense regards as objects. It follows that what the proper names of natural language (henceforth 'ordinary names') apply to are not objects and hence that they are not names in the strict logical sense. I am not at present asking about Russell's reasons for holding this view: the unequivocal nature of his statement makes it safe to proceed on the assumption that it *is* his view, and that is all we need at present. Ordinary names do not, therefore, fit Russell's notion of a logically proper name.

Turning now to Frege, on whose view, too, proper names are strictly correlative to objects,[3] the impossibility of regarding ordinary names as logically proper is not as immediately clear as it was with Russell, but it nonetheless follows from tenets he is well known to have held. To take account of Frege's terminology it must be stressed that what follows is confined to objects *other than truth values and value ranges.* Thus with regard to Frege our claim needs to be rephrased as follows: even when those kinds of names (which can only tell *against* the identification) are excluded, there is still no fit between the ordinary and the logical notions.

Frege, as is well known, held senses to be immutable, but it has hardly been observed that this entails that referents must be indestructible. The objects that ordinary proper names are names of not only endure change, but are also created (or come into being) and perish: people are born and then die, buildings are erected and demolished and so on. Moreover, it seems plausible to maintain that for *any* object of the kind ordinary names apply to, there was a time when there was no such object.

Given that the property of determining the referent it does is internal to a sense (and by implication, so is its determining something), it follows that a referent's coming to be or passing away should coincide with a change in

---

3 There has been some debate over the direction of fit: are proper names those expressions, whatever they may be, which pick out members of an independently identifiable category of objects, or are objects whatever is picked out by members of an independently identifiable category of proper names? After attributing the latter to Frege in FPL (pp. 55 ff.), Dummett came to admit (IFP: Chapter 12) that no evidence could be found for this in Frege's writings, and ended up claiming that it was only 'in Frege's spirit'. On the view I advocate the whole dilemma appears misconceived, on grounds which will emerge towards the end of the present chapter.

any sense which determines it: from being one which has no referent to one which does or vice versa. But this is clearly incompatible with holding that senses are immutable.[4]

A manoeuvre open to Frege, in principle, is to exploit the fact that being *wirklich* (or existing, as it was called in Chapter 3 above) is a property on a par with any other, and to explain the destruction and creation of objects as losing or gaining that particular property. Such change would, on these assumptions, be no more mysterious than any other change. However, this cannot work for the purpose at hand, because the objects bearing ordinary names do *not* come into being or perish as wholes in a single stroke – switching, as it were, between mere possibility and actuality *tout court*. If the creation and destruction of ordinary objects is incompatible with their being the referents of immutable senses, then their names cannot be logically proper on Frege's terms.[5]

Once we recognize that the theoretical, or 'logically proper', notions of object and proper name in Russell and Frege are prima facie distinct from those of common sense and natural language, we are set to ask, 'how, then, are the two related?'. Since proper names are correlative to objects, the answer is to be sought in discovering what are logically proper objects. To anticipate, I will argue that it is a highly programmatic notion whose nature can only be properly understood in the broader context of what I will call 'generic metaphysics'. Before launching the move towards the explanation of this notion, however, let us address what seems to be prima facie evidence against the view taken above.

III What morals can we draw from illustration?

What is to be made, if the above view is correct, of the numerous examples, in both Russell's and Frege's writings, in which names like 'Socrates', 'Etna' or 'the morning star' appear to be regarded as proper names? With the exception of one important kind of case (to be discussed shortly), I contend that

---

4 Such a change *in* the sense needs to be contrasted with Frege's view on grasping or expressing a sense which effects no such change (see 'Logic' in PW: p. 138). Other accounts of the creation and destruction of common-sense objects which are compatible with the immutability of senses are, of course, possible, but bearing in mind that anthropocentric distinctions between 'long' and 'short' durations are logically irrelevant, they seem to militate against the supposition that common-sense objects are indeed objects in the logical sense. They may, for instance, be construed as events, but this shifts objecthood to the entities these events involve. They could be construed as time-slices of common-sense objects. Such moves concede, in effect, that common sense objects are *not* objects in the logical sense, because they shift objecthood to some other kind of entity.

5 For the pre-SuB period we might cite Gl. § 62: 'If we are to use a symbol *a* to signify an object, we must have a criterion for deciding in all cases whether *b* is the same as *a*, even if it is not always in our power to apply this criterion'. It seems hardly plausible to suppose that Frege thought that our ordinary names satisfy this standard.

taking such examples as a guide to what Russell or Frege took to be proper names is to mistake what is put forth merely for the purpose of illustration for a paradigmatic case.

The correct interpretation of such illustrations, it seems to me, is along the following lines. Where, for example, 'Socrates is wise' serves to illustrate a subject–predicate proposition, it is *tacitly assumed, for the sake of illustration*, that Socrates is a definite immutable, indestructible object, and (similarly) that the concept expressed by 'is wise' has absolutely sharp boundaries. 'Socrates is wise' can then be taken to express a subject–predicate proposition. *But it is no part of the theory that any of these assumptions is true.* In fact we are quite certain they are false, but this can be ignored because the point of these illustrations is neither to make nor imply any substantive claim regarding Socrates (or wisdom). Examples and illustrations are there to fulfil a heuristic role, and the non-logical objects and concepts to which they appeal form no part of the theory's subject matter. It is simply assumed *for the sake of illustration* that they satisfy certain requirements. Upon reflection the point seems to me so obvious that it should go without saying, and yet, having literally gone without saying in so many instances, it is very easily lost sight of, and the temptation to think that Russell and Frege were speaking of ordinary names creeps in.

There is, however, an important exception to what has just been said regarding illustrations. Its importance lies not just in its being an exception, but perhaps more in its providing a contrast which illuminates the *grounds* for taking natural language illustration in the manner just proposed. *Mathematical* illustrations *should* be taken at face value. On Frege's terms, we are entitled to assume that points in a geometrical construction, or numerical equations, involve genuine (logically proper) names and objects, and similarly that pairs of expressions like '2 + 5' and '3 + 4' can be said, strictly and literally, to express distinct senses which have the same referent. The reason is obvious: in this department of knowledge, unlike any other, both Russell and Frege had carefully worked back to ultimate foundations, which involves settling which notions were primitive and which defined (and, regarding the latter, *how* they are to be defined). In such a context theoretical commitments to a particular entity's being an object or a concept, as the case may be, are substantial, and not merely illustrative.

This contrasts markedly with the situation regarding empirical knowledge, for which Russell at that time had not even begun, and Frege never would begin, a similar undertaking. Before any commitment to something's being a concept or an object could be counted as substantial, a scheme of a similar nature to that devised for arithmetic would have to be devised for the domain of empirical knowledge.[6] It is fairly clear that statements about

---

6 If one is tempted to think that whether something is an object or a concept is too obvious a matter to require abstruse consideration, he might consider Frege's discussion in Gl. § 57. In

Socrates will involve *some* non-logical constants, but no attempt had been made (for Russell we might add, 'at that time') to address the difficulties involved in settling what they are. Moreover, when a stab in that direction was made, however rudimentary, the one thing that became immediately clear was that nothing remotely resembling Socrates would be a proper object, and hence that nothing like 'Socrates' would be a logically proper name.

We can now turn to the somewhat broader question of how we are to interpret analytic forms proposed by Russell or Frege which contain, as they often do, occurrences of ordinary names and concept-words. The question is essentially the same for cases as simple as a disjunctive statement like 'either it is raining or it is not', or as complex as the analysis of 'the author of *Waverley* was Scott'. Our reply needs to take heed of the fact that, unlike when we enquired whether 'Socrates' in isolation could be counted as a name and Socrates as an object, the analytic forms we are concerned with contain both a logical component and non-logical words.

As for the logical component (expressed, as Russell or Frege often expressed it, with natural language words like 'or', 'and' or 'all') the answer is fairly straightforward. The words should be understood as having the precise logical sense, namely as standing for the logical constant in question, whether or not we think of this as a faithful rendition of the natural language word as we normally use it. But for the non-logical words (such as 'Scott', 'author of' and '*Waverley*') the matter is not so simple, because we have no independently established strict sense to appeal to, and yet we must presume, if the analysis is to hold good, that the words in question behave as if they were 'logically proper'.

The answer can, I think, be found in applying what may be seen as a form of selective attention to such words and the entities they are supposed to stand for; regarding them, that is, as 'temporary symbols' (to use Frege's phrase) or 'relative individuals' and correspondingly 'relative names' (to use Russell's phrase). When summing up the demands a concept-script ought to satisfy (in the 1882 essay 'On the Scientific Justification of a Conceptual Notation'), Frege addressed the following paradox: 'It is impossible, someone might say, to advance science with a conceptual notation, for the invention of the latter already presupposes the completion of the former' (CN: p. 88). For this reason what we require from the concept-script strictly applies only to the logical relations, while

> the symbols for denoting [non-logical] content are less essential. They can be easily created as required, once the general [logical] forms are

which the consideration of cardinal numbers seems initially to lead to the conclusion that they are *properties* of classes, a view which is eventually discarded in favour of the view that they are objects. Frege's decision to regard the true and the false as objects may not be an obvious choice either.

available. If the analysis of a concept into its ultimate components does not succeed or appears unnecessary, **we can be content with temporary symbols**.

(CN: p. 88)

Although Frege might be judged over-optimistic about the ease of supplying non-logical contents, the point relevant to our discussion is his appeal to 'temporary symbols', whose temporariness need not hamper progress made with regard to the logical structure. Russell makes a similar point when, as a side remark made in the course of introducing the theory of descriptions in his *Introduction to Mathematical Philosophy,* he appeals to the notions of an individual and a name. At this point he adds,

> If, as may be the case, whatever *seems* to be an 'individual' is really capable of further analysis, we shall have to content ourselves with what may be called 'relative individuals,' which will be terms that, throughout the context in question, are never analysed and never occur otherwise than as subjects. And in that case we shall have correspondingly to content ourselves with 'relative names'.[7]

This makes essentially the same move, in relation to objects (here spoken of as 'individuals') and names, that Frege makes, in relation to concepts and their corresponding words. In both cases we are advised not to regard the use of non-logical words as committing the author to their actually being what the illustration seems to suggest they are.

The effect thus obtained is similar to that of assuming for the sake of illustration that a name used in an example is logically proper: by deciding that it will remain unanalysed *throughout the present context*, we simply ignore everything that would tell against a name or concept-word being 'logically proper'. I submit that this is the underlying reasoning of Russell's and Frege's appeal to natural language locutions when illustrating analyses of the kind mentioned.

Perhaps even more important than acknowledging that Frege and Russell were not advancing theories about natural language is the recognition that, for their purposes, the question of applicability to natural language is an *additional* one, and whatever answer is given to it, if any, will not affect the theories' success in fulfilling their primary role. Even though remarks do occur which seem to express views on these matters, they ought not to be regarded

---

7 Bertrand Russell, *Introduction to Mathematical Philosophy* (London: George Allen and Unwin, 1919) pp. 173–4. Despite the fact that this passage, from 1919, falls outside time boundaries I have set for Russell in this study, citing it here seems to me appropriate. Its content has nothing to do with the changes in Russell's position that led us to draw the line at about 1910, and I can think of no substantial reason why he might not have said it in 1900.

as part and parcel of the logical theory – they belong to a different level altogether. The logical theory, to be precise, neither asserts nor denies a relation to what would appear to be the corresponding natural language expressions. It is essentially indifferent to this question. Even if we do think an analysis captures the logical essence of some form of expression in natural language as well, we must still recognize that whether or not it succeeds in this task is, from Russell's and Frege's points of view, quite a *different* question from whether it will do for the concept-script.

Finally on this theme, if what has been said so far suggests that the theoretical notion of a proper name has nothing whatsoever to do with the intuitive, ordinary, notion, then this needs qualifying in a way which does show some roundabout relevance after all. Here we might begin from Dummett's comment, which comes in response to Tugendhat's interpretation of Frege's notion of reference as entirely programmatic. Dummett writes that Tugendhat's interpretation 'entirely misses the point of Frege's appeal, in his introduction of the notion of reference, to various intuitive, pre-systematic concepts which we have, such as that of the relation of name to bearer' (FPL: p. 406). For once I find myself in agreement with Dummett about the name–bearer prototype's having some role to play – pending, however, further clarifications of what precisely being a prototype implies.

If it is understood as committing Frege to the view that any particular ordinary name is a proper name in the strict logical sense (or even that ordinary names 'by and large' are), then, I think, we get the wrong idea. The appeal to our pre-systematic notion should, I suggest, be interpreted rather along the following lines. Whatever objects, and (correspondingly) proper names ultimately are, their *valency* (i.e. what other kinds of propositional, and correspondingly sentential, constituents they can combine with) is approximated to by that of ordinary names and common-sense objects. Similarly, the *relation* of proper names to their bearers approximates that of ordinary names in that their use would effect speech *about* them. This prototype has an important, arguably indispensable, heuristic role, but to mistake it for the very subject matter of Frege's discussion is a gross misunderstanding. It is this restricted sense of a 'prototype' which might also explain why Russell and Frege used 'proper name' (or *Eigenname*) as a label for the theoretical notion. Natural language proper names are the most natural (though ultimately, perhaps not the best) candidates for being logically proper names *inasmuch as anything in natural language is;* similarly for concept-words. They are by far the best approximations available among our pre-theoretic notions.

One might, of course, argue that the picture of logical names I have drawn is a chimera, on the grounds that any understanding we might have of what is meant by Russell's and Frege's theoretical notion is essentially dependent upon the appeal to the ordinary language notion. But such a line must be dismissed – it is irrelevant even if true. A fundamental tenet that Russell was emphatic about (and Frege even more so[8]) is that the psychological prerequisites for acquiring a concept are not to be confused with its content. It may well be that to understand cardinal numbers we need, as a matter of fact, first to master the practice of counting, but that does not render the theoretical notion of a cardinal number dependent upon the practice of counting – analysis reveals, in fact, that it is the other way around.[9] One could of course take a different view on this question of principle (e.g. along verificationist lines), but even if such a view is ultimately the right one, and the Russell–Frege view of meanings as independent of us ought to be dismissed as a myth, taking such a line is to argue *against* Russell and Frege, while our present concern is only with what can plausibly be attributed to them. I turn next to the attempt to provide a positive characterization of the revised (i.e. logical) notions of object and proper name. This involves broadening our view to encompass more general features of the enterprise in the course of which they are invoked.

IV The revisionary nature of the Russell–Frege enterprise

In his introduction to *Individuals*, Peter Strawson draws a distinction between descriptive and revisionary metaphysics: the former is characterized as 'content to describe the actual structure of **our** thought about the world', as opposed to the latter which is concerned 'to produce a better structure'.[10] Although no more than a moment's reflection is needed to place both Russell and Frege squarely in the 'revisionary' camp,[11] much more careful attention is required to establish, first, the precise manner in which their enterprise was 'revisionary' and, second, how they came to be, and in what manner precisely were they (if at all) metaphysicians.[12] I introduce Strawson's vision of descriptive metaphysics because its contrast with Russell's and Frege's enterprise strikes me as capable of illuminating the latter.

A clearer picture of this terrain is the key to understanding what Russell and Frege mean by 'object' and hence by 'proper name'. But obtaining such a picture is by no means a straightforward task. This is due to the fact that the metaphysical dimension of their logicist pursuit dawned upon them, as

---

8 E.g. Gl.: § 40.
9 See PoM: §§ 109 and 129.
10 P. F. Strawson, *Individuals* (London: Methuen, 1959) p. 9.
11 At any rate, when Strawson's phraseology is taken at face value. Ultimately, however, Russell's and Frege's enterprise might have a claim to the epithet 'descriptive', though not of *our* thought – this will be explained below.
12 For Russell's case we may add 'at that stage', in view of the fact that later in his career (e.g. starting most conspicuously in 'The Philosophy of Logical Atomism' (1918), in Marsh, pp. 177–281) he did engage in metaphysics in a very straightforward manner.

we shall see, only gradually and, in a curious way, *ex post facto,* while at the same time it was prescribed, more or less from the start, by their conception of logic. Part of the difficulty, for us, is to appreciate that in their enterprise revision proceeds 'simultaneously' in logic, mathematics, language (in a sense to be elaborated) and metaphysics. The enterprise is pitched at a level of generality which is oblivious of these boundaries. We, on the other hand, are more accustomed to regarding these as quite distinct, albeit related, domains. Understanding the exact manner in which the enterprise was revisionary will provide insight into its relation to natural language as well, but our inquiry into 'revision' needs to begin from mathematics itself.

Neither Russell nor Frege had set out to revise mathematics itself in any straightforward sense, and the accepted methods and results of mathematics were regarded by them as by and large correct, i.e. as embodying genuine knowledge. At the same time they were struck by what appeared to them as nothing short of a scandal: the answers to foundational questions about mathematics ('what is number?', 'what is the nature of mathematical propositions?') proposed by philosophers and mathematicians of their day seemed to them confused and, in general, radically unsatisfactory.[13] Mathematics, in a word, lacked a proper foundation. In Russell's words,

> The Philosophy of Mathematics has been hitherto as controversial, obscure and unprogressive as the other branches of philosophy. Although it was generally agreed that mathematics is in some sense true, philosophers disputed as to what mathematical propositions really meant: although something was true, no two people were agreed as to what it was that was true, and if something was known, no one knew what it was that was known. So long, however, as this was doubtful, it could hardly be said that any certain and exact knowledge was to be obtained in mathematics.
>
> (PoM: § 3)

Frege's view of the scandal seems to have been, at least initially, more narrowly focused on questions such as 'what is the nature of mathematical judgements?' and 'what is the nature of the number 1?' In the introduction to Gl. he writes,

> is it not a scandal that our science should be unclear about the first and foremost of its objects, and one which is apparently so simple? Small hope, then, that we shall be able to say what number is. If a concept fun-

---

13 Russell, despite sharing Frege's critical viewpoint, was less prone to the kind of polemical writing so characteristic of Frege. He was content to note that such views were untenable (with an occasional, 'local', discussion in relation to particular topics) and then to go on with his own business.

damental to a mighty science gives rise to difficulties, then it is surely an imperative task to investigate it more closely until those difficulties are overcome.

(Gl.: p. ii)

His more persistent and fundamental complaint, however, concerns the absence of clear standards of *proof*. As he explains in the preface to Bs., in setting out to decide whether the ultimate justification of arithmetic was dependent at any point upon anything experiential, Frege needed first to test how far one could get in mathematics by means of logical deductions alone. In the course of this attempt,

> So that something intuitive [*anschauliches*] could not squeeze in unnoticed here, it was most important to keep the chain of reasoning free of gaps. As I endeavoured to fulfil this requirement most rigorously, I found an obstacle in the inadequacy of the language; despite all the unwieldiness of the expressions, the more complex the relations became, the less precision – which my purpose required – could be obtained. From this deficiency arose the idea of the 'conceptual notation' presented here.
>
> (Bynum: p. 104)

The conceptual notation is, on this view, first and foremost a *tool* (and not an end in itself) to help carry out a job.[14] The job, i.e. the logicist enterprise, was conceived of not as introducing anything genuinely new, but rather as uncovering what is already there – making explicit what had hitherto been left implicit. The more fundamental drive seems to be not to prove any particular thesis about the nature of arithmetic, but rather to discover its nature *whatever it may be*. The enterprise may be construed as an immensely complex *experiment* to test a particular hypothesis, namely that the whole of arithmetic could be derived from purely logical premises.[15] The rigour is due, therefore, not only to the nature of the subject matter or the particular foundational hypothesis at stake, but rather to its very foundational nature.

Before we consider revisionary moves specifically associated with the logicist enterprise, it is useful to consider revision in mathematics proper – regardless of any particular foundational agenda. Here, too, we meet the same question as in the cases we are concerned with: 'how does the revised notion

---

14 See in this connection Frege's analogy, in the preface to Bs., between the concept-script and the microscope (Bynum: p. 105), and the penultimate paragraph of 'On the Scientific Justification of a Conceptual Notation' (Bynum: p. 89).

15 This perspective on the logicist enterprise, only dimly hinted at in the last quotation from Frege, was further elaborated upon by Russell in a number of places, and forms the principal theme in his 'The Regressive Method of Discovering the Premises of Mathematics' of 1907 (Lackey: pp. 272–83).

relate to what preceded it?'. Broadly speaking, mathematics in the period leading up to Russell's and Frege's work was characterized by a move towards greater rigour. Progress is embodied in giving precise definitions to familiar notions whose use had been governed only by intuitive recognition, and in providing formal proofs of tenets whose truth had been widely accepted. Such proofs reveal the grounds on which those tenets rest, and allows results which had been applied only to a limited domain to be extended to their utmost generality. Consider the following remark by Russell about Cantor and the continuum:

> The notion to which Cantor gives the name of *continuum* may, of course, be called by any other name in or out of the dictionary, and it is open to every one to assert that he himself means something else by the continuum. But these verbal questions are purely frivolous. **Cantor's merit lies, not in meaning what other people mean, but in telling us what he means himself** – an almost unique merit, where continuity is concerned . . . **This notion was presupposed in existing mathematics, though it was not known exactly what it was that was presupposed.**[16]
>
> (PoM: § 335)

Despite the specifically mathematical nature of the case at stake, this statement is a quintessential expression of the conception of revision which guided both Russell and Frege, first and foremost in logic, but which informs their revisionary enterprise in (what would naturally be regarded as) other areas as well. This statement seems to me so striking and clear that no exegetical comment could add to it.

Moving on to the logical constants, a view similar to Russell's is manifest in Frege's response (in a letter to Husserl) to the complaint that by rendering sentences containing 'all'-phrases, in a manner that avoids any existential import, he diverges from the manner in which such sentences are normally understood:

> Linguistic usage cannot be absolutely decisive here, since we need not be concerned with what linguistic usage is. Instead we can lay down our lin-

---

16 Remarks in a similar vein, though not in relation to a specifically mathematical notion, occur in Frege's polemical reply to Benno Kerry in 'On Concept and Object' (G&B: p. 42), where he says:

> The word 'concept' is used in various ways; its sense is sometimes psychological, sometimes logical, and sometimes perhaps a confused mixture of both. Since this licence exists, it is natural to restrict it by requiring that when once a usage is adopted it shall be maintained. What I decided was to keep strictly to a purely logical use; the question of whether this or that use is more appropriate is one that I should like to leave on one side as of minor importance.

guistic usage in logic according to our logical needs. The reason for the usage I have laid down is simplicity.

(PMC: p. 71)

Similarly, Frege shows in Bs. that he is fully aware that his theoretical notion of a conditional (roughly, material implication), differs from what is customarily expressed by 'if . . . then . . .' locutions, in that they would not be used in the absence of an assumption of a causal relation between the two components, and hence that one would not be inclined to admit that such a conditional was true solely on grounds of the antecedent's being false.[17]

Russell's and Frege's aim with regard to the logical constants, as with revisions in mathematics proper, is *not* (to borrow Russell's phrase) 'to mean what other people mean', but rather to tell us what they themselves mean. For Russell and Frege it went without saying that the chief aim was to mean something which would be of use in providing an account of mathematics. Any bearing the theoretical notions may have on previous usage and on the expressions of natural language are thus quite inessential from their theoretical point of view. The enterprise is thus clearly 'revisionary' in Strawson's terms. What is meant by the common-sense pre-systematic locutions is regarded as not sufficiently definite and therefore inappropriate for theoretical purposes. What is proposed in its place is simply laid down, and recommended chiefly for its precision and utility for the theoretical task at hand.

There is, however, an inherent tension, in that, after all, we do need to end up with something which can make a plausible claim to be mathematics, or logic. More generally, despite the deliberate indifference to what is meant by the corresponding natural language locutions, there is a loose assumption that the revised notion is, after all, what was really intended all along (as Russell often puts it – 'unconsciously'[18]). The looseness of these assumptions is prescribed by the nature of the case. Given a pair of notions, one of which is vague and the other precise, it can hardly be expected that the difference between them can be made precise.

V Logic as metaphysics

So far, revision seems not to involve us in anything expressly metaphysical, and might be perceived as confined to mathematics and logic (and thus,

---

17 A remark in similar vein (which was cited earlier, in Chapter 3) occurs in PoM § 19 when Russell distances his defined notions of disjunction and negation from those in general use.

18 A good example is Russell's comment upon his own definition of pure mathematics which opens PoM, saying that it 'professes to be, not an arbitrary decision to use a common word in an uncommon signification, but rather a precise analysis of the ideas which, more or less unconsciously, are implied in the ordinary employment of the term' (PoM: § 2).

indirectly, to the languages employed in their articulation). This might well have been all there was to it if Russell's and Frege's conception of logic was the one we are accustomed to today. This, however, is not the case.

When describing Russell's and Frege's overall aim as that of reducing mathematics to logic, or of showing mathematics to be a branch of logic, it must be borne in mind that for them this was a means of answering the foundational question 'what *is* mathematics?'. If a similar question can arise for logic itself, then the whole enterprise will have been in vain, because instead of an answer we will have merely pushed the question back, agreeing (to use Russell's phrase) that logic is true, but not knowing what it is that is true.

Another way of bringing out the same point would be to consider a hypothetical position which held mathematics to be reducible to logic (perhaps even endorsing the same formulae as Russell or Frege would), but which then went on to hold a psychologist, formalist or conventionalist account of logic itself. Surely, such a position, though it might perhaps be called 'logicist' in a sense, goes against the grain of Russell's and Frege's logicism. This suggests that Russell and Frege regarded the question of the nature of logic as something to which the answer was firmly established in advance, at least in outline – and this answer was essential to their logicism. What is in question here has little to do with the choice of axioms and theorems. It is concerned, rather, with the *significance* of the laws of logic, whatever they may turn out to be. It is at this point that the Russell–Frege view diverges profoundly from those which have since become current.

We might bring out this strand in their conception of logic by considering their view of its place in relation to other sciences. The matter is not addressed in a systematic way, but we do have a number of disparate remarks which make their view clear, namely the view that logic is distinguished from other sciences primarily in degree of generality, and that the only difference between the propositions occurring in logic and those in other sciences is the occurrence in the latter of (non-logical) constants.[19]

Another angle on the relation between logic and the other sciences is provided by Frege's notorious remark that if logic is said to embody the laws of thought, then this is not intended in the sense of a *description* of the way we do, as a matter of fact, think, but rather as a *prescription* for how we ought to think. Frege continues, however,

19 The clearest example of this is geometry. Both Russell and Frege regarded it as falling outside the scope of the logicist thesis, because it involves non-logical (and intuitive) constants (see in Frege's 1882 essay 'On the Scientific Justification of a Conceptual Notation' in Bynum p. 88). Russell's position is essentially the same, but it cannot be so straightforwardly stated because of the manner in which he distinguished between 'pure' and 'applied' geometry (see PoM § 5) – only the latter would coincide with what Frege meant by that term.

Any law asserting what is, can be conceived as prescribing that one ought to think in conformity with it, and is thus in that sense a law of thought. This holds for laws of geometry and physics no less than for laws of logic. The latter have a special claim to the name 'laws of thought' only if we mean to assert that they are the most general laws.[20]

(Gg.: p. 12)

So there is a sense in which logic might be said to be descriptive after all. Not of *our* thinking, as in Strawson, but of the world as it is independently of us. However, particularly in Frege's early phase of the enterprise, one observes a certain duality between what may be described as a 'low-key' view, according to which the concept-script does no more than supplement the existing formal language of arithmetic, and a more ambitious one, which regards its absolute generality as giving it some philosophical significance. Both strands are manifest on the same page of his 1882 essay 'On the Scientific Justification of a Conceptual Notation' (Bynum: p. 89). This brings us to the metaphysical dimension of logic.

Let us begin by making clear that the Russell–Frege view is ontologically committed to whatever is assumed to have being, regardless of whether it exists (in the sense roughly equivalent to 'concrete entity', earlier labelled 'exist$_1$'). The positing of senses by Frege, and of denoting concepts by Russell, exemplify such commitments. On their view, but not on the more modern view, such commitments are part of the business of *logic* – which draws one's attention to the fact that the difference between their characteristic use of this term and the current one is no mere matter of nomenclature.

Except for the logical constants – about which there was no question in either Russell's or Frege's mind of their being specific entities[21] – any other ontological commitments Russell and Frege may have had are of a highly programmatic nature. We are told what *kinds* of entities there must be but,

---

20 In a similar vein is Frege's talk of the visionary Leibnizian *lingua universalis* as a method of notation which 'fits things themselves' (Bynum: p. 105); as well as remarks on the first page of the introduction to the 1897 essay 'Logic' (PW: p. 128). Such remarks suggest that Wittgenstein's opposition to theories in which 'the logical proposition acquires all the characteristics of a proposition of natural science' (L. Wittgenstein, *Tractatus Logico-Philosophicus*, translated by D. F. Pears and B. F. McGuinness (London: Routledge and Kegan Paul, 1961) 6.111), though arguably exaggerated, has a solid source in Russell's and Frege's conception of logic.

21 This may not be immediately apparent from the manner in which they are introduced in Bs. (though it is implied by the assumption, inevitable in that context, that the symbols in question have *content*) but it becomes clear in Gg., where each logical constant is expressly secured a referent (Volume I § 31). In Russell's case the same point is implicit in his remark that the logical constants are the only constants (i.e. non-variables) occurring in mathematical propositions (PoM: § 1).

except in a very restricted class of cases, no instances of those entities are, strictly speaking, given.[22]

The distinction between concepts and objects, which is essentially common to Frege and Russell, exemplifies this programmatic nature. Except for the logical constants (and whatever is defined by their means) we are not told whether anything in particular is a concept or an object; and we have to make do with a characterization in terms of other, similarly programmatic, notions.

That these notions rather than others come to the fore is, of course, because they are required for the theory of deduction. But now let us ask what, on this view, is an inference. It concerns generic propositions (rather than sentences or beliefs), but bearing in mind that these are objective entities, the laws of inference are just very general laws concerning relations between these entities.[23] Thus they have no more to do with language than, say, the laws of physics – it is just that they are more general.

In view of all this, I propose we go further than some writers have, when proclaiming (particularly in relation to Russell) that logic has a 'metaphysical import', or 'metaphysical presuppositions',[24] and say that logic just *is* a very generalized form of metaphysics: what I shall call 'generic metaphysics'. It is distinguished by its strictly a-priori nature, and hence by its disregard for existence (in the sense delineated earlier as correlative with 'concrete' or 'actual').

Before further elaborating upon the notion of generic metaphysics, two remarks need to be made. First, there is no tension between admitting that this is the *nature* of the notions occurring both in Russell's and Frege's theories, and admitting substantial differences between them with regard to their specification. That Russell and Frege disagreed on whether, for example, concepts can occur as subjects, or on whether generic propositions might contain objects of level 0, or on whether truth and falsity are objects – none of these facts tells against the view that they were engaging in the same kind of pursuit. Second, the generality of the notions in question ought

---

22 This might seem to be controverted by Frege's contention that the cardinal numbers are specific objects. But the programmatic element remains, because the definition of the cardinal numbers involves quantification over all objects, without its having been specified what objects there are. The programmatic nature of 'object' thus affects anything specified by appeal to the individual variable.

23 This is more immediately clear in Russell's case (see e.g. PoM: § 37); but in Frege's case, too, it must be remembered that ultimately arguments and proofs consist of *thoughts,* not sentences or formulae (see Frege's 'Logic in Mathematics' (1914) in PW: p. 206), and that the prevailing manner of speech, which seems to suggest the contrary, is, upon scrutiny, only a convenient abbreviation (see e.g. note in 'On Schoenfliess: *Die Logischen Paradoxien der Mengenlehre*' (1906) in PW: p. 178).

24 See e.g. Hylton, *Russell*, p. 170.

not to be mistaken for vagueness. To specify them further would be to go against the generality of logic. Logic would not embody the 'laws of thought' (on Frege's view) unless it applied to abstract and concrete entities alike.

The following passage is a poignant articulation of the point of view which gives rise to generic metaphysics, as well as of other fundamental assumptions Russell and Frege shared:

> Presentations, judgements and assumptions . . . always have *objects;* and these objects are independent of the states of mind in which they are apprehended. This independence has been obscured hitherto by the 'prejudice in favour of the existent' (*des Wirklichen*), which has led people to suppose that, when the thought has a non-existent object, there is really no object distinct from the thought. But this is an error: existents are only an infinitesimal part of the objects of knowledge. This is illustrated by mathematics, which never deals with anything to which existence is essential, and deals in the main with objects which *cannot* exist, such as numbers. Now we do not need first to study the knowledge of objects before we study the objects themselves; hence the study of objects is essentially independent of both psychology and theory of knowledge. It may be objected that the study of objects must be coextensive with *all* knowledge; but we may consider separately the more general properties and kinds of objects, and this is an essential part of philosophy . . .
>
> This subject is not identical with metaphysics, but is wider in its scope; for metaphysics deals only with the real, whereas the theory of objects has no such limitation. The theory of objects deals with whatever can be known *a priori* about objects, but knowledge of reality can only be obtained by experience. The theory of objects is not psychology, since objects are independent of our apprehension of them. It is also not theory of knowledge; for knowledge has two sides, the cognition, which belongs to psychology, and the object, which is independent. The theory of objects . . . is also not to be identified with pure logic, since logic [on this opinion], is essentially practical in its aim, being concerned with right reasoning. (On this point opinions will differ; but the question is in any case only one of nomenclature.) The conclusion is, that the theory of objects is an independent subject, and the most general of all philosophical subjects. Mathematics is essentially part of it, and thus at last finds a proper place; for the traditional division of sciences into natural and mental left no room for mathematics, because it took account only of the existent. Grammar may be a guide in the general theory of objects, as mathematics in more special parts of the theory.

(Lackey: pp. 77–8)

This passage – first published in the same number of *Mind* as OD – opens Russell's review of a volume by Meinong and his disciples, and provides a summary of the viewpoint Meinong had labelled *Gegenstandstheorie* (translated as 'theory of objects' above). In view of the low esteem in which Meinong's ontological views are often held it may be worth stressing, before going any further, the distinction between the specific metaphysical views which Meinong endorsed – which were rejected by Russell, as they would most probably also have been by Frege – and the general conception of the programme, which is independent of these specific views. The programme and underlying tenets described above by Russell fit, with only minor alterations, the kind of theoretical enterprise that Russell and Frege were ultimately engaged in. I am not suggesting this was their conception of it at the outset, but rather that it provides a good *retrospective* account of what the enterprise (or rather, its non-technical aspects) had become in the course of its development. In Russell's case, at any rate, we have some direct evidence for this.

In the long passage just quoted, Russell speaks on Meinong's behalf. But in a letter he wrote to Meinong some months earlier, he speaks of the volume, from the review of which we have just quoted, as follows:

> I find myself in almost complete agreement with the general viewpoint and the problems dealt with seem to me very important. **I myself have been accustomed to use the word 'Logic' for that which you call *Gegenstandstheorie*** and the reasons you cite against this use . . . appear to me hardly decisive.
>
> I am in complete agreement with the view that mathematics is *Gegenstandstheorie*. This is in fact one of the main theses of my *Principles of Mathematics* . . . Its entire first part is explicitly concerned with questions concerning *Gegenstandstheorie*. Of course there are many discussions whose purpose is purely formal, that is, serving only to lead into technical mathematical procedures. Yet the general (non-technical) questions are the essential matters treated there.[25]

Barring the difference over the application of the term 'logic' (which is also hinted at in the review), Russell appears to be in full agreement with Meinong. This difference, however, seems to me not quite as purely verbal as Russell makes it out to be, because (like Frege) Russell regards the theory of deduction in the narrow sense – which is supposedly what Meinong wishes to exclude – as continuous with mathematics, and hence as part and parcel of the theory of objects. From Russell's, and even more clearly from Frege's, use of 'logic', it is plain that they thought of it as covering a broader domain

---

25 The German original appeared in A. Meinong, *Philosophenbriefe*, pp. 150–1. The English translation is by Janet Farrel Smith (from whom I have diverted by replacing the original German in some instances), and appears as an appendix to her paper 'The Russell–Meinong Debate'.

than the theory of deduction, and in particular as including matters such as theories of denoting and the distinction between sense and reference.

VI The latency of the metaphysical facet

As stated earlier, I am not proposing that 'generic metaphysics' was Russell's or Frege's view of the enterprise at the outset; and despite Russell's unequivocal testimony (which, it may be noted, is retrospective), the assimilation of Part I of PoM with a theory of objects is, I must confess, by no means obvious. (It is even less obvious that 'one of the main theses' of PoM was that mathematics is part of the theory of objects.) The manner in which their enterprise might be construed as a form of the theory of objects requires explanation, therefore, not only in Frege's case, but also in Russell's. In this and the next and final section, I shall try to provide a sketch of such an explanation, and then to exploit the angle it provides on the enterprise as a whole to illuminate the theories discussed in the earlier chapters.

The reason why the metaphysical dimension of the inquiry, so crisply expressed by Russell in the passage quoted in the last section, remains mostly tacit in Russell's and Frege's writings is, I suggest, that it only dawned upon them very gradually (in Frege's case it never became completely explicit); and the reason for this is, in a nutshell, that the nature of the logicist enterprise changed as it unfolded. It became philosophical in a manner that far exceeded the confines of the philosophy of mathematics and the logicist thesis. The point was already touched upon, obliquely, when we noted Frege's ambivalence as between the 'low-key' view, and a more ambitious one concerning the significance of the concept-script; and when noting Russell's changing views concerning the boundary between the philosophical and the technical–logical parts of the enterprise in the final section of Chapter 3 above. Despite the fact that Frege never expressed the kind of retrospective view we quoted earlier from Russell, I think that grouping Russell and Frege together on this question is ultimately justified. In terms of the development to be described shortly, Frege's starting point seems to have been further back than Russell's, and his mature view never obtained the kind of explicit metaphysical character Russell would arrive at later. Nonetheless, both seem to have travelled along essentially the same route; and the absence of full awareness of these matters is, on my reading, an essential ingredient of the tale.

Both Russell and Frege seem to have begun with a chiefly technical enterprise in mind: the non-technical questions associated with the symbols' meaning seemed to them capable of being settled in a few brief remarks to the effect that every symbol (in the concept-script) must be supposed to have content (the entity it stands for). In the case of complex symbols capable of being true or false, this content was a generic proposition. This goes no further than anyone with a broadly Platonist view of mathematics would admit, and can hardly be regarded as seriously engaging in metaphysics. This is the kind of picture that emerges, for example, in Bs., and probably in the earlier versions of PoM (on this, see below).

The philosophical concerns appear to have been initially confined, first, to the discontent with alternative views on the nature of number and mathematics; second, to an acute awareness that to prove logicism right was to prove Kant's view that arithmetic is concerned with a form of intuition wrong; and third, to some rather vague declaration of allegiance to Leibniz's vision of a *lingua universalis*.[26] That the philosophical significance of the enterprise seemed at first to be restricted in this manner is suggested, *inter alia*, by the fact that earlier versions of PoM did not contain anything corresponding to Part I of that work as we now know it;[27] and by the very narrow view Frege takes of his own enterprise in the introduction to Bs., where he seems to regard his logical innovations as essentially technical, and to be only very tentative about their having a broader philosophical significance.

The principal impetus to the enterprise's becoming more philosophical, and hence to its authors' greater (though still partial) metaphysical self-awareness, was, I suggest, no other than the developments discussed in the first two parts of the present work, and in particular the positing of denoting concepts and senses. So long as one preserves the very simple semantic assumptions that Frege and Russell began with (excluding denoting concepts), one is hardly inclined to consider oneself as engaging in metaphysics. But finding the need to admit entities of a kind *not* formerly admitted – as happened with Russell's first theory, but only with Frege's second – tends to make one more aware that one has engaged in metaphysics. The discussions of denoting and of reference drew them into questions of general philosophy of a kind which they had not envisaged at the outset they would need to deal with.

What initially seemed like rather marginal problems in an essentially technical pursuit drove each to devise his respective 'first' solution. This, in turn, led to replacing each of the first two theories with their respective ultimate solutions, and those moves eventually affected the nature of the whole enterprise they were engaged in. It had become more philosophical, engaging in problems which are by no means special to the philosophy of mathematics. This change is evidenced, in Russell's case, by the contrast between PoM itself and his retrospective remarks on it in the letter to Meinong, and continues, in a more obvious manner, after 1910. In Frege's case, we have the

26 See Frege's remarks in the preface to Bs. (Bynum: p. 105), and Russell's in PoM, both at the outset (start of § 5) and in the summary of Part VI (§ 436).

27 The attempt to make this statement precise (regarding which manuscript is to be counted as 'a former version of PoM') would take us too far afield. This much, however, is fairly clear: what is known as 'the draft of 1899–1900' (item 1 in Volume 3 of Russell's *Collected Papers*) reveals that nothing corresponding to PoM Part I occurs in that draft, and that the first draft of Part I (which occurs as item 2 in the same volume) was written only a year later.

increasingly central place that questions associated with the sense/reference distinction came to hold in his writings, a distinction which may be said to have begun life as an extended footnote to Gg. This development continued into Frege's final years, when such questions seem to have acquired an interest in their own right.

Although, as we saw, an essential part in all this was played by *epistemological* considerations – I will say more about this in the next section – it is worth noting that this development was *not* prompted, as one might have expected, by issues in the more philosophical regions of the enterprise, such as the debate with other views on the nature of mathematics or logic, or mathematical knowledge. Rather, in each case the problem sprang from, and was intimately linked to, logicism's *formal* development: as with the identity-sign in Frege, or general propositions in Russell. They arose from the attempt to reconcile the demands of a perspicuous notation with the simple-minded semantic conception they had at the outset. At this point it may also be remembered that the problem which drove Russell to the discovery of the theory of descriptions arose from an attempt to devise a *notation* which would reflect the duality of denoting concepts. If it had not been for these demands of a perspicuous notation these problems might well have remained buried, and the theories which came in response to them would never have been contemplated.

This is no more than a crude sketch of a development a full account of which would require, *inter alia*, more careful attention to the differences between Russell and Frege. However, I think it can serve nonetheless, first, to explain (in part) why the metaphysical dimension was mostly tacit; second, to challenge the view which simply takes the general philosophical significance of these theories for granted and fails to appreciate their debt to the logicist enterprise; and third, to provide the setting for what I propose is a more correct perspective on the nature of those theories themselves.

VII Concluding remarks: the nature of the enterprise

Although we already considered (in Chapters 1, 2 and 4) the inner workings of the processes which led the way in the developments outlined above, I shall begin the present section by recounting the tale very briefly. Then, by emphasizing a particular strand of it, I will raise a question the answer to which provides an overview of the process as a whole. Following our discussion in Chapter 6, I will use both 'sense' and 'acquaintance' in a generic sense. 'Generic' both in encompassing both Russell's and Frege's views, and in the sense of 'generic metaphysics' explained earlier.

The consideration that led Russell to posit denoting concepts may be outlined thus: we cannot possibly be acquainted with infinite totalities, yet we do grasp propositions about them; hence something other than the infinite totalities must occur in the propositions we grasp. These 'other things' are

denoting concepts.[28] In Frege's case the considerations are essentially similar. The possibility of true informative identities leads to the conclusion that
when grasping such generic propositions we cannot possibly be directly
grasping, or acquainted with, what those identities are about, and hence that
something else (i.e. other than the referent) must determine the generic
proposition's identity.[29]

From both these processes it emerges that if the positing of senses is to
provide even a prima facie solution to the problems it was meant to solve, it
is absolutely crucial that senses be accessible to acquaintance,[30] at least in the
case of simple senses. Otherwise the problem senses were designed to solve
could reappear – this time regarding them. It is likewise essential that they
be aboutness-shifters – because otherwise our knowledge, or understanding,
would end up being *about* something other than we presumed at the outset.

If we ask where in Russell's writings there is anything to secure, or make
it so much as probable, that acquaintance with simple denoting concepts is
possible, or, on Frege's view, that senses will be graspable (in a manner in
which referents are held not to be), then we find nothing, or next to nothing.
We are told effectively nothing about what is involved in grasping senses by
Frege, nor about what is involved in being acquainted with denoting concepts by Russell. The relations themselves seem barely intelligible. On the
face of things, then, both Russell and Frege appear to have failed to provide
an explanation at the very point where it is most needed. The fault is so
blatant and fundamental that it suggests either that they were extremely
bad philosophers, or that the expectation is based on some misconception.

As soon as we form the correct picture of the nature and place of the
epistemic considerations sketched above, however, the apparent lacuna disappears. This is because Russell and Frege did not set out on an epistemic
inquiry in its own right, and their true course seems to me more aptly

28 It is worth noting that this line of reasoning tacitly assumes, in effect, something along the
lines of the *contrapositive* of Russell's notorious 'principle of acquaintance' (to wit: every
proposition we understand must be constituted wholly of constituents with which we are
acquainted). From the impossibility of something's being an object of acquaintance together
with the assumption that understanding does occur, we derive the conclusion that something
other than the inaccessible object must take its place in the object of understanding. The
principle can thus be seen to have played a role long before its first explicit formulation. I
think that something along these lines can plausibly be said to underlie Frege's route to positing
senses as well (see below), but a full articulation of this claim would carry us too far afield.
29 To admit that a principal role of the notion of sense is to be an object of cognition does *not*
imply that they are conceptually dependent upon cognition. On Russell's and Frege's view,
the very opposite follows, because the object of genuine knowledge must be independent of
the knowing mind.
30 As noted earlier, despite the fact that Russell's discussion in OD relates only to *complex*
senses (where acquaintance with the complex is not essential), his position in PoM allows
there to be simple senses as well (in which case their accessibility to acquaintance would
be essential). As for Frege, I argued in Chapter 6 that on his view there is no escape from
admitting simple senses of some sort.

described along the following lines.[31] They both began by assuming, at least implicitly, a rather simple view of cognition, and a correspondingly simple semantic view, according to which understanding and knowledge consist in a direct relation between a mind and the object which the knowledge, or understanding, was about. Such a view must be presumed to have *preceded* the respective *first* theory of each, because these theories embody fairly local modifications to it. The consideration of identity-statements and infinite totalities, however, showed that such a view was *obviously* false.

In view of this, the motivation that needs to be attributed to Russell and Frege to explain their diversion to epistemic considerations is no more than the desire to provide a sketch, which is not *obviously* false, of what makes formulae meaningful. This minimal standard, moreover, is all the more plausible in view of the predominantly technical nature of the pursuit. Obtaining this minimal standard, however, proved not at all easy, and the job of avoiding this patent falsity ultimately forced them to make major changes.

Let us return now to the apparent lacunae with respect to our acquaintance with senses and denoting concepts, and with respect to their feature of aboutness-shifting. The chief merit of these entities appears to be that they are *not referents*, and hence that there are no compelling grounds – as there were for referents – *against* our being acquainted with them (at least in the problematic cases). My proposal is that this is all Russell and Frege provide us with, and that it is all they need provide us with. The somewhat surprising answer to the problem of the alleged lacunae is, in short, that there simply *is* no answer. To the questions 'how do they shift aboutness?', or 'how are they guaranteed epistemic accessibility?', the answer is, 'they just do (or are)', and that is all there is to it.[32]

Lest this view of the matter make the postulation of such entities seem frivolous, it is worth noting that, at least in Russell's case, it was acknowledged that an additional logical constant was required (which is a substantial price to pay), and that such devices can lead, as we saw in Chapter 2 above, to inextricable tangles, or even to contradictions. Such devices were posited only as a last resort, and (as with Russell) abandoned as soon as an alternative solution emerged.

To sum up, there are, in my opinion, no secrets that Frege did not share with us either about the nature of sense, or about what it is to grasp a sense, nor are there secrets regarding acquaintance which Russell knew but did not impart. *These notions are determined to the precise degree that the relevant*

---

31 A quintessential expression of the opposing view is found in Dummett, when he says that Frege's 'original concern [leading to the sense/reference distinction] was to explain the general notion of the cognitive value of a statement'. I am not denying, of course, that this is something Frege *ended up* doing (though note reservations below), but to suggest this was what he had set out to do from the outset strikes me as a grossly misleading.

32 Contrast this with Dummett's view in 'Frege's myth of the third realm' (FOP: pp. 251–2). See also FPL: p. 227.

theories determine them, and to pose further questions is simply a misunderstanding of their generic natures. This is *not* to say that one cannot study the implications of positing them, argue for or against the plausibility of such implication, or question their consistency. But this is not the same as to further determine their very identities.

Russell and Frege were not sitting in a logical observatory and passing on to us some of the most striking things they saw. They were theoreticians who, when faced with a problem they were unable get around by other means, postulated a theoretical entity satisfying certain requirements. It so happened that, alarmed by a fault Frege was unaware of (and thanks to his observing a distinction between simple and complex names), Russell was led to the discovery of a theory in which such entities were no longer necessary.

The answer with regard to proper names is the same as that with regard to objects, concepts, senses, and acquaintance. They are all *generic* terms which hang together, and Russell and Frege may not have known any more about what they are than they told us in their writings. This helps to illuminate the relation of Russell's and Frege's concerns with language: a relation we have been seeking to understand in this chapter. Asking whether the answer to 'what is a proper name?' ought to determine the answer to 'what is an object?' or vice versa, can now be seen as futile. Given Russell's and Frege's technical use of these terms, the strict correspondence of names and objects is as good as an analytical truth – it is no substantial thesis at all. Perhaps part of the misunderstanding here is due to the fact that these questions get easily confused with others – to wit, do *we* first identify something as an object and then decide to apply a proper name to it, or does it happen the other way around? I contend that Frege neither asked these latter questions nor needed to say anything about them.

We are accustomed to accounts which provide a far more colourful picture of these notions, but whether or not such a picture is justified in the light of later developments, I think it is important to recognize how these notions were initially conceived, because it directs our attention to their most essential features, which happen also to be their *least* 'pictorial' and intuitive.

The suggestion that the theory of descriptions and the theory of sense and reference were essentially extended footnotes to the *Principia* and Gg. respectively has been rejected – in the Fregean case, as a diminution of Frege's achievement.[33] But I think that if we take this remark not as a form of tacit evaluation, but merely as a rough description of their place in the broader theoretical setting, we will not be far off the mark, and will have gained some important insights into their natures.

---

33 The point was made by Dummett in response to Sluga's remark that the sense/reference distinction is 'an appendix to a philosophy of mathematics' (IFP: pp. 36–7), but I think that it diverts attention from the question of the theory's place in Frege's agenda, to the quite different one of its intrinsic value and interest.

Appendix A

The text of the obscure passage from 'On Denoting'

(*A*) The relation of the meaning to the denotation involves certain rather curious difficulties, which seem in themselves sufficient to prove that the theory which leads to such difficulties must be wrong.

(*B*) When we wish to speak about the *meaning* of a denoting phrase, as opposed to its *denotation*, the natural mode of doing so is by inverted commas. Thus we say:

> The centre of mass of the Solar System is a point, not a denoting complex;
> 'The centre of mass of the Solar System' is a denoting complex, not a point.

Or again,

> The first line of Gray's Elegy states a proposition.
> 'The first line of Gray's Elegy' does not state a proposition.

Thus taking any denoting phrase, say *C*, we wish to consider the relation between *C* and '*C*', where the difference of the two is of the kind exemplified in the above two instances.

(*C*) We say, to begin with, that when *C* occurs it is the *denotation* that we are speaking about; but when '*C*' occurs, it is the *meaning*. Now the relation of meaning and denotation is not merely linguistic through the phrase: there must be a logical relation involved, which we express by saying that the meaning denotes the denotation. But the difficulty that confronts us is that we cannot succeed in *both* preserving the connexion of meaning and denotation *and* preventing them from being one and the same; also that the meaning cannot be got at except by means of denoting phrases. This happens as follows.

(D) The one phrase C was to have both meaning and denotation. But if we speak of 'the meaning of C', that gives us the meaning (if any) of the denotation. 'The meaning of the first line of Gray's Elegy' is the same as 'The meaning of "The curfew tolls the knell of parting day",' and is not the same as 'The meaning of "the first line of Gray's Elegy" '. Thus in order to get the meaning we want, we must speak not of 'the meaning of C', but of 'the meaning of "C",' which is the same as 'C' by itself. Similarly 'the denotation of C' does not mean the denotation we want, but means something which, if it denotes at all, denotes what is denoted by the denotation we want. For example, let 'C' be 'the denoting complex occurring in the second of the above instances'. Then

$$C = \text{'the first line of Gray's Elegy', and}$$

the denotation of C = The curfew tolls the knell of parting day. But what we *meant* to have as the denotation was 'the first line of Gray's Elegy'. Thus we have failed to get what we wanted.

(E) The difficulty in speaking of the meaning of a denoting complex may be stated thus: The moment we put the complex in a proposition, the proposition is about the denotation; and if we make a proposition in which the subject is 'the meaning of C', then the subject is the meaning (if any) of the denotation, which was not intended. This leads us to say that, when we distinguish meaning and denotation, we must be dealing with the meaning: the meaning has denotation and is a complex, and there is not something other than the meaning, which can be called the complex, and be said to *have* both meaning and denotation. The right phrase, on the view in question, is that some meanings have denotations.

(F) But this only makes our difficulty in speaking of meanings more evident. For suppose C is our complex; then we are to say that C *is* the meaning of the complex. Nevertheless, whenever C occurs without inverted commas, what is said is not true of the meaning, but only of the denotation, as when we say: The centre of mass of the solar system is a point. Thus to speak of C itself, i.e. to make a proposition about the meaning, our subject must not be C, but something which denotes C. Thus 'C', which is what we use when we want to speak of the meaning, must be not the meaning, but something which denotes the meaning. And C must not be a constituent of this complex (as it is of 'the meaning of C'); for if C occurs in the complex, it will be its denotation, not its meaning, that will occur, and there is no backward road from denotations to meanings, because every object can be denoted by an infinite number of different denoting phrases.

(G) Thus it would seem that 'C' and C are different entities, such that 'C' denotes C; but this cannot be an explanation, because the relation of

'C' to C remains wholly mysterious; and where are we to find the denoting complex 'C' which is to denote C? Moreover, when C occurs in a proposition, it is not *only* the denotation that occurs (as we shall see in the next paragraph); yet, on the view in question, C is only the denotation, the meaning being wholly relegated to 'C'. This is an inextricable tangle, and seems to prove that the whole distinction of meaning and denotation has been wrongly conceived.

(H)   That the meaning is relevant when a denoting phrase occurs in a proposition is formally proved by the puzzle about the author of *Waverley*. The proposition 'Scott was the author of *Waverley*' has a property not possessed by 'Scott was Scott', namely the property that George IV wished to know whether it was true. Thus the two are not identical propositions; hence the meaning of 'the author of *Waverley*' must be relevant as well as the denotation, if we adhere to the point of view to which this distinction belongs. Yet, as we have just seen, so long as we adhere to this point of view, we are compelled to hold that only the denotation can be relevant. Thus the point of view in question must be abandoned.

Appendix B

Russell's example in the latter half of paragraph (D) of the obscure passage

Russell's illustration, in the latter half of paragraph (*D*) of the obscure passage, of the second of the twin phenomena mentioned on page 35 in Chapter 2, is best explained, like its twin, with the help of a graphic depiction. This illustration is more complex than that of its twin, and matching each phrase in Russell's text with its corresponding pictorial element may require some effort. It also requires adding the following two graphic conventions to those used in Figures 1, 2 and 3 in Chapter 2: The *logical* relation of denoting (between a complex and its denotation) is represented by an unbroken diagonal line, and the relation for which Russell uses 'the same as' by '='. For the sake of clarity, Figure 4 also contains boxes, i.e. phrases, which are not mentioned in Russell's text, but which are indispensable for understanding what he says about those which are. His illustration of the second of the twin phenomena can now be read thus: 'Similarly "the denotation of *C*" does not mean the denotation we want [i.e. α], but means something [i.e. γ] which, if it denotes at all, denotes what is denoted by the denotation we want [i.e. β].

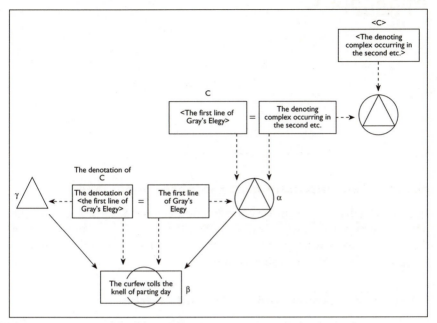

Figure 4

Appendix C

Some recent discussions of the obscure passage

In this appendix I comment very briefly on three previous discussions of the obscure passage which were available when this study began, and discuss in detail three others which appeared in print only later. It is no attempt at a comprehensive survey of such accounts.

1 Searle, Blackburn and Code, and Hylton

My chief complaint against the accounts which were available when this study began is simple enough: even if it is granted that everything they say about the text is true, large portions of it remain obscure, and this alone seems to cast doubt on their validity. Of course, the unaccounted portions may ultimately be found not to be so important, but failing to make sense of them is hardly suitable grounds for supposing so. To maintain that the passage (or its most difficult parts) is so deeply confused that no coherent interpretation of it is possible strikes me as an easy way out.

One of the earliest attempts to interpret the passage, by Searle,[1] effectively accounts for only one half of a single paragraph ((D)) of the eight. Blackburn and Code,[2] who seem to account for much more, start on a wrong footing by taking the passage to be a dilemma between a use horn and a mention horn (which is plainly a misunderstanding of Russell's use of inverted commas) and fatally assimilating proper names and denoting phrases. What is worse, they simply ignore the most perplexing parts of the text. A third, more recent, interpretation by Peter Hylton[3] boils down – once *his* views on what is wrong with the theory are separated from those he ascribed to Russell

1 Searle, 'Russell's Objections'.
2 Blackburn and Code, 'The power of Russell's criticism'.
3 Hylton, *Russell*, Chapter 6, especially pp. 248 ff.

– to the claim that Russell is advancing an infinite-regress argument – a view for which there is simply no evidence in the text (and against which there is strong circumstantial evidence).[4] Michael Dummett, whose remarks do not purport to account for the text in detail, comes sometimes closer than most to the view presented in Chapter 2 above; but his account does not keep the attempt to understand Russell and the attempt to refute him sufficiently apart. Since Dummett reads the passage as an attack on Frege's view, the discussion of his account, and his proposal for circumventing Russell's difficulty, have been incorporated into Chapter 5.

Turning now to the three more recent accounts of the passage, by Pakaluk, Kremer and Noonan, my intention is to provide the reader, who may be baffled by the variety of extensive and rather involved accounts of the same text, first, with some guidance as to what distinguishes each of these accounts from the one proposed in Chapter 2, and second, with a glimpse of the kind of polemical response which may be adduced, regarding the disputed matters, from the vantage point articulated in Chapter 2. This provides, *inter alia*, a useful opportunity to further clarify and refine my own view. All three papers embody, to my mind, an advance over the earlier accounts just mentioned in at least some respect, be it in the attention given to the PoM background or in that given to the textual detail of the passage itself. Since I could not possibly address every issue deserving attention within the confines of an appendix, my course will be to drive straight at the principal matter. I focus almost exclusively on each writer's account of the portion beginning with 'this cannot be an explanation', which is both the most difficult to explain and acknowledged by all as the point where the whole of Russell's case comes to a head. With one's perspective thus narrowed, there is one feature which is shared (in one form or another) by all three writers, and which can be noted at the outset as distinguishing their accounts from mine: they all regard the notion of *acquaintance* as playing an essential role in Russell's argument. I will try to explain why I think this is a mistake. Whether or not the discussion establishes that my account fares better than the alternatives, I think it clearly establishes that they differ from it, each in its own way, quite markedly. Despite much agreement over what may be described as 'scene-setting' and what I have called the symbolic round, our respective perceptions of Russell's core argument differ substantially and not merely in emphasis of this element or that. I take up each of these writers in turn, following the order in which their essays were published.

---

4 This should not be confused with the infinite regress argument found in Russell's later essay (and mentioned in footnote 14 of Chapter 2 above) which, though relating to the same theory, is quite a different regress from the one proposed by Hylton.

II Pakaluk

Pakaluk's discussion,[5] in the form of a commentary, marks a considerable advance over its predecessors in attention to textual detail, in its clear view of the need to account for the text in its entirety, and in advancing a good presentation of the position Russell is attacking. The most important question, though, is what Pakaluk makes of the statements beginning with 'but this cannot be an explanation'. Pakaluk seems to regard this portion, as I do, as the culmination of the chief argument, but his account of its content has little in common with mine – though this may not be obvious at first sight.

Since the remarks we are concerned with reflect on the finding that <C> and C are different entities such that the former denotes the latter, our question is 'what fault, on Pakaluk's reading, does Russell find in this result?'. His reply, encapsulated in two paragraphs on pp. 56–7, begins as follows (the view Pakaluk labels '(ii)' is essentially the same as the one I delineated as underlying the 'substantial round'; I translate his notational conventions into mine): 'The defender of (ii), as we have seen, now simply asserts that what "<C>" indicates denotes what "C" indicates. But he admits that, in this assertion, both "<C>" and "C" indicate denoting complexes.'

So far so good. But he continues (to avoid confusion, I translate Pakaluk's notation into mine, replacing his use of boldface to indicate mention with inverted commas, and Russell's 'meaning quotes', as before, with '< >'),

> Hence, on this view, what these complexes denote does not enter into the proposition he asserts. It follows, then, that when the defender of (ii) says '<C> denotes C', the relation of denoting that is asserted to hold between <C> and C also does not enter into the proposition. Thus the relation is 'wholly mysterious'.
>
> (p. 56)

That 'what these complexes denotes does not enter into the proposition' is no more than a truism of the theory of denoting,[6] but to continue 'it follows . . . [that] the **relation of denoting** . . . does not enter into the proposition' is, in the first place, false because it does *not* follow, and in any case Pakaluk's ground for maintaining that it does remain a mystery. Furthermore, the conclusion is patently false. The theory of denoting prescribes – which is also made clear by the second sentence of (*F*) – that the predicate in a proposi-

5 M. Pakaluk, 'The interpretation of Russell's "Gray's Elegy" argument' in A. D. Irvine and G. A. Wedekind (eds), *Russell and Analytical Philosophy* (Toronto, Buffalo and London: University of Toronto Press, 1994).
6 Though not quite true of the particular proposition at stake, because of the two complexes occurring in it one is the denotation of the other, so one of the denotations *does* enter into the proposition.

tion containing a denoting complex is held to be true of the denotation (rather than of the complex). This is what it means to say that it is *about* the denotation. I see no reason to suppose this changes with the move from a one-place predicate to a relation, or when the relation involved happens to be that of denoting.[7] Third, even if it was the case that denoting did not occur in the said proposition, why would this make the relation 'wholly mysterious'? Pakaluk's paper provides no answer.

It seems that Pakaluk had not thought through the implications of what he says about '<C> denotes C'. He claims that the relation of denoting does not occur in it, but seems to forget that unless *some* relation does occur – and he proposes no other – we do not have a proposition at all. He then proceeds to offer what is presented as an alternative statement of the same point:

> for any claim of the form '<C> denotes C', we would not be acquainted with the denotation relation there asserted; hence a claim of this form expresses a proposition that could not be apprehended or understood. Russell is urging, in effect, that even if it were possible to speak of meanings as claimed, it would not be possible to speak of that which related them to denotations.
>
> (ibid. pp. 56–7)

But which proposition, supposedly *not* containing denoting, is he speaking of? Not only is denoting's absence from a proposition quite a different matter from our lack of acquaintance with it, but the relation between the two is in fact quite the opposite of what Pakaluk leads one to think. If denoting does *not* occur in a proposition, then (given other Russellian assumptions) that would make acquaintance with it *irrelevant* to its comprehension – not imply that it was incomprehensible. Pakaluk does not explain why he thinks acquaintance with denoting is any more problematic than with any other relation. Not only does Russell say nothing in the passage or elsewhere to suggest that it is, but general considerations concerning both denoting and acquaintance clearly point to the opposite conclusion.[8] The whole course of Pakaluk's interpretation at this crucial juncture strikes me as both

---

7 Pakaluk's wording ('the relation of denoting **that is asserted to hold between <C> and C** does not enter'; 'we would not be acquainted with the relation of denoting **there asserted**'; p. 56) raises the suspicion that he may be thinking of a *particular* relation in each case, as distinct from the general relation of denoting. But such a line would run contrary to Russell's explicit view that 'relations do not have instances, but are strictly the same in all propositions in which they occur (PoM: § 55).

8 Russell's recognition of denoting as an indefinable means that we must take acquaintance with it to be a settled matter. (This is, in fact, the epistemic corollary of its having this status). The plausibility of maintaining that we are acquainted with denoting (and other logical constants) may, of course, be challenged on other, non-Russellian, grounds, but even if successful this would be no help in reconstructing *Russell's* argument.

implausible as an account of the text in question, and rather weak, as a piece of reasoning in its own right. It does not, to sum up, amount to any plausible argument (Russellian or not) against the theory of denoting.

With regard to the second charge ('where are we to find the denoting complex <C> which is to denote C?') Pakaluk comes closer to the mark when he says that 'the objection is that there simply seems to be no predicate from which any such complex can be constructed'. Barring the conflation of there *being* no such predicate, and us not *knowing* any such predicate, this comes fairly close to what I have called the epistemic charge. But this grain of truth is, in Pakaluk's reconstruction, only one step in a much broader argument which does not, so far as I can tell, fit the text.

The alleged argument starts from the premise that denoting complexes 'can exist only if they can be arrived at by some method of construction from simpler constituents'. This, to begin with, suggests that Russell has set out to establish that some kind of denoting complexes do not *exist* – which strikes me as being far off the mark. He then supports his claim for the unavailability of the required predicate by appeal to his earlier conclusion that 'the relation "denotes" is certainly not available to us' (p. 57). But denoting, as explained earlier, is something Russell assumes *is* available to us, and its availability, moreover, is at the foundation of his fresh attack on the problem (discussed in the final section of Chapter 2 above), a text Pakaluk completely ignores. If what he says about (Russell's claim regarding) denoting was right, such a course would have been unthinkable.

The above difficulties are in part only symptoms of a more fundamental problem underlying the interpretation here. It is worth laying it bare because it will resurface in the next section as well. Pakaluk takes Russell's statement 'but this cannot be an explanation' to be pointing to some (apparently hidden) fault with the statement that C2 is a denoting complex, distinct from C1, which denotes C1. Given this assumption the interpreter's task is to uncover the fault. But Russell (as I understand him) is *not* faulting the statement itself: he does not argue that it is false, incoherent, incomprehensible or unknowable, and the whole idea that the statement is being put forward in the way Pakaluk's discussion takes it to be seems to me wrong. Russell's point, as he plainly puts it, is that this statement cannot be an *explanation* – an explanation *of what we mean by '<C>'*. So it is *as an explanation* that it is being tested, not as a proposition we ought to know, or understand, but fail to do so (though that may be the case as well). The broader implicit charge is that the theory provides us with *nothing more* than this non-explanation of C2, and that this renders the theory untenable.

Pakaluk's account of the third charge (from 'moreover' in (*G*) to the end) strikes me as very peculiar. After an inconclusive attempt to elucidate the text – the difficulty being that, on the proposed reading, one is at loss to say what precisely is the problem – our attention is shifted to *another* text. 'I think it is evident', Pakaluk writes, 'that he [i.e. Russell] is pointing here to the regress problem that is explicitly developed in KAKD' (p. 57). The regress argument is, of course, aimed at the same theory as the argument in question, but Pakaluk's contention that this is what Russell is 'pointing to' in the third charge is laid down as being 'evident' without a shred of either textual evidence or argument to support it. Russell was quite capable of stating a regress argument when he saw fit, but fails to either mention or hint at any regress in stating the third charge. To pick one salient difference: it is an essential feature of the third charge that it appeals to epistemic contexts, but the regress argument in KAKD has nothing to do with such contexts. By marrying these two arguments Pakaluk appears to be offering an account of this difficult piece of text, but even a cursory reading of the two sources will suffice to establish that they articulate two quite different arguments.

Pakaluk claims that 'the chief advantage of my interpretation over those previously proposed is that I am able to read the passage in such a way that **every** sentence has a philosophical and argumentative point . . . I do not find it necessary to pick and choose among the sentences of the passage to find an argument' (p. 37). I wholeheartedly endorse this stand on the importance of the merit of completeness, and it is to Pakaluk's credit that, unlike other writers, he acknowledges it as an essential requirement and strives towards it. But I remain unconvinced, particularly in view of his account of the third charge, that he has achieved this goal.

To sum up, although I find it hard to pin Pakaluk's account of the cardinal problem down to one clear claim, his account of Russell's central statements seems to regard the absence of *acquaintance* with the relation of denoting as playing a crucial role in the argument. For my part I fail to see any of this in Russell's text. So despite agreement over much of the preliminaries, when it comes to the crunch Pakaluk's account and mine have little in common. I turn next to Kremer's account.

III Kremer

Kremer's paper[9] does not confine itself to reporting what the passage actually says; it regards its argument as part of a broader exercise revolving around *the principle of acquaintance* (the principle, that is, that to understand a proposition one must be acquainted with each of its constituents). Only by reference to the principle, Kremer contends, does the whole point of the passage come to light. The argument, he says,

> shows that the attempt to use the theory of denoting concepts to handle apparent counterexamples to the PoA [principle of acquaintance] is

9 Michael Kremer, 'The argument of "On Denoting" ', *Philosophical Review* 103 (1994) pp. 249–97. My comments relate, almost exclusively, to pp. 287–90.

ultimately self-defeating; for the theory of denoting concepts, turned on itself, *undermines* the PoA. The GEA [Gray's Elegy Argument] argues that *if* the theory of denoting concepts is true, we can *know* this only by knowing propositions which *cannot* be composed only of constituents with which we are acquainted – propositions about denoting concepts themselves.

(Kremer, 'The argument': p. 268)

Lest this be thought a dispensable feature of his interpretation, Kremer returns to it after his discussion of the text, stating that the argument

reveals a basic conflict between the theory of denoting concepts and the PoA. **This is Russell's main argument against the theory of denoting concepts** – while the theory was intended to support the PoA, it in fact undermines the principle, and should be rejected.

(p. 290)

The above citations articulate what may be described as the global component of Kremer's interpretation. The more local component, i.e. Kremer's account of what the passage actually *says* (rather than implies) is, accordingly, that the fault Russell points out is indeed the absence of *acquaintance* with second-level complexes.[10]

In view of the account of this matter set out in Chapter 2 above, it will be no surprise that I confess that I do not recognize any of this in the passage (it is the argument in the passage, not just any argument Russell might have made, that we are after). Kremer's view that the principle of acquaintance is relevant to the theory of denoting *in general* seems plausible enough, but that does not guarantee it a role in the argument made against it in the passage. That neither acquaintance nor any cognate Russellian notion is ever mentioned in the passage makes this reading, to my mind, prima facie suspect.

The argument proposed by Kremer has a fairly clear hierarchical structure. At the base we have 'no acquaintance' (with second-level complexes); hence – given the principle of acquaintance – no knowledge of propositions

---

10 For the most part Kremer speaks of acquaintance with the complex itself, but at times this requirement seems to shift to acquaintance with the complex's constituents (and sometimes, as in Pakaluk, also to acquaintance with the *relation* of denoting; see pp. 283 and 289). But since the former would seem to presuppose the latter, acquaintance with the constituents would be required in any case. To avoid tiresome prolixity I conduct the discussion primarily in relation to the constituents, on the understanding that what is said applies *mutatis mutandis* to the complex itself. Kremer also seems to oscillate between the ideas that the required acquaintance is simply not available, and that it is impossible (see p. 289). Though important in themselves, I shall leave these matters to one side because they do not affect my principal claim against Kremer's view.

of the form 'C2 denotes C1'; hence the theory cannot be true. This structure is convenient for my purpose because the demolition of any single claim brings down all those which depend upon it. If it can be shown that Russell is *not* concerned with lack of acquaintance (either with second-level complexes or with their constituents), this will sever the purported link to the *principle* of acquaintance, and thus undermine Kremer's whole interpretation.

As with Pakaluk earlier, the heart of the matter must be sought in the account of the remarks beginning with 'but this cannot be an explanation'. After rejecting Hylton's idea of an infinite regress argument,[11] Kremer explains Russell's point as being twofold: first, (unlike a first-level denoting complex) with a second-level complex 'we have no idea what its constituents are or how they're put together'. Second ('{{C}}', and '{C}' mean the same as my 'C2' and 'C1' respectively),

> Given our inability to grasp the inner complexity of {{the teacher of Plato}}, we can get no grip on the relation between it and {the teacher of Plato}. We can posit such a relation, but we cannot explain it in terms of any entities **with which we are acquainted**.
>
> (pp. 287–8)

Although I agree, of course, with some of the things said here, I will focus on the feature with which I disagree. (Since Kremer regards these features as *essential* to Russell's argument, this disagreement is crucial.) I wish to question, first, whether it is indeed *acquaintance*, rather than some other epistemic relation, that is in question, and second, whether the core problem is indeed epistemic.

Although some epistemic deficiency is at the very least *associated* with the fault Russell brings out, I think it a mistake to identify it with (the lack of) acquaintance. To explain why, we need the distinction between being *acquainted* with a complex (or with its constituents), and *knowing what* a complex is (or what its constituents are). I use 'acquaintance' in the familiar Russellian sense; but wish to *introduce* 'knowing what' (which has no similarly established technical sense) as having a definite sense as follows.

Consider the MRTJ's characterization of a judgement to which a given fact corresponds. It tells us that the judgement is another fact, consisting of all of the first fact's constituents related, together with a mind, by the multiple relation of judging. Such a characterization appeals to the general notion of a mind, but not to any particular one, and its intelligibility does not, therefore, presuppose acquaintance with any mind – nor with any particular

---

11 Rightly, I believe, and in much greater detail than I provided at the beginning of this appendix. This is *not* the same regress that was mentioned earlier, and which Pakaluk associated with the third charge.

fact or constituent, yet it imparts, in the relevant sense, the *knowledge what* such a (second-level) fact is. It is true, of course, that the principle of acquaintance dictates that such *knowing what* will involve acquaintance with the constituents of the description employed (in this case such class concepts as 'mind', 'multiple relation' and 'fact') but this is quite a different matter from acquaintance with either the fact or with its constituents. (*Knowing what* is a species of *descriptive knowledge*, but not quite identical with it.)

That these two epistemic states are independent of each other, with regard to any particular object, is shown by its being possible to know, in the required sense, *what* the constituents of a complex are, *without* being acquainted with any of them (this could be the case even when acquaintance is ruled out *on principle*); and by its being possible that one might *happen* to be acquainted with all the constituents of a complex without knowing what the complex is. What is lacking in such a case is the knowledge that they are the constituents of the said complex – as when one knows someone's uncle without knowing he is the uncle.

I would like to think that as soon as this distinction is drawn, it becomes evident that it is the absence of *knowing what* (with regard to the second-level complex) rather than of *acquaintance* that Russell is concerned with. But there is also a matter of logical priority. The question of acquaintance with constituents can only be raised *after* it has been settled *what* they are. I counter Kremer's view, therefore, not by maintaining that we *do* have the acquaintance which he (on Russell's behalf) says we do not, but rather by contesting that we are even in a position which allows the question to arise. Kremer provides no reason to suppose – and for my part, I tend to think there is none – that constituents of second-level complexes form a distinct class from those of first-level complexes, nor, therefore, that acquaintance with them raises any special difficulty. From the fact that in a particular case we do not know *what* those constituents are, it by no means follows that we are not *acquainted* with them (nor, of course, that such acquaintance is impossible).

The contrast between Kremer's reading and mine can now be encapsulated by appeal to two hypothetical situations. In the first we *have* an explanation of what C2 is, but it implies that acquaintance with its constituents is impossible (because they involve, say, some special constituent knowable to us only by description). This would, on my reading, *resolve* Russell's actual difficulty (while of course creating another); on Kremer's reading it would not. In the other situation, theoretical considerations somehow *guarantee* our acquaintance with all the constituents of such complexes (or at least, those denoting complexes we apprehend). This would *not* alleviate the difficulty on my reading (because it does not tell us what these complexes are), but it would on Kremer's.

I turn now to the question of whether the core difficulty is indeed, as Kremer maintains, epistemic. Let us begin by asking, 'who are the "we" whose epistemic failure is at stake?' I take Kremer to be using 'we' in the same sense as Russell does when saying 'where are **we** to find . . .'. But what precisely does *Russell* mean? Who is acquaintance, or 'knowledge what', required of? Here, again, the reply requires a distinction. A theory may impose epistemic requirements upon a *knower*, and it may impose requirements upon the *theorist*. The distinction is conveniently illustrated by the theory of denoting – though it is by no means special to it.

Together with the principle of acquaintance, the theory of denoting prescribes that a *knower* who apprehends a proposition whose expression involves a denoting phrase must be acquainted with the denoting concept's constituents (which may, if the concept is simple, be identified with the concept itself).[12] The knower's grasp of the proposition *constitutes*, on this view, his thinking *about* the denotation – no inferential process is involved. It does *not* follow from this that he needs to know, not even 'implicitly', that the denoting concept denotes the denotation, or even that he needs to be aware of this relation (let alone be acquainted with it). For *the statement of the theory*, on the other hand, no acquaintance with particular constituents is required, but acquaintance with the relation of denoting is, because (given its indefinability) without it the statement of the theory could not be comprehensible.[13]

By 'knower' in the present context I mean a subject who *apprehends* a particular proposition containing a denoting complex, and who can therefore be supposed to apprehend the denoting complex itself. While the conjunction of the principle of acquaintance and the theory of denoting prescribes

---

12 Kremer contends that Russell's terminological shift from 'denoting concept' (in PoM) to 'denoting complex' (in the intermediate manuscripts and in OD) signifies his abandoning the commitment to such concepts being *always* simple in favour of a view whereby they are always complex (this is supposed to have come in response to difficulties which Kremer speculates about without a trace of evidence that Russell ever considered them. See Kremer, 'The argument', pp. 270–2). I profoundly disagree with this proposal. In the first place, it is plainly belied by Russell's use of *both* these terms throughout OF. Russell's PoM position was *not* that denoting concepts are invariably simple, but only that they are *no more complex* than the concept from which they derive, i.e. that they *can* be simple. Nor does he maintain later that they are invariably complex. I think a much simpler explanation, which is also more consonant with the textual evidence, is possible. Denoting complexes are a sub-species of denoting concepts. In PoM Russell did not set the complex case aside for special treatment, but in the intermediate writings he came to focus upon them because they give rise to questions (familiar with respect to propositions) regarding the substitution of constituents, which he discusses at great length in OF.

13 That Kremer is far from clear about this distinction is evidenced by the first of the passages cited above. His argument there moves from a requirement that the theory be known to be true, via a requirement that a (particular) proposition about denoting concepts be known, to the requirement of acquaintance with the constituents of such propositions. A similar conflation occurs in his discussion of the difficulties, alluded to in the previous footnote, which are alleged to have motivated Russell's terminological shift from 'denoting concepts' to 'denoting complexes'.

that he be acquainted with all the complex's constituents, what does it imply regarding his relation to a complex *denoting* the one he apprehends? The answer is, I think, very clear: *nothing* follows regarding his relation either to the second-level complex or its constituents. So the mere fact that he is not acquainted with these entities tells nothing against the principle of acquaintance. If an epistemic relation to the second-level complex is to be required at all, it is surely not required of the knower, and Russell's 'we' cannot therefore be understood as applying to the knowing subject. But what precisely is it to require knowledge of 'the theorist'? This question is best approached via the intermediate or 'mixed' type of case.

The knower I have been appealing to was assumed to lack any knowledge of the theory, and the theorist, correspondingly, to lack any acquaintance with particulars. But what Kremer probably has in mind, which is also what lends credence to his formulation, is, I suspect, a mixed case. If we think of the theorist as apprehending some *particular* first-level complex (or of a knower who also knows the theory, or if we put ourselves, who know the theory, in a knower's place) and ask him 'what second-level complex denotes *it*?', his inability to answer is surely *related* to the problem at stake, because had he known, as theorist, what such a complex must in general be (how its structure and constituents relate to those of the first-level complex), his apprehension, as knower, of the particular first-level complex, *would* equip him epistemically to determine such a second-level complex. This is indeed true enough, and is perhaps the best way of getting a first glimpse of Russell's problem, but a closer look suggests that it conflates elements which are truly essential to the problem with others which are not.

Reflection upon the mixed case reveals that the *particular* element in the situation, i.e. the knower's input, is playing no real role. It is a mere heuristic device to help focus our minds on an abstract problem by reference to a particular example. What we are after is something like a formula, a rule – not anything a knower could be expected to supply.

Having dismissed the knower in favour of the theorist, it is time we asked what precisely 'the theorist' means. It appears that, in this context, what the theory determines and what the theorist knows are one and the same (and similarly for what is *not* determined and *not* known). Imagine a theory of deduction which failed to capture some intuitively valid inference; we could, if we wished, phrase our objection to it by saying, 'but how do we *know* whether the said inference is valid?', but this is no grounds for regarding the problem as epistemic. Another example might be Frege's objecting (Gl.: § 56) to a proposed definition of the step from any given number to the next, on the grounds that it does not tell us whether, for example, Julius Caesar is a number. That a problem can be put in epistemic terms is not in itself sufficient to establish it as an epistemic problem.

Personifying the theory as 'the theorist' has served us well in setting aside 'the knower', but it transpires that it is no more than a literary device for making statements about the *theory*. Once this is acknowledged, any semblance of the problem's being *epistemic* in nature disappears into thin air. The difficulty is that the theory does not determine the said complex, and Russell's 'where are we to find . . .?' uses 'we' in the manner just described. It is for this reason that I insisted that the core problem is *not* epistemic, though I do admit there is a (derivative) epistemic problem as well, which plays a useful heuristic role.

Kremer contrasts Hylton's view of the fault, which he labels 'metaphysical', with his own, which he labels 'epistemic'. By contrast with both, my construal of Russell's problem may be labeled '*logical*'. The epistemic deficiency is only a way of bringing out the *theory's* failure to provide a satisfactory explanation for a symbol it has introduced. Despite my disagreement with much of what Kremer says about the core difficulty, the challenge of articulating the disagreement was, I must confess, very instructive indeed, and helpful in clarifying my own position, not least to myself.

IV Noonan

Harold Noonan's paper,[14] deals with exactly the same texts and set of problems as do Pakaluk's and Kremer's, but he shows relatively little concern for textual detail, and makes no attempt at a comprehensive account of the text. He presents three arguments, two of which he maintains *are* successful against the theory but cannot be read into Russell's text, and one which he thinks *is* in Russell's text, but which he maintains is incomplete. The argument he attributes to Russell runs as follows:

(1) If denoting concepts exist it must be possible to speak about them.
(2) Denoting concepts cannot be spoken of except by using denoting phrases; they cannot be referred to by name.
(3) Denoting phrases which contain *mention* of other denoting phrases *may* provide a way of speaking of denoting concepts, but given the ontological status of denoting concepts (qua concepts), this cannot be the *only* possibility if such concepts exist.
(4) A denoting concept cannot be spoken of by *using* the phrase which expresses it *unembedded* in a use of a larger denoting phrase.
(5) A denoting concept cannot be spoken of by *using* the phrase which expresses it *embedded* in a use of a larger denoting phrase.
(6) There are no other possibilities.
(7) Therefore, denoting concepts cannot exist.

(Noonan, 'The "Gray's Elegy" argument', p. 93)

14 H. Noonan, 'The "Gray's Elegy" argument – and others', in A. Palmer and R. Monk (eds), *Russell and the Origins of Analytical Philosophy* (Bristol, Thoemmes Press, 1996).

Although the inner steps, (2)–(6), can, barring some reservations,[15] be plausibly read into Russell's passage, the outermost steps, and the proposed conclusion in particular, cannot be right. In the first place, the passage never mentions the issue of the *existence* (or any cognate term) of denoting complexes, and Noonan does not tell us where precisely *in the text* he derives this idea from (this strand occurs in Pakaluk as well, but not in quite the central position it has in Noonan's reading). Second, step (1) implies that inability to *speak* about something might (at the very least) count against its very *existence*, but Noonan offers nothing to recommend this assumption, either in its own right or as one to be attributed to Russell. Moreover, the idea that Russell might have sought to establish that denoting concepts can *never* be spoken about is belied by an example Russell himself provides in the passage (namely 'the denoting complex occurring . . .' in (*D*)). I contend, therefore, that the conclusion of Russell's argument cannot be what Noonan holds it to be.

Noonan is surely right to observe that Russell faults a number of apparent possibilities for speaking about denoting complexes, but the difficulty is to say how precisely this leads to undermining the whole theory. The text's structure strongly suggests that the answer is to be sought in the statements beginning with 'but this cannot be an explanation', but Noonan's reading simply *ignores* these crucial statements, and indeed all the remainder of the text.[16] His reading thus ends up evading the chief difficulty in interpreting the passage. It is true enough that *if* one could establish that denoting concepts cannot exist, this *would* be a conclusive argument against the theory, but this is hardly grounds for ascribing this line of argument to Russell. Noonan's account, to sum up his proposed reconstruction, puts forward an argument which is untenable as an interpretation of Russell's text. So much for the argument Noonan attributes to Russell.

As mentioned earlier, Noonan also presents two further arguments which he maintains *are* effective against the theory, though he admits that they *cannot* be attributed to Russell. I will comment on the first of these only briefly, as it is not a contender for what Russell is arguing in the passage, and ignore the second because it would take us too far afield. In its general thrust the argument resembles what Kremer regards as the principal argument in the text, namely that the theory is incompatible with the principle of acquaintance. When discussed in relation to Kremer this proposal was rebutted on the grounds that it was not supported by the text, but in Noonan's case such a retort is no longer to the point.

---

15 With regard to the latter half of (2), my objection will become clear shortly. Regarding (3), I do not see Russell making any such partial concession to the appeal to mention. It is a possibility dismissed at the outset which does not feature in the body of the argument.

16 Which, given his account of the argument, is asking us in effect to believe that they mean something like 'denoting complexes do not exist'. For my part this is asking too much.

Noonan's version differs from Kremer's by putting the weight not on epistemic difficulties regarding 'C2 denotes C1', but rather on the (alleged) impossibility of *naming* denoting complexes. (This line also occurs in Kremer, 'The argument', p. 289, but rather like an afterthought.) Noonan lists four propositions which he thinks Russell is committed to, and which are jointly inconsistent:

(1) Any object of acquaintance can be given a logically proper name,
(2) denoting concepts are objects of acquaintance,
(3) whatever has a logically proper name can be spoken about by using that name,
(4) denoting concepts cannot be spoken about except by using denoting phrases.

(Noonan, 'The "Gray's Elegy" argument', p. 81)

The set is indeed inconsistent, but I do not think Noonan is correct in committing Russell to all four. The only proposition I fully agree about is (4), though I do not think its significance for Russell is what Noonan takes it to be, i.e. as involving a denial that denoting complexes can be *named*. I am not at all sure what 'object of acquaintance', so prominent in (1) and (2), is intended to exclude, and hence whether Russell is committed to these claims. Fortunately, this matter can be left aside, since my case can be made by appeal to (3) alone. It *seems* very plausible to think that Russell is committed to it. Probably because denoting complexes were a relatively transient feature of his philosophy (compared to acquaintance and naming) and being a very unusual kind of entity, they are easily overlooked in the statement of such principles. Ultimately, however, I think Russell is not committed to (3) as a *universal* principle – the exception being, of course, denoting complexes.

The line of argument via names is clearly inspired, as in Kremer's case, by Russell's remark 'the meaning cannot be got at except by means of denoting phrases'. But I think that taking this as invoking the contrast with naming – which, as I will show shortly, is not even relevant – is a misunderstanding. Russell's point is, rather, that – unlike any other kind of entity whatsoever, including propositions – to obtain a proposition about a denoting complex requires *another* complex. Despite the talk of phrases, the linguistic angle is not essential to Russell's remark, and ultimately it is misleading.[17]

To see this let us assume, for the sake of argument, that we *have* named a denoting complex. Now a sentence in which this name occurs will express a proposition in which the name's bearer occurs – this is what names invariably

---

17 Similar statements may also be found in OF p. 363 and OMD p. 322. The contrast is not with naming, but rather with the result, for other kinds of entities, of putting something in a subject position in a proposition.

do. It follows that the proposition expressed – paradoxical as this may seem – will *not* be about the complex (but rather about its denotation). So even if naming complexes were possible, it would be of no help in speaking about them. The question of whether complexes can be named is one which, upon reflection, we have no reason to enter into – it is simply irrelevant. Needless to say, it is no foundation for an argument against the theory. My final verdict on (3), therefore, is that though clearly true of everything *except* denoting complexes, its appearing as a universal truth is owed to the (perhaps understandable) inclination to overlook their special case. The set of four propositions listed by Noonan is thus not one Russell can be held committed to, and its inconsistency, therefore, does not tell against his theory.

Rodriguez-Consuegra, F. A. 46n

Sainsbury, M. 3n
Salmon, N. 85n
Searle, John; on the obscure passage
  from OD 24n, 127n, 208; on semantic
  facts 98n
sense 81ff.; ancestry in Bs. 90ff.;
  'determine' modeled on concepts
  121–5; determines reference
  absolutely 117–21, 130; epistemic
  accessibility of 200–2; generic notion
  of 142–3; immutability of 118; and
  indirect speech 109–11; inevitability
  of simple 161n, 200n; language
  inessential to identity of 124–5,
  138–9; language not involved in its
  relation to reference 138; novelty of
  notion compared to that of reference
  107; relation to the reference 104;
  route model of 112–17; thoughts
  about 127ff.; whether all expressions
  have 151–5; whether all names have
  149–50; without reference 112–17,

125–7 (see also Sense/reference
  distinction, Bestimmungsweise)
sense/reference distinction; for complete
  sentences 107; for concept-words 108,
  122–3; priority of names 106–9, 111,
  123
Sluga, Hans 90n, 95, 100n, 202n
Smith, J.F. 60n, 196n
Strawson, P.F. 187, 191, 193

Tarski, A. 1
Taschek, W.W. 85n
'the'-phrases 13, 17, 21, 61, 69, 77,
  165ff., 169ff.
truth 11, 22–3, 119, 128, 140, 194
Tugendhat, E. 186

variable, the 34n, 46n, 50, 57, 76–7,
  151n, 166–7, 173, 194n (see also
  'any')

Wiggins, David 95–6
Wirklich 165, 182, 195 (see also Being)
Wittgenstein, L. 4, 93n, 152, 193n

Bibliography

For abbreviations, see list of abbreviations following table of contents. Post-humous works by Russell and Frege are placed according to their surmised date of composition.

I Russell

(i) Collections

(1993) *The Collected Papers of Bertrand Russell, Volume 3*, edited by G. H. Moore, London and New York: Routledge and Kegan Paul.

(1994) *The Collected Papers of Bertrand Russell, Volume 4, Foundations of Logic 1903–05*, edited by A. Urquhart, London and New York: Routledge and Kegan Paul.

(1973) *Essays in Analysis*, edited by D. Lackey, London: Allen and Unwin.

(1956) *Logic and Knowledge: Essays 1901–1950*, edited by L. C. Marsh, London: Allen and Unwin.

(1949) *Mysticism and Logic*, edited by G. H. Moore, London: Allen and Unwin (originally published 1917).

(1966) *Philosophical Essays*, edited by G. H. Moore, New York: Simon and Schuster/ London, Allen and Unwin (Originally published 1910).

(ii) Individual works

(1903) *The Principles of Mathematics*, London: Allen and Unwin (2nd edn 1937, London: Allen and Unwin).

(1903) 'On the Meaning and Denotation of Phrases', in CPR, Volume 4.

(1903) 'Points about Denoting', in CPR, Volume 4.

(1903) 'On Meaning and Denotation,' in CPR, Volume 4.

(1904) 'Meinong's Theory of Complexes and Assumptions', in Lackey.

(1905) 'The Existential Import of Propositions', in Lackey.

(1905) Review of A. Meinong, *Untersuchungen zur Gegenstandstheorie und Psychologie*, in Lackey.

(1905) 'On Fundamentals', CPR, Volume 4.

(1905) 'On Denoting', in Marsh, also in Lackey.

(1905) 'The Nature of Truth', CPR, Volume 4.

(1905) 'Necessity and Possibility', in CPR, Volume 4.

(1906) 'On the Substitutional Theory of Classes and Relations', in Lackey.

(1907) Review of A. Meinong, *Über die Stellung der Gegenstandstheorie im System der Wissenschaften*, in Lackey.

(1907) 'The Regressive Method of Discovering the Premises of Mathematics', in Lackey.

(1910) 'The Nature of Truth and Falsehood', in Russell (1966), *Philosophical Essays*.

(1910) (with Whitehead, A. N.) *Principia Mathematica*, Volume 1, Cambridge: Cambridge University Press (2nd edn 1925, Cambridge: Cambridge University Press).

(1911) 'Knowledge by Acquaintance and Knowledge by Description', in Russell (1949), *Mysticism and Logic*.

(1912) *The Problems of Philosophy*, Oxford: Oxford University Press, 1974.

(1913) *Theory of Knowledge*, London: Routledge and Kegan Paul, 1993.

(1918) 'The Philosophy of Logical Atomism', in Marsh.

(1919) *Introduction to Mathematical Philosophy*, London: Allen and Unwin.

(1959) *My Philosophical Development*, London: Allen and Unwin.

II Frege

(i) Collections

(1984) *Collected Papers on Mathematics, Logic, and Philosophy*, edited by B. McGuiness, Oxford: Blackwell.

(1972) *Conceptual Notation and Related Articles*, edited by T. Bynum, translated by the editor, Oxford: Clarendon Press.

(1980) *Philosophical and Mathematical Correspondence*, edited by G. Gabriel, H. Hermes, K. Kambartal *et al.*, abridged for the English edition by B. McGuiness and translated by H. Kaal, Oxford: Blackwell.

(1979) *Posthumous Writings*, edited by H. Hermes, F. Kambartel and F. Kaulbach, Oxford: Blackwell.

(1960) *Translations from the Philosophical Writings of Gottlob Frege*, edited by P. T. Geach and M. Black, 2nd edn, Oxford: Blackwell.

(ii) Individual works

(1879) 'Conceptual Notation', in Bynum.

(1882) 'On the Scientific Justification of a Conceptual Notation', in Bynum.

(Before 1884) 'Dialogue with Pünjer on Existence', in PW.

(1884) *The Foundations of Arithmetic*, translated by J. L. Austin, 2nd edn, Oxford: Blackwell, 1986.

(1885) 'On Formal Theories of Arithmetic', in CPF.

(1891) 'Function and Concept', in G&B.

(1892) 'On Concept and Object' in G&B.

(1892) 'On Sense and Reference', in G&B.

(1892) 'On Mr. Peano's Conceptual Notation and My Own', in PW.

(1892–5) 'Comments on Sense and Meaning' in PW.

(1893) *The Basic Laws of Arithmetic*, translated and edited by Montgomery Furth, Berkeley, CA: University of California Press, 1964.
(1897) 'Logic', in PW.
(1904) 'What is a Function?' in G&B.
(1906) 'On Schoenfliess: *die Logischen Paradoxien der Mengenlehre*', in PW.
(1906) 'Introduction to Logic', in PW.
(1918) 'Thoughts', in CPF.

III Works by other writers

Ayer, A. J. (1971) *Russell and Moore: The Analytic Heritage*, London: Macmillan.
Ayer, A. J. (1972) *Russell*, London: Fontana/Collins.
Baker, G. and Hacker, P. (1984) *Frege: Logical Excavations*, New York: Oxford University Press, and Oxford: Blackwell.
Bell, D. (1979) *Frege's Theory of Judgement*, Oxford: Clarendon Press.
Blackburn, S. and Code, A. (1978) 'The power of Russell's criticism of Frege: "On Denoting" pp. 48–50', *Analysis* 38, 65–77; reprinted in Irvine, A. D. and Wedekind, G. A. (eds) *Russell and Analytical Philosophy*, Toronto, Buffalo and London: University of Toronto Press, 1994.
Bynum, T. W. (1976) 'The evolution of Frege's logicism', in Schirn, M. (ed.) *Studies on Frege*, 3 vols, Stuttgart and Bad-Cannstatt: Frommann-Holzboog, Volume I, pp. 279–86.
Cartwright, R. (1987) 'On the origins of Russell's theory of descriptions', in Cartwright, *Philosophical Essays*, Cambridge, MA: MIT Press.
Coffa, J. A. (1985) 'Russell as a Platonic dialogue: the matter of denoting', *Synthese* 45, 43–70.
Dummett, M. (1975) 'What is a theory of meaning?', in Guttenplan, S. (ed.) *Mind and Language*, Oxford: Clarendon Press.
Dummett, M. (1978) 'Frege's distinction between sense and reference', in Dummett, *Truth and Other Enigmas*, London: Duckworth.
Dummett, M. (1981) *Frege: Philosophy of Language*, 2nd edn, London: Duckworth.
Dummett, M. (1981) *The Interpretation of Frege's Philosophy*, London: Duckworth.
Dummett, M. (1991) 'Frege's myth of the third realm', in FOP.
Dummett, M. (1991) 'Which end of the telescope?', in FOP.
Evans, G. (1982) *The Varieties of Reference*, Oxford: Clarendon Press.
Hylton, P. (1980) 'Russell's substitutional theory', *Synthese* 45, 1–31.
Hylton, P. (1989) 'The Significance of "On Denoting"', in Savage, C. W. and Anderson, C. A. (eds) *Rereading Russell* (Minnesota Studies in the Philosophy of Science, Volume 12), Minneapolis: University of Minnesota Press.
Hylton, P. (1990) 'Logic and Russell's logicism', in Bell, D. and Cooper, N. (eds) *The Analytic Tradition*, Oxford: Blackwell.
Hylton, P. (1990b) *Russell, Idealism and the Emergence of Analytical Philosophy*, Oxford: Clarendon Press.
Kaplan, D. (1970) 'What Is Russell's theory of descriptions', in Yourgrau, W. and Beck, A. D. (eds) *Physics, Logic and History*, New York: Penlum Press.
Kaplan, D. (1975) 'How to Russell a Frege-Church', *Journal of Philosophy* 72, 716–29.

Kremer, M. (1994) 'The argument of "On denoting"', *Philosophical Review* 103, 249–97.

Linsky, L. (1969) *Referring*, London: Routledge and Kegan Paul.

Meinong, A. (1965) *Philosophenbriefe*, edited by R. Kindinger, Graz: Akademische Druck- und Verlagsanstalt.

Mendelsohn, R. L. (1982) 'Frege's *Begriffsschrift* theory of identity', *Journal of the History of Philosophy* 20, 279–99.

Noonan, H. (1996) 'The "Gray's Elegy" argument – and others', in Palmer, A. and Monk, R. (eds) *Russell and the Origins of Analytical Philosophy*, Bristol: Thoemmes Press.

Pakaluk, M. (1994) 'The Interpretation of Russell's "Gray's *Elegy*" argument', in Irvine, A. D. and Wedekind, G. A. (eds) *Russell and Analytical Philosophy*, Toronto, Buffalo and London: University of Toronto Press.

Quine, W. V. O. (1961) 'On what there is', in Quine, *From a Logical Point of View*, 2nd edn, New York: Harper and Row.

Quine, W. V. O. (1972) 'Russell's ontological development', in Pears, D. (ed.) *Bertrand Russell: A Collection of Critical Essays*, New York: Doubleday (originally published 1966).

Sainsbury, R. M. (1979) *Russell*, London: Routledge and Kegan Paul.

Sainsbury, R. M. (1983) 'On a Fregean argument for the distinctness of sense and reference', *Analysis* 43, 12–14.

Salmon, N. (1986) *Frege's Puzzle*, Cambridge, MA: MIT Press.

Searle, J. R. (1958) 'Russell's objections to Frege's theory of sense and reference', *Analysis* 18, 137–43.

Searle, J. R. (1964) 'How to derive "ought" from "is"', *Philosophical Review* 73, 43–58.

Sluga, H. (1980) *Gottlob Frege*, London, Boston and Henley: Routledge and Kegan Paul.

Smith, J. F. (1985) 'The Russell–Meinong debate', *Philosophy and Phenomenological Research*, 45, 305–50.

Strawson, P. F. (1959) *Individuals*, London: Methuen.

Taschek, W. W. (1992) 'Frege's puzzle, sense, and information content', *Mind* 101, 76–91.

Wiggins, D. (1976) 'Frege's puzzle of the morning star and the evening star', in Schirn, M. (ed.) *Studies on Frege*, 3 vols, Stuttgart and Bad-Cannstatt: Frommann-Holzboog, Volume II, pp. 221–56.

Wittgenstein, L. (1961) *Tractatus Logico-Philosophicus*, translated by D. F. Pears and B. F. McGuinness, London: Routledge and Kegan Paul.

Index

about and aboutness shifting 12, 17–18, 25, 49, 153, 22, 111, 118, 127, 142, 144, 211, 217
acquaintance 17, 153n, 154; distinction from 'knowing what' 215–16; generic sense of 146–7, 199–202; in Kremer 214–19; in Noonan 221–2; in Pakaluk 211; principle of 200n, 213–14, 217–18; relevance to passage from OD 209
any 68–9, 77, 174
Ayer, A.J. 53n

Baker, G. and Hacker P. 95
being; contrast with 'existence' 56–8, 193; contrast with 'is' 67; denial of 57, 71, 73, 165
Bell, David 151–2
Bestimmungsweise (BW) and *Art des Gegebensein*s (AdG) 90–4, 97n, 102–4, 111n, 112, 117, 130n, 160, 163, 175
Black, Max; translation of SuB 94n, 97, 99n
Blackburn, Simon and Code, Alan 24n, 27n, 208

Campbell, John 39n
Cartwright, Richard; on comparing Russell and Frege 137–9; on OF §40, 45ff.
class concepts 174–6 *passim*; acquisition of 186–7; determination of extensions 121–2; in Frege's post-SuB terminology 122–3, 171; generic notion of 194; must have sharp boundaries 115, 180; ordinary vs logically proper 183, 190n; in Russell 15, 19, 25–6, 50–1, 67

classes 21; extensional and intensional view of 15; infinite 14–15, 16, 113n, 141, 143, 144, 145, 173, 199, 201; the null 15, relation of a member to a 41–2, 51, 67
Code, Alan *see* Blackburn
Coffa, A. 3n
combinations 13, 18, 40n, 180n
compositionality; of judgeable content 84–6; of thoughts 106, 107
conceptual content (Frege) 82ff.; bipartite notion of 102; contrast with colouring 87, 89; contrast with 'our way of looking' 92n; objectivity of 104; and relevance to logic 92–3

definition 16–17, 47n, 63, 168n; contextual 68–9, 167; Frege on 84, 93; mathematical v. philosophical 78
denoting concepts/complexes 18n., 217n; abolition of 70; acquaintance with 221; acquaintance with constituents of 215–19; as exception to the simple sense of 'having meaning' 139; existence of 219–20; infinite hierarchy of 28; and propositional complexes 43–5; relation to class concepts 165; second-level 27, 28, 38, 40; simplicity of 20; speaking/thinking about 21, 22–3, 32, 34, 220–1
denoting, relation of; acquaintance with 210–12, 217; and 'about' 18; compared with other logical relations 41–2; and definition 16–17; and determining 15; and identity statements 17, 36; as 'forward road'

to denotation 47–8; logical character of 18–19; many–one 18; single or many 13; symbol for 14n

Dummett, Michael 29n, 94–5, 114n, 181n, 201n, 202n; on Frege's admitting empty senses 153–4; on Frege's interest in cognitive content 201n; on name-bearer relation 186; on the obscure passage from OD 209; on Russell's criticism of Frege 130–1; on sense and indirect speech 109; on sense as a route 112–13, 116–17

'empty' names and description 2–3, 52, 54, 58–9, 61–4, 78, 112–17, 125–7, 164–5, 172, 178

epistemic contexts 17, 33, 87, 109–11, 128, 199, 213

Evans G. 98n; on Frege 88–9, 112–17; on Russell 3n, 4n

existence see 'being'

facts 120–1, 140

formal implication 14–15, 68–9, 77, 166n

Hacker, P. see Baker G.

Hylton, Peter; account of passage from OD 208–9; on the role of language 74–6; on Russell's ontological change 54–68

identity statements, informative 17, 32, 83–9, 104, 110–11, 118, 141, 142, 149–50, 154, 157

infinite regress 37n, 209n, 213, 215

Kant, I. 198

Kremer, M. 209, 213–19, 220, 221

language 4, 6, 7; content independent of 83; and Frege's puzzle 86; generic propositions independent of 141; indifference of logic to 18, 190, 194; irrelevant to the relation between sense and reference 116, 124–5; natural (and the concept-script 82; defect of 116; logical rendition of expressions in 167, 172; place in the Russell–Frege enterprise 179–91; transparency of 67, 74–5)

Leibniz, G.W. 193n, 198

Linsky, L. 3

logical constants 14, 68n, 162, 171; role in account of denoting phrases 174ff., 184, 190, 193n

logicism 4, 50, 78, 81–2, 141, 187ff., 192, 196–9

mathematics 19, 21, 54, 56–7, 62, 68n, 69, 78, 82, 84, 91n, 93n, 141–2, 170, 183, 191n, 193n, 195–7; philosophy of 13–16 passim, 188–90, 192, 198–9, 202n (see also logicism)

Meinong, Alexius; ontology of 4, 52–6, 78; Russell's case against 58–65, 78; theory of objects 195–8

Mendelsohn, R. L. 103

mentioned expressions 24, 34, 37, 61n, 101, 128, 219

multiple relation theory of judgement 29–31, 40, 41, 71, 76, 215

Noonan, H. 209, 219–22

Pakaluk, M. 209–13

Peano, G. 126n, 166n, 176n, 180n

proper names 135, 202; approximation of theoretical notion 186; availability of simple senses of in Frege 162–4; of denoting concepts 23, 221–2; lexical vs logical simplicity of 157–60; logically proper 157; logically proper vs ordinary 179–82; 'relative' 185; Russell's and Frege's different taxonomies 155–64, 169, 173, 177n; senses of 142, 145, 147; whether logically prior to objects 181n, 202 (see also empty names and descriptions)

propositional functions 48–50, 56, 69n, 73n, 76, 153n, 173n

propositions 11–12; as complexes 21; with Frege's content 83; generic 139 (constituents of 149; as epistemic objects 153); as incomplete symbols 71–2, 76; in mathematics and in ordinary language 16; resemblance Russellian and Frege's thoughts 135

Quine, W.V.O. 61, 65, 109; on every word having some meaning 66–7; on Russell's ontological development 53–60